FORTS or FOLLIES?

THE STORY OF PLYMOUTH'S PALMERSTON FORTS

FREDDY WOODWARD

HALSGROVE

First published in Great Britain by Devon Books, 1998

ISBN 1 874448 12 4

Cataloguing in Publication Data

CIP record for this title is available from the British Library

HALSGROVE
PUBLISHING, MEDIA AND DISTRIBUTION
Halsgrove House
Lower Moor Way
Tiverton
Devon EX16 6SS

Tel: 01884 243242
Fax: 01884 243325
www.halsgrove.com

Printed in Great Britain by Bookcraft Ltd, Midsomer Norton

IN

MEMORY OF

JANE

WHO DID NOT

LIVE TO SEE THIS

FINISHED

Frontispiece: *The gateway, Crownhill Fort, and a gunner dressed in the style of the 1880s.* (Western Evening Herald ©)

FOREWORD

In recent years the fortifications of Plymouth have received much more attention than they have had previously, and their historical importance in consequence has become better recognised. Not before time it might be said. The defences of Portsmouth, Dover and those of the Thames and Medway first gained attention about a generation ago and in consequence have achieved a reasonably successful record of conservation. That the situation in Plymouth has now changed from former ignorance and neglect is due substantially to the initiative and writings of Freddy Woodward. In 1987, his *Citadel: A History of the Royal Citadel, Plymouth* was published, opening up the story of the great fortress on the Hoe from its beginnings as a late Elizabethan fort to its replacement by the baroque, pentagonal fortress of the late seventeenth century which still dominates the skyline above Sutton Harbour. This pioneering book was followed in 1990 by a general review over the course of time of Plymouth's defences; an introduction for the general reader. In its essentials this served as the precursor for the more extensive commentary on, and gazetteer of, the defence sites in and around Plymouth from the Tudors up to 1945 and their present condition in which Freddy Woodward collaborated with Andrew Pye under the title of *The Historic Defences of Plymouth* (1996). This comprehensive review has given a greater detailed awareness and understanding of Plymouth's defence heritage to planners and conservation bodies at national as well as local level.

Plymouth's defences from sea and land attack have evolved over the course of five centuries as the effectiveness of the weapons likely to be used against them has also developed both in range and destructiveness. In this Plymouth and Devonport have been no different from the other major English naval dockyards in the progressive expansion of their protective skins. Like them, in terms of geographical spread and the sheer numbers of forts and batteries built over the course of a decade during the middle years of the nineteenth century, this period of construction was the high point in the development of protective measures against external attack. Because the Dockyard and the Sound were the critical areas to defend, this meant the fortification of the Antony peninsula and Whitesand Bay on the Cornish side and the Staddon Position on the opposite coast as well as immediately adjacent defences, especially following the introduction of rifled guns whose increased range enabled a bombardment of the Dockyard from afar. Since it is axiomatic that the way to neutralise coastal batteries was to land a force nearby and attack them from the rear, this also meant a closing of the ring by the line of detached forts of the North Eastern Defences of which Crownhill Fort is the key. In this respect Plymouth paralleled the pattern of defensive rings round Portsmouth and Chatham.

The fortification programme, set in motion during the 1850s, modified and formalised in the report of the Royal Commission on the Defences of the United Kingdom published in 1860, was a staggering sleight of hand on the part of the military in alliance with key political figures such as Lord Palmerston. This exploited popular fears during the three great invasion 'panics' of the 1840s and '50s and supported the hypothesis of a Royal Navy drawn out of position on distant seas leaving the English Channel coast open to a French invasion force. Combined with a leak in the *Morning Post*, these fears were used to stimulate public concern. They were also symptoms of the national self doubt that was beginning to trouble a country with the most powerful navy in the world and still commanding commercial and industrial predominance. The Parliamentary debates following the Royal Commission Report barely touched on the fundamental question of the necessity for such expenditure on defence when there was no hard evidence of hostile preparations on the part of France. Instead, there was niggling criticism of the proposals relating to Portsmouth which then expanded into wider controversy stimulated by the 'Blue Water School' who claimed that there was no necessity for fixed defences when the navy could deal with any invading force. In the meantime, with the sacrifice of the proposed forts in advance of Saltash on grounds of economy, the fortifications of Plymouth were confirmed.

In retrospect, the Royal Commission forts were regarded as a triumph for British military engineering by fellow European practitioners such as the Belgian engineer, Brialmont. While work on the 'Palmerston Forts' was under way, the hero of the defence of Sebastopol during the Crimean War, General Count Todleben, was allowed to inspect their progress and offer his comments. His visit in 1864 to Plymouth brought him to Tregantle where he approved the presence of the keep and the general design of the fort. In respect of the North Eastern line the General

was full of praise, 'and that the desired result of commanding the ground was obtained in a far higher degree than he should have thought possible from first glance at the undulating character of the country'. As a fortified place the General preferred Plymouth to Portsmouth, 'for the positions looked finer and the girdle of works more complete'. This comment was subsequently qualified by Burgoyne, the Inspector General of Fortifications, as meaning that, 'the remark was more in connection with general appearance than with the comparative strength of the two places'.

Plymouth's ring of Victorian forts have therefore to be seen as part of a massive programme of national defences not simply as a local phenomenon. They do, however, have their own distinctive characteristics when compared with those of Portsmouth and Chatham but in their essentials they share common design concepts and form part of the broad strategy of defending the main Royal Dockyards and the land bases of the navy. It is the topographical considerations of Plymouth that have led to the adoption of different solutions. That they now, for the first time, have their champion, and that their significance and interrelationships as well as the details of construction are identified in this book satisfies a long felt need.

Andrew Saunders
Chairman, Fortress Study Group

CONTENTS

LIST OF ILLUSTRATIONS

List of Maps

ACKNOWLEDGEMENTS

I doubt if this book would have been finished without the help and encouragement of Andrew Pye and I am most grateful for this. In particular he read and commented on the first draft.

Andrew Saunders was kind enough to write the Foreword, and also to read one of the early chapters which I felt was a little outside my field, a fact which was confirmed by his comments. Paddy Griffith kindly read the first draft of 'The battle at Bowden Battery' and commented. I hope he approves the final version.

One has help from time to time from the staff of many libraries and institutions, including the Public Record Office, the British Library, the MOD Whitehall Library, the Library of the Royal Artillery Historical Trust, the Royal Engineers Corps Library and the libraries of the Royal United Services Institute, and the National Army Museum. The latter and the National Portrait Gallery have allowed me to use copies of portraits of Palmerston and Burgoyne respectively and Timothy Crick in Canberra obtained the copy of the print of Jervois. We are fortunate to have such a helpful staff, now sadly reduced, at the West Devon Record Office and also at the Local Studies Library in Plymouth.

I am grateful to Exeter Archaeology, Cornwall Archaeological Unit and Frances Griffith of Devon County Council for permission to use their photographs, especially the aerial photos. Devon Archeological Society have also allowed me to use a plan of the Drake's Island magazines and Landmark Trust a panorama of Crownhill Fort. Andrew Perry came round with me in the early days and took a lot of photos which later came in very useful. He drew the drawbridge at Polhawn after helping in its reconstruction.

Ian V. Hogg sent me the notes he had made earlier on the Plymouth defences and allowed me to use his sketch of the Picklecombe shields. Roger Serpell's collection of early postcards has provided some interesting illustrations and Dennis W. Quarmby produced the photograph of Picklecombe just after it was completed. Members of the Fortress Study Group have provided information on particular points and so have the Palmerston Forts Society, particularly David Moore, through its magazine *Redan*.

One is lucky to have Austin C. Carpenter living close by as I can turn to him for advice on guns, though he cannot be held responsible for all I have said on the subject! Members of Fortress Study Group South West helped in the early stages, especially Tom Hitchins, Keith Rawlings, John Symons, Ian Angus and Reg Erskine. Many other people should be thanked: James Barber, Janet Cambridge, Michael Chapman, Arthur Clamp, Cynthia Gaskell-Brown, Crispin Gill, Molly Godfrey, John Goodwin, John Kinross, Norman Litchfield, Keith Ray, Chris Shorter, and Bob Thomas.

The occupiers of the forts have kindly allowed me to go round them from time to time. In particular, I have had a lot of help from John Wickstead at Polhawn, Paul Newton at Bowden, Alan Bax at Bovisand, Paul Roberts and the staff at Crownhill, as well as from Lt-Col. A. H. Clark, commanding Devon and Cornwall Training Areas, and successive MOD wardens at Tregantle. Sally Alexander has once again produced the maps and plans and I am most grateful for her skill and care.

Years ago, or so seems, Jilly Macdonald typed the numerous early drafts, for which I owe her many thanks. She must be as surprised as I am that it has finally come to fruition. Finally, I remember with much gratitude the patience and support of my wife Jane.

INTRODUCTION

In the Foreword to *Plymouth's Defences* I said there were two more books to be written on the subject. Since 1990 much has changed, and so have my plans. Early in the following year English Heritage agreed to sponsor a survey of the Plymouth defences and this was done over the next five years by Andrew Pye of Exeter Archaeology. The results were published in the gazetteer to the *The Historic Defences of Plymouth* in 1995, with chapters on conservation by Rob Iles of English Heritage and on the historical background by myself.

Meanwhile, Groundwork Plymouth Area have produced several leaflets on 'Walks about Forts' and are working on the development of the Rame Heritage Trail, whose first three-year phase has been completed. The Palmerston Forts Society have since covered a number of the forts on their Fortlog system. The proposed book on 'What to see' was not needed.

I started on the second book under the title 'The Last Hundred Years' of the defences - from 1844. But it soon became clear that the story of the Plymouth Palmerston forts formed a subject on its own and one which would dominate the book anyway. So I decided to write about this alone and try to present it in all its aspects.

Halfway through the work I came across the typescript of a lecture entitled 'Palmerston's Folly' by the late Stanley Goodman, for many years secretary of the Old Plymouth Society. He began by explaining that this was 'the name given to the imposing, expensive and quite useless ring of fourteen (land) forts built around Plymouth between the years 1862 and 1870'. This was so limited a view, based mainly it appeared on the information in Appendix B, that it was a challenge.

In writing an historical account of the background to the 'Palmerston Forts', I have tried to make it in the first place readable to those interested in Plymouth's history, and added information on the fortification of the period and on the individual forts at Appendices C and D. I have kept the references in the text to a minimum and limited the Bibliography to books special to the subject and to the main documentary sources. Secondly, I have tried to show the place of the Plymouth forts in the development of the fortification of the period. Finally, in order to bring the subject to a point I have suggested in Chapter 8 how the defences might have reacted to the type of attack for which they were prepared.

Within its period the book is complementary to *The Historic Defences of Plymouth* which contains basic information about individual forts. In going beyond this base I have had to venture into specialist fields. If I am proved wrong in detail I hope that members of Fortress Study Group will correct me with their customary courtesy.

Incidentally, I am unrepentant in my use of Imperial measure when referring to fortifications or gunnery. It was used at the time and to most of my readers an 8-inch cannon, a 2 foot embrasure or a 30 foot ditch convey more than the metric equivalent.

There is much more work still to be done on the papers of the Defence and Fortification Committees and on the political background to the development of the whole programme of fortification over fifteen years. I have been primarily concerned with the end product at Plymouth alone, so have referred mainly to official reports and memoranda. This book is in many ways only a start on the subject and I hope someone else will complete the work.

During the time I have been writing - there was a gap of eighteen months from January 1995 - other people have been working on parallel subjects. John Kinross completed his MA dissertation on 'The Palmerston Forts in the South West - why were they built?' in 1994 and I have recently read this. He covers in particular the debates in Parliament on the report of the Royal Commission and the eventual financial position in greater detail than I have done, and I recommend his paper (in the History Department, Exeter University). In Canberra, Timothy Crick has been working on 'Ramparts of Empire, the life and times of Sir William Jervois' which is now under consideration for publication. Andrew Pye's forthcoming paper on 'The Inner Defences of Devonport Dockyard'* is the first study of this involved subject so I have said little about Devonport Lines in this book.

In 1990 I drew attention to the lack of a policy of conservation for the Plymouth defences as a whole. Though a policy has since been outlined by Rob Iles of English Heritage there is little evidence of it being imple-mented in detail by Plymouth City Council. Both Caradon and South Hams District Councils have shown their aware-ness of the need for conservation of their fortifications but there is not much to show for it so far.

Plymouth has however benefited from the appointment five years ago of a City Archaeologist. As a result the work initiated by the Plymouth Development Corporation at Mount Batten and Mount Wise has included the recording and where possible the conservation of the defences on these sites, and later will include their interpretation. To complete the picture, interpretation should also be provid-ed at Western King in the middle of the waterfront.

Much work remains to be done on the conservation of the Palmerston forts generally and on the restoration of gateways in particular. The Ministry of Defence have done a lot to clear and secure Tregantle, especially the keep, and there are plans to re-asphalt and then re-decorate the latter. Many visitors now come each year to the Heritage Weekends held there in September. No development appears to have been carried out on Drake's Island since its change of ownership three years ago. But provisional plans have recently been shown and described in the local press, involving a centre for conferences and functions with interpretation displays in the main magazine and in the casemates covering periods in the Island's history.

On this rather more optimistic note about the future of Plymouth's defences it would be only right to mention the continuing work done by Landmark Trust at Crownhill Fort and a unique development which should be complet-ed there by the time this work is published.

---

* 'The Inner Defences of Devonport Dockyard'. Andrew Pye in Ray, K. (Ed) 1997 *Archaeological Investigation and Research in Plymouth. Vol. II*: 1997. *Plymouth Archaeological Occasional Publications No.4.*

1
THE EARLIER DEFENCES

To plunge into the story of the remarkable develop-ments in Plymouth's defences from 1844 onwards without some account of their growth over the preceding 400 years would be confusing. This growth was mainly a reaction to recurring threats of invasion, and as defences are expensive to build and costly to maintain these sudden periods of activity were followed by years of neglect in peacetime.

The natural harbour in Sutton Pool was adequate for the handful of fishing boats that sheltered there in early Norman times, when, on the top of the tide, merchant vessels could reach Plympton with its important Priory and Castle. As the Plym estuary silted up ships began to anchor in Plym Mouth, which we now know as the Cattewater. Increasingly Plymouth became a centre for trade with the King's possessions in France, which by the second half of the twelfth century extended from Normandy down to the Pyrenees.

In the fourteenth century Plymouth was used for the first time as a base for the King's expeditions to his French possessions which were by then limited to south-western France. As a result of its growing importance the town suffered a series of raids from northern France, starting in 1338. The most destructive of these was in 1403 when much of the town north of Sutton Pool was burnt. This expedition landed at Cattedown because by then there was a chain across the entrance to Sutton Harbour which was

Plate 1: *The Artillery Tower, Firestone Bay.* (ANDREW PERRY)

raised whenever the alarm was given. A further raid by the Spanish in 1405 was driven off by cannon fire, probably from cannon mounted temporarily on the east end of the Hoe. To strengthen the defence of the harbour further, a substantial four-towered castle was completed in about 1400 on the lower slopes of Lambhay Hill, known as the Castle Quadrate (Map I).

In about 1490 the first limestone blockhouse, or Artillery Tower as it is called now (Plate 1), was built in the middle of Firestone Bay, the best landing beach on the north shore of the Sound and one which leads directly to the village of Stonehouse, then defended by a wall.

Plate 2: *Devil's Point Blockhouse.* (AUTHOR)

With Henry VIII increasingly at odds with the rest of Europe in the 1530s, the Corporation and some leading citizens bought guns and built bulwarks (earthworks) on the Hoe and raised stockades along the shore. By 1540 blockhouses had also been built at Fishers Nose, either side of Millbay, and at Devil's Point (Plate 2). This local initiative probably explains why when Henry VIII in 1539 began to build a chain of castles from Deal to Falmouth he did not build one at Plymouth.

A new war against the French in 1548-49 resulted in pressure from the Privy Council to improve its defences further and to build a small fort on Drake's Island. Once cannon had been developed with a range of over 1000 yards the capture of the Island would have closed the port. From this time onwards the Island was vital to the defence of Plymouth, and later of the Dockyard, and whenever the defences of Plymouth were improved so were those of Drake's Island.

From 1585 onwards, it became clear that a Spanish invasion was likely and that Plymouth could be one of its targets, so the Crown began to take a hand in the coast defences. More bulwarks were built on the Hoe in 1585 and in the following year instructions were issued to Lords Lieutenant giving the defensive measures to be taken in the maritime counties. In 1587 Sir Richard Grenville was instructed to survey the defences of the South West The positions of 29 heavy guns, and their arcs of fire, are shown on a map[1] of the time, as are the places where a total of nineteen hundred soldiers of the militia were to be stationed.

Two years after the Armada, in 1590, the Corporation of Plymouth strongly supported by its MP, Sir Francis Drake, petitioned the Queen to build a fort on the Hoe and to surround the town with a wall. When the Queen's engineer, Robert Adams surveyed the town two years later he reported that it would be 'a hard matter without millions to environ it with a royal strength'.[2] As a result, although a fort (Plate 3) on the east end of the Hoe was

Plate 3: *Plymouth Fort, a sketch.* (WEST DEVON RECORD OFFICE)

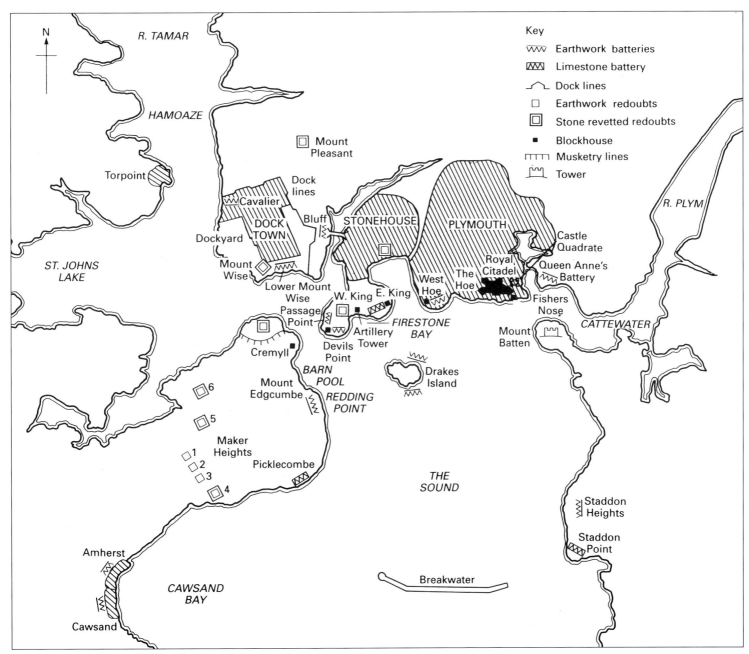

N

R. TAMAR

HAMOAZE

Torpoint

ST. JOHNS
LAKE

Mount
Pleasant

Dock
lines

Cavalier

DOCK
TOWN

Bluff

Dockyard

Mount
Wise

Lower Mount
Wise

Passage
Point

Cremyll

Mount
Edgcumbe

6

5

1

2

3

4

Maker
Heights

Picklecombe

Amherst

Cawsand

CAWSAND
BAY

STONEHOUSE

W. King E. King

Devils
Point

Artillery
Tower

BARN
POOL

REDDING
POINT

West
Hoe

Drakes
Island

THE
SOUND

Breakwater

PLYMOUTH

FIRESTONE
BAY

The
Hoe

Royal
Citadel

Castle
Quadrate

Queen Anne's
Battery

Fishers
Nose

Mount
Batten

CATTEWATER

R. PLYM

Staddon
Heights

Staddon
Point

Key

ᗺᗺᗺ Earthwork batteries

ᗺᗺᗺ Limestone battery

⌐⌐ Dock lines

☐ Earthwork redoubts

▣ Stone revetted redoubts

■ Blockhouse

ᒍᒍᒍ Musketry lines

⛫ Tower

Map I: *Plymouth's early fortifications up to 1850.*

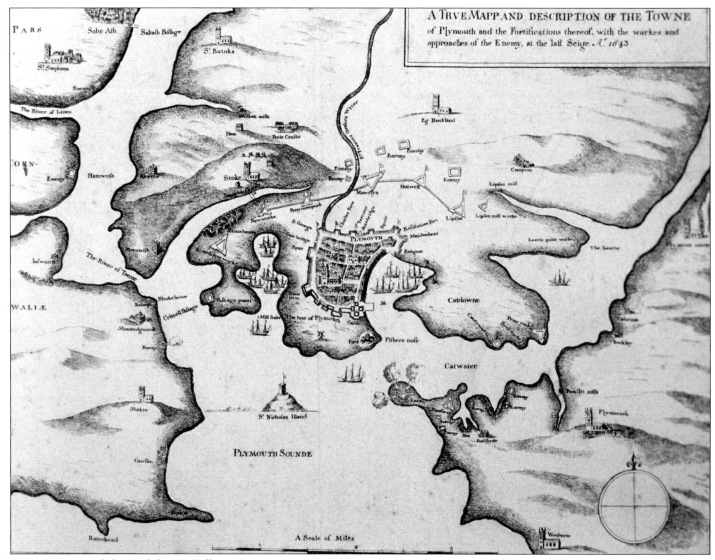

Plate 4: *Siege map of Plymouth by W. Hollar, 1643.*

completed by 1595 nothing more was heard of the town wall. From this time onwards the entrance to the Cattewater was guarded principally by the guns on the shore below the fort itself - referred to as the Lower Fort.

Since the Spanish were known to be still planning an invasion, the defences of the Sound were manned from time to time when the alarm was raised, and these included defences on the Cornish side of the Sound.

16

In 1642 Plymouth declared for Parliament when most of the West Country was for the King. In addition to taking over command of the Fort and Drake's Island the Corporation made strenuous efforts to put the town into a state of defence from July 1643, and it was eventually surrounded by a ditch and stone-revetted rampart up to 18 feet high with numerous bastions or spurs from which guns could cover the ditch.

A line of triangular redoubts, linked eventually by a ditch, were built along the ridge which runs through North Hill and dominates the town. The redoubts ran from Lipson through Holiwell, Mawdlyn and Pennycomequick to Newworke, overlooking Millbridge. In addition, isolated redoubts covered likely landing places from Cattedown, through Prince Rock and Laira and round to Stonehouse and Passage Point to the south west (Plate 4).

At some time in the following years the round gun tower was built at Mount Batten (Plate 5). The importance of this position had been emphasised during the siege when the outlying redoubt at Stamford had been taken by the

Plate 5: *Mount Batten Tower.* (EXETER ARCHAEOLOGY ©)

Royalists and held for several months, causing the shipping in the Cattewater to take refuge in Millbay. A map of 1646 suggests that the tower, named after the commander of the Commonwealth naval forces during the siege, was built immediately after the end of the Civil War.

The last commander of the Royalist forces besieging Plymouth was the young Prince Charles, and soon after his restoration to the throne in 1660 as Charles II he ordered a survey of the defences of the South West. He began to make plans for a fortress on the Hoe at Plymouth, which would not only secure the anchorage in the Cattewater against the Dutch, but would protect the Dockyard which he planned, at that time, to build at Hooe Lake. It would also ensure the loyalty of the town.

The Royal Citadel was begun in February 1665, a month before the beginning of the Second Dutch War, and its building was supervised by a special commission, appointed by the King, under John Grenville, Earl of Bath, who was governor of Plymouth and Lord Lieutenant of Cornwall. Because of the likelihood of a raid by the Dutch, a threat which materialised in 1667, the new Citadel was temporarily joined to the old fort whose ramparts on the south side were only realigned later. The new fortress was sufficiently impressive to deter the Dutch fleet from attacking when it anchored in the Sound in July 1667.

Charles II inspected his Royal Citadel for the first time in 1671, approving what had been done and ordering the building of a New Harbour where the Royal Plymouth Corinthian Yacht Club now stands. The Citadel was eventually completed and fully armed with 153 guns by the year 1680. It is the most impressive seventeenth century fortification in the country (Plate 6).

The proposed Royal Dockyard which the Citadel was to protect was not begun until 1690, in the reign of William and Mary, when work started at a new site at Point Froward

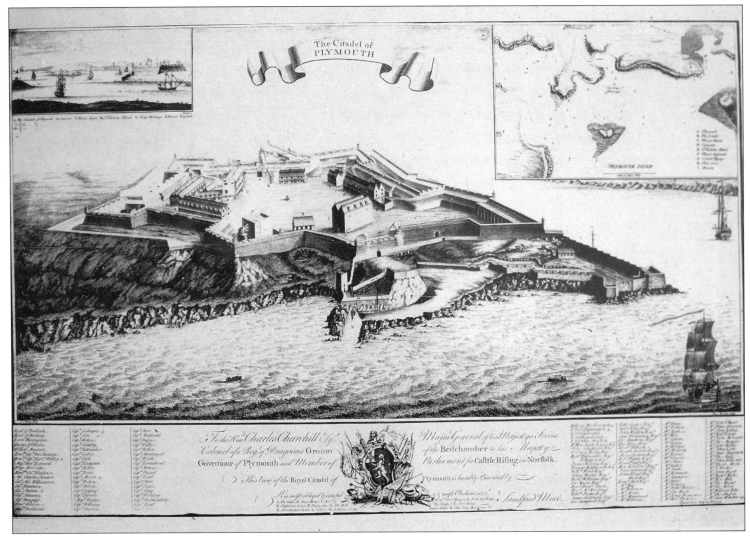

Plate 6: 'The Citadel of Plymouth', 1737, an engraving by Sandford Mace.

on the Hamoaze. As the channel to the Dockyard ran between Drake's Island and the Hoe the importance of the Island and the Citadel for its defence was clear. In 1700 plans were made for further batteries to be built to cover the channel closer to the Dockyard. A large battery was built near Redding Point below Mount Edgcumbe, an additional one on Drake's Island and another on Western King, immediately east of Devil's Point. At this time there was a

18

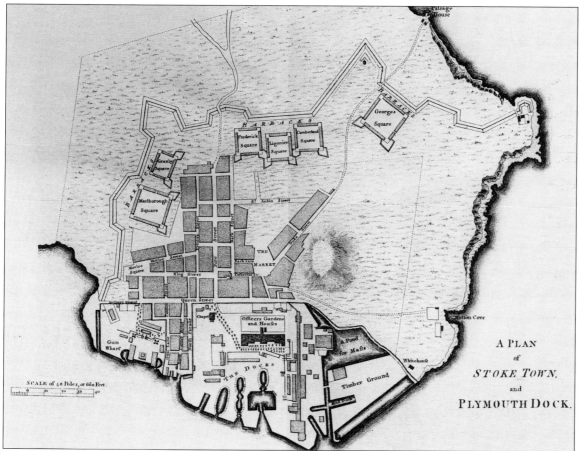

permanent battery at Cawsand and the gun position at Queen Anne's Battery, built during the emergency in 1667, was stone-revetted and permanently armed.

After the end of the War of Austrian Succession in 1748 it became clear that there would be a further conflict with France which had by then become our rival overseas in trade and colonisation, as the Dutch had been a century before.

The energetic governor of the Royal Citadel, Sir John Ligonier, modernised and extended its defences and in particular built three new batteries in the Lower Fort, facing west so as to take enemy men-of-war in the stern as they passed between West Hoe and Drake's Island.

In the 1750s before, and at the beginning of, the Seven Year's War the battery at Redding Point was strengthened and a new one built at Kingsand (Amherst). A year after the outbreak of war work began on a rampart and ditch around the growing Dockyard, enclosing the six new barrack squares which were being built for the garrison. But Dock Lines, as they were called, were neither well designed nor substantial enough to withstand a siege at this stage (Plate 7).

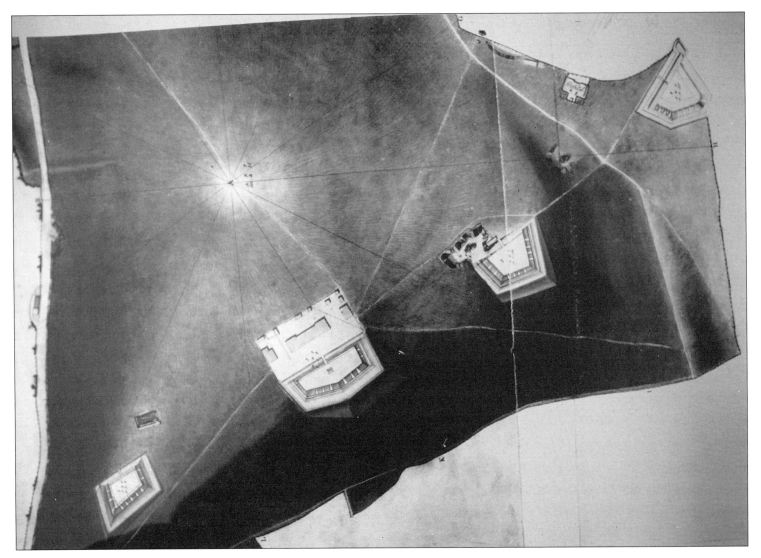

Plate 8: *Maker Redoubts, 1808.* (PRO/WO 78/396 MR 1209)

The outbreak of the War of American Independence in 1775 gave the French an opportunity to develop their plans for an invasion of England. This they had been preparing since the end of the Seven Years War, as most of our army and navy became involved in the conflict in America. The combined Franco-Spanish fleet was to clear the Channel and convoy an army which had been collected in the Low Countries to the Sussex coast. It was also intended that Plymouth and its Dockyard should be put out of action if possible on the way.

Urgent work began at Plymouth in 1778 on a plan to strengthen the defences and create a string of earthwork redoubts, several of which were improved after the end of the war and became permanent defences. On the other hand several of the smaller redoubts and batteries shown on the original plan[3] by Lt-Col Dixon, Chief Engineer Western Division, in January 1780, do not appear to have been completed.

Work had already begun in 1778 on redoubts at Mount Wise and Western King. In the following year three earthwork batteries to complete the defence of Cawsand Bay were built at Minadew Brake, Cawsand Redoubt and Sandway, and a powerful new battery of 32-pounders was built on Drake's Island facing south. Five earthwork redoubts were also thrown up in a line along Maker Heights (Plate 8), facing Cawsand, by the regiments of Foot and of Militia which were in camp there. To support these troops a redoubt and a musketry position were built covering the landing place at Cremyll from which they would have to withdraw to the Dockyard if they were driven off the Heights.

To protect the Dockyard further a battery was built at Lower Mount Wise and one at Bluff Battery to cover the entrance from Stonehouse. A new battery at Passage Point above Devil's Point was completed and earthwork batteries built at Eastern King and West Hoe. One of two proposed redoubts on Stonehouse was finished. Further out an important redoubt on Mount Pleasant which overlooks the Dockyard was begun, and this was to be supported by two smaller redoubts to the south and west which do not seem to have been completed. On the westernmost bastion of the north section of the Lines, Cavalier Battery was built to cover the New Gun Wharf below. There is no sign that the

proposed redoubt on Windmill Hill within the Dockyard was completed, or the ones at Mount Batten and Torpoint. These defences were sufficient to deter the Franco-Spanish fleet, already weakened by ten weeks at sea and the resulting sickness and shortage of supplies, from attacking when it did anchor in Cawsand Bay in August 1779.

In 1782 a battery was built on Staddon Heights for the first time, facing over the sound. In the years after the end of the war in 1783, the redoubts at Mount Pleasant, Western King, Mount Wise and Cawsand were revetted with brick or stone. No.4 Redoubt on Maker Heights overlooking the sea was strengthened and No.5 Redoubt, similar in strength to No.4 and covering the road from Millbrook to Cremyll, was completed. A later proposal by the Duke of Richmond, then Master-General of the Ordnance, to build two large forts, one on Maker Heights and one near Antony, was defeated in Parliament by the casting vote of the Speaker in 1786.

During the French Revolutionary Wars beginning in 1793, and the later wars against Napoleon I ending in 1815, the defences of Plymouth were progressively improved in detail. Larger guns were mounted in the coast batteries, and shot furnaces for heating red hot shot were added at the Citadel, and at the batteries covering the channel to the Dockyard. Mortars were mounted at the Citadel and Mount Wise. A sixth redoubt on Maker Heights was built at Empacombe overlooking St John's Lake and a barracks built for the whole garrison on the Heights. The battery on top of Drake's Island was extended and armed with 32-pounders, and the battery on the promontory above Devil's Point, known as Passage Point was rearmed and known as 3-Gun Battery.

On either side of Mount Wise redoubt five earthwork gun batteries were built, and a mortar battery, to be manned by sailors from the Naval Barracks behind it. In

1804 the two small redoubts (the second completed in 1784) on Stonehouse Hill were incorporated into a strong limestone redoubt and in 1810 work began to improve Dock Lines. This work was finally abandoned in 1816 after the north and west sections of the Lines had been rebuilt, to a point north of George's Bastion, with a deeper ditch and with higher stone-revetted ramparts.

The defeat of Napoleon in 1815 removed the threat of invasion. Guns were left in the coast batteries and in the principal redoubts but many of the others were disarmed. Care of the guns in the Plymouth defences was in the hands of two master gunners and a dozen invalid gunners, with such help as could be obtained from the artillery company quartered within Dock Lines. After a number of years the state of the guns, more particularly of the wooden carriages, can be imagined.

In 1830 a sudden revolution in France resulted in the overthrow of the Bourbon Monarchy for the second time and its replacement by the 'Citizen King' Louis Phillipe.

But it was not until 1844 that politicians in this country became concerned again about a possible threat from France. In that year the first of a series of invasion scares occurred, resulting in a review of the state of Plymouth's coast defences.

References

[1] The Defence of Plymouth Sound proposed by Sir Richard Grenvyle, 1587. (PRO.MPF6).
[2] *History of the King's Works* Vol. IV Part II p. 486
[3] Report and map of the existing and proposed defences of Plymouth by Lt-Col. Matthew Dixon, January 1780. (BL Kings Top XI 79)

Note: For details and plans of individual sites referred to in this chapter see *The Historical Defences of Plymouth*, Chapter 3 – Gazetteer.

2
STATE OF THE ART OF FORTIFICATION, GUNNERY AND COAST DEFENCE

From 1847 onwards, over some thirty years, the largest programme of fortification against both sea and land attack in the history of Britain was completed. Unlike the continental countries, we had not endured land warfare in this country, other than the rebellions of 1715 and 1745, since the Civil War. Cities and towns had not been fortified against attack but our principal naval ports had earlier been well defended against both sea and land attack. However at Plymouth the modernisation of Dock Lines was still uncompleted.

Britain had built no major fortifications since 1815 and her experience of field defences was limited to the Peninsular War and the campaigns in North America. So one needs to know something of the history and development of fortification in Europe, and later in the United States, to appreciate the design of the defences created in Plymouth in the mid-nineteenth century.

The introduction of gunpowder to warfare in the late fourteenth century resulted in the introduction of gunports in fortifications. By the mid-fifteenth century the French had shown in the latter stages of the Hundred Years War that large calibre siege guns, such as the early bombards, could demolish the high but relatively thin walls of the castles held by the English. Such castles had for centuries been the principal form of static defence. Later, in 1494, Charles VIII proved in Northern Italy that with a well-organised siege train it was possible to destroy

any castle that opposed him. In future walls would have to be backed by earth ramparts to absorb the heavy shot from the besiegers. To keep the earthworks stable, walls tended to be lower and therefore easier to scale. So the protection of deep ditches or moats became even more important and the walls (scarps) must be swept by gunfire to prevent them being carried by escalade.

Experiments in new forms of fortification, notably gun-towers, appeared at Berwick, and in Scotland as far north as Dunbar at the end of the fifteenth century. But the first considered reaction in this country to the threat of both land and sea attack by cannon was in the time of Henry VIII who as a result of his wars on the continent had learnt something of the new ideas on fortification. When invasion threatened in 1539-40 he built a chain of castles along the South coast from Deal in Kent to Pendennis in Cornwall. These castles had a strong central tower either surrounded by a low curtain on which the guns were emplaced, as at Pendennis, or from which half round bastions, like squat towers, radiated as at St Mawes.

Their main object was still coast defence and their principal armament was the culverin with its 18-pound shot and the demi-cannon (32-pdr). These cannon were at that time mounted on a variety of carriages: some were still on the earliest bedstocks, others on two-wheeled carriages with a wooden trail, or on the truck carriages which became standard later. They could fire their cast iron shot up to about 2000 yards. As the ships which were likely to attack them mounted guns that were no heavier than culverins the defenders could expect to drive off an attacker using fewer but heavier guns on a stable platform.

During the early sixteenth century the Italians developed the angle bastion system which in various forms was the basis of fortification against artillery for nearly 300 years. The bastion trace (design) provided around the town or strongpoint a continuous rampart and ditch which was defended in such a way that throughout its length both the face of the ramparts and the ditch itself could be swept by the close range fire of cannon. This was achieved by a series of four-sided projections from the main line of the rampart - bastions - which were a development from the earlier gun tower. The two sides forming the point or salient were called faces and fired directly on an approaching enemy. It became the practice during the sixteenth and early seventeenth centuries to set the inner sides, or flanks, of the bastion at right angles to the curtain wall which joined them to the next bastion, and they were armed with guns which could fire grape and cannister shot not only along the curtain wall and ditch but across the face of the next bastion.

An early example of the bastion system was Plymouth Fort, completed in 1595, but the principle can be seen in its developed form in the two western bastions of the Citadel (Plate 9). The bastion trace, with all its later elaborations in and beyond the ditch to give defence in greater depth, was in origin a geometrical one though it could be adapted to some extent to the ground on which it stood. As it became increasing complex so it became more expensive and required an ever larger garrison.

It was eventually proved that a continuous line of defense was not essential and so the line of detached redoubts was adopted in places in the eighteenth century.

By the first half of the nineteenth century large permanent detached works were used to defend even the most important sites. These works were irregular in shape (polygonal) and adapted to the ground on which they stood and which they covered by fire. New methods were being used to cover the ditch with fire.

Early in the Civil War, in 1643, Plymouth was encircled with a revetted (stone-faced) rampart and ditch with spurs which acted as primitive bastions (see Plate 4). As these ramparts were only 15–18 feet high and the ditch about 6 feet deep it was fortunate that this part of the defences was never seriously attacked. The main fighting took place around the triangular earthwork redoubts, joined by a ditch, which lined the ridge of North Hill. These were armed with guns on field carriages (two large wheels and a wooden trail) which could be towed into position wherever they were required. On occasions during the siege the Royalists overran one or other of the redoubts or penetrated between them. Then the townspeople in their companies sallied forth and drove the Royalists back. Counter attack by reserves held behind the line of fortifications was an essential part also of the tactics associated with the later Palmerston forts.

The defences of the Royal Citadel, owing partly to the uneven site, are not as large or as elaborate as many that were built in Western Europe in the next thirty years. One limitation of the bastion system was that in its original form it was a regular one which made it less adaptable to the needs of the defence of a particular site. Towards the end of the eighteenth century alternative systems began to be developed, several of them by Frenchmen. Montalembert developed the idea of 'perpendicular fortification' in which gunfire could be concentrated where it was needed by building huge towers in which many guns mounted on two or three levels fired from within case-

Plate 9: *The western bastions of the Royal Citadel, Plymouth.* (AUTHOR)

Plate 10a and b: *Caponiers at Crownhill Fort.* (AUTHOR)

mates (bomb-proof vaulted chambers with an embrasure for the gun). Circular or crescent-shaped batteries on this principle were adapted for coast defence to counter the broadsides of 50–60 guns which were mounted by men-of-war by the end of the Napoleonic Wars.

In applying his theories to land defences, Montalembert maintained that the curtain walls between the bastions were so vulnerable as to be useless when attacked by direct gunfire. He recommended that defensive fire should be concentrated from strong towers within a *tenaille* trace based on a series of redans joined a right angles so as to produce a saw-toothed front of defence. He developed caponiers (Plate 10a and b) - galleries for rifles and later guns - which jutted out into a ditch so deep that the caponiers themselves were covered from the direct fire of an attacker. A caponier appears for the first time at Plymouth in a plan drawn in 1781 entitled 'a casemated gallery with loopholes' but whether it was built and in which redoubt is not known. Elaborate caponiers were built at Fort Monckton, west of Gosport, in the mid-1780s in what was otherwise a conventional bastion trace.

During the Napoleonic Wars the defences of Portsmouth, Dover and Chatham were strengthened to meet the threat of invasion. At Dover the defences of the Castle and of the Western Heights were extensively modernised by the addition of 'bastions' which were in fact ditched irregular earthworks pushed out in front of the main line of defence and relying on caponiers to cover the ditch around them. At Portsmouth, Fort Cumberland was re-built, still on the bastioned principle but including guns on the flanks of the bastions, in casemates as well as on the ramparts, covering a wide and relatively shallow ditch.

Andrew Saunders has pointed out the importance of Forts Monckton and Cumberland in the modification of the earlier bastion system and in developments based on Montalembert's ideas.

'The move towards separating offensive fire from defensive, which implied the conscious identification of ditch defences, was the main characteristic of both forts; also, the adoption of bombproof casemates for guns as well as for barrack purposes. The outworks were... to protect the rampart scarp from direct fire'.[1]

By the time the principal land forts of the Plymouth defences of the 1860s were built the value of towers and even keeps had been questioned in land defences. However powerful the fire of their guns in defence, towers and keeps could in turn be the target for deliberate and concentrated fire from an attacker using the more powerful guns then being developed. Partly for this reason and also because of the additional expense, only one Plymouth fort had an independent keep. Two of the works (Ernesettle and Staddon) do incorporate the idea of another Frenchman, Carnot, who advocated the use of batteries of mortars protected from above by vaulted casemates.

Artillery towers with very thick walls of brick continued to be used in coast defences - especially likely landing beaches where they were not liable to such accurate fire - well into the nineteenth century and three gun towers were completed at Pembroke Dock as late as 1851. At this time some continental coast defence systems featured huge round gun towers mounting up to three tiers of guns firing both from casemates and from the roof. The nearest to this type of design in Plymouth was Breakwater Fort, originally planned in 1860 to be built of stone entirely, with 33 guns in two tiers and seven guns on top. In their final form Breakwater Fort and similar sea forts built at Spithead, all with a single tier of guns, represent the ultimate development of the large round gun tower in this country, eventually rendered obsolete by the power of modern guns which made it essential to disperse and conceal coast batteries. But in the 1860s the need to meet ships attacking up a channel with heavy fire from muzzle-loading guns which were slow to load and traverse resulted in the defence of our naval bases being by a series of casemated batteries each laid out in a wide arc. These had a single tier of guns except for the most important batteries at Picklecombe and Garrison Point, Sheerness, with two tiers.

The earthwork redoubts thrown up in 1779 at Plymouth were four-sided and because on Maker Heights it was necessary to adapt them to the uneven ground they were covering, they were irregular in shape (see Plate 8). Such redoubts were developed much further in the Peninsular campaign in the Lines of Torres Vedras in 1810. There the British built a series of irregular many-sided (polygonal) redoubts adapted to the hills on which they stood, and unconnected with each other by any general rampart or ditch. This system proved effective in deterring the French who were weakened by lack of supplies. Since British engineers had given up using a continuous bastion trace, it was natural that the irregular polygonal trace should be used again in the hilly and often steep countryside around Plymouth when the land forts and batteries were built in the 1860s.

During the first half of the nineteenth century a number of elaborate systems of fortification were developed in Germany, Austria and Poland based on experience during the Napoleonic Wars. In most of these systems the guns were mounted inside casemates to protect them from the latest developments in artillery: the plunging fire of mortars and howitzers and shrapnel from bursting shells. The disadvantage of casemates was the confined space in which the gunners had to work, the effect of blast, the dense acrid smoke from the black powder then used and the limited field of fire. Where guns were sited for coast defence close to the shore and to the channel along which attacking ships would pass, casemates had fewer disadvantages and gave additional protection from sharp shooters in the rigging of the ships and from case shot. But to bring a heavy fire on ships either moored off, or moving across the face of, the battery required a large number of guns.

The coast fortifications built in the 1860s were designed to prevent a hostile fleet bombarding the Dockyards. Since it had been shown over the years that such batteries were more likely to be taken from the rear than from the sea, they required defended gorges. The threat to the land defences of Plymouth was of a strong raid intended to put the Dockyard out of action and did not include the possibility of deliberate and prolonged siege by a well equipped army on a continental scale. The principle was adopted of a general line of fortification, using the lie of the ground, and consisting of forts and batteries with from four to seven sides supporting one another by fire, with the principal forts capable of sustained all-round defence. These forts were similar to contemporary continental design and were even by some considered superior.

The forts were surrounded by deep and relatively narrow ditches covered by the fire of both guns and rifles from caponiers. The latter were built out into the ditch and covered one or more sections of it with fire. But their effectiveness became limited if the scarp wall was brought down by bombardment, and the rubble masked the ditch beyond the fall from their fire.

Sometimes parts of the ditch were covered by fire from musketry galleries in the counterscarp and sometimes the 'caponiers' were no more than musketry galleries themselves - without guns.

At Tregantle, designed in the late 1850s, there is a self-defensible keep, surrounded by a ditch with a counterscarp gallery all round it. This was designed to be a 'keep of last resort' in which a garrison could hold out for several hours after the fort itself was taken and until relief came. This principle had been abandoned at Plymouth by the time the later major forts, such as Crownhill, came to be built, partly due to the need to economise since a number of keeps were built at Portsmouth.

Incorporated in the Plymouth forts was the latest experience gained from two overseas wars in the 1850s and early 1860s. During the Crimean war, 1854-56, the stubborn defence of Sebastopol by General Todleben showed the effectiveness of earthwork defences, often hurriedly improvised, manned by determined and well-led regular troops. Earlier, in 1832, the siege of Antwerp which had been reduced to rubble by fire of mortars and howitzers showed the effectiveness of these weapons and this was proved again at Sebastopol. Experience in the American Civil War, 1861-65, where the new rifled guns with their greater range, accuracy and penetrating power were used for the first time, emphasised the effectiveness of 'bombproofing' by covering the gun casemates and magazines with six foot or more of earth and rubble. It was also proved again that fewer guns separated by earth traverses (banks) were in the end more effective than many more guns close together on an open rampart.

Although the theory of fortification had continued to develop, guns which in the 1840s were the main defensive weapon, were the same in principle, though much larger, than those which had been used in Henry VIII's time. Admittedly cast iron, smooth-bore, muzzle-loading cannon had become more reliable and accurate. By 1815 the main armament on Drake's Island was the 32-pounder and the Citadel mounted some of the largest cannon of those days - 42-pounders - facing over the Sound. These cannon normally fired solid cast iron balls whose weight gave the gun its classification. The muzzle velocity was relatively high but owing to the poor aerodynamic shape and limited accuracy of a cannonball the effective range of the larger cannon was little more than 2000 yards at 5 degrees elevation and the extreme range in practice was just over 3000 yards.

Plate 11: *18-pdr cannon on a garrison standing carriage at the Royal Citadel, Plymouth.* (AUTHOR)

Plate 12: *24-pdr cannon on a traversing siege carriage at the Royal Citadel, Plymouth.* (AUTHOR)

The opening range of engagement by the defenders was normally 500–1000 yards both against land targets and against ships, though for different reasons. In forts, though the guns were capable of engaging fixed targets in a deliberate siege, in the event of an attack in the open there was the problem of hitting a relatively small advancing body of troops with a cannon whose garrison carriage had four cast iron truck wheels and which had to be traversed and elevated with the help of handspikes (levers) (Plate 11). Aiming was normally by means of graduations from 0–3 degrees, marked on the breech ring, which enabled the gun captain to aim at the target with the help of a notch on the muzzle. These can be seen on the guns facing over the Hoe on the ramparts of the Royal Citadel. Later, guns there were fitted with tangent sights by which the range was set on a vertical scale mounted on top of the breech.

Against ships, a much larger target, the range was kept relatively short because of the need to produce the maximum hitting power from the shot. Guns used for coast

defence were often faced by a target which could move once it had fired a broadside at the defences and it was not until the development of the traversing garrison carriage (Plate 12) in the late eighteenth century that coast guns were able to engage a moving target relatively effectively.

There had been developments over the years in the type of shot which cannon fired. Even the single cast iron shot was made more effective against wooden ships by heating it red hot in one of the shot furnaces which were built at Plymouth and elsewhere during the Napoleonic Wars. On land extensive use was made of grape (8-10 smaller balls in a cluster) and short range cannister shot, producing a hail of bullets, against attacking troops as they approached. These types of shot were also used by cannon in the flanks of bastions to sweep the ditch, the curtain wall and the face of the opposite bastion when they were attacked by infantry.

There were two developments in gunnery in the preceding years which were to have an influence on the coast and land fortifications of the 1860s. Cannon fire was in effect horizontal fire; effective against vertical targets such as walls and ramparts but not against whatever was behind them. From about 1720 onwards howitzers designed to fire shells - hollow balls filled with explosive and with a primitive fuze - were developed. They used a smaller charge so as not to fracture the ball on firing so they were shorter and lighter in the barrel than the normal cannon.

The development of progressively more reliable fuzes also made mortars more effective and they were used in large numbers at the siege of Sebastopol. Mortars are mounted at a fixed elavation of 45 degrees and the range is varied by the amount of powder in the charge, making them relatively inaccurate in range and therefore only really effective against a large target. On the other hand the bomb descends almost vertically and can penetrate the target before exploding.

During the Napoleonic Wars 10-inch and 13-inch mortars were sited at Mount Wise and on Drake's Island, and the Citadel had both mortars and the earliest howitzers in its armament (Plate 13).

Plate 13: *10-in mortar at the Royal Citadel, Plymouth.* (AUTHOR)

In the Crimean War, shells were extensively used by both field and siege guns, using the improved Boxer fuze. Sea service mortars, normally 13-inch, were fitted in specially designed ships for the bombardment of harbours and coast defences. In a word, the coast and land defences of the 1860s had to be prepared for bombardment not only by horizontal fire but also by plunging fire, both types using explosive shells.

These developments were minor compared with the effect on the design of both coast and land forts of the development from 1858 onwards of new generations of rifled guns, first breech-loading and then muzzle-loading. The former trebled the range of existing guns and gave improved accuracy, and greater explosive and penetrating power, whilst the latter resulted in guns of much larger calibre. These will be discussed in detail in the following chapters.

'Coast defence, as a distinct branch of fortification engineering, received little recognition prior to the nineteenth century'.[2] Yet coast defence has always been important to England with its many ports and estuaries and its proximity to France. That importance has varied in the eyes of successive governments according to their confidence in the ability of the Royal Navy to dominate the seas around Britain at any particular time. Loss of command of the Channel resulted in threats to Plymouth in 1667 and 1690, and a well-justified panic in the town in August 1779 when a Franco-Spanish fleet anchored in Cawsand Bay. On each of these occasions temporary batteries were hurriedly thrown up and naval guns moved into position to supplement the permanent batteries. These batteries consisted of a line of guns firing either through stone-revetted embrasures in earth parapets or, as can still be seen at Lower

Plate 14: *9-pdr battery sited en barbette, Lower Mount Wise.* (AUTHOR)

Mount Wise, over a low parapet (*en barbette*) (Plate 14). It was not until the late 1840s that guns in the coast defence role were mounted in casemates at Plymouth.

At the start of every major war with France during the eighteenth century attention turned again to the coast batteries. The wooden carriages of their guns had mostly stood exposed to wind, rain and sea spray since the last emergency and often had to be hurriedly repaired or renewed. This problem was due not so much to any inefficiency on the part of the Master Gunners who looked after them as to the extreme parsimony of the Board of Ordnance who provided the money and stores.

The job of a Master Gunner was 'to see that the Ordnance, Carriages, Ammunition and Stores are preserved in good order and report defects: to keep the batteries clean, to fire salutes where ordered, and hoist the flag: also to render quarterly and annual accounts of the Ordnance and Stores in their charge to the Principal Storekeepers Office at the Tower'.[3]

The manning of coast guns was considered to be something which was quickly learned. It was also considered that it could be done by invalid soldiers, up to six companies of whom were stationed at the Citadel from 1715 onwards, with a detached company on Drake's Island. However, this principle was largely dictated by the savings resulting from the employment of Invalids who only had to be paid 'fire and candle' (6d a day) in place of regular troops. In emergency dockyard men or other volunteers were drafted in (in 1779 Cornish tinners were called in to man guns in Dock Lines and at the Citadel) under the instruction of trained gunners.

After 1815, William Edmonds, Master Gunner at the Citadel, had five invalid gunners under him, forming a part of what was called the Invalid Detachment which had its headquarters at Woolwich. George Mahon, Master Gunner on Drake's Island, had no Invalids so he either had to employ civilians or borrow men from the artillery companies in the Artillery Barracks (the original Granby Barracks) within Dock Lines. There was only one 'garrison company' of artillery in Plymouth and Devonport for most of the first half of the nineteenth century though significantly by 1850 it had been increased to three.

Although the organisation of which they formed a part changed from time to time, the Master Gunners continued to be responsible for the care and maintenance of coast guns and their increasingly complex equipment until 1956 when Coast Artillery in the British Army came to an end.

The guns mounted for coast defence were ones which had in the first instance been designed for the Royal Navy since the Navy was first priority for the armament developed by the Board of Ordnance. The main difference was that guns for coast defence were mounted on garrison carriages with iron truck wheels rather than the wooden wheels used on ships. When in the 1860s huge numbers of guns were required for the recently built coast defences and land forts, coast batteries were second in priority after the Navy for the new rifled breech-loaders (RBL) and later, when the former proved unsatisfactory, for rifled muzzle-loading (RML) guns. It was not until the 1880s that there were sufficient of both types of guns, many of them already obsolescent by then, to arm the land defences properly. In the meanwhile the coast batteries as they were completed in the early 1860s were temporarily armed with the last generation of smooth-bore guns developed in the 1840s, 68 pounders and 8-inch shell guns, which were gradually replaced by RMLs.

Coast defences have almost always been able to repel attack from the sea for reasons discussed below. When they were put out of action it was normally due to a land attack, often using surprise or the cover of darkness. This is the reason for the all round defences, in the form of gorge (rear) walls covered by guard houses and even ditches, which had been developed as a result of experience.

Wooden sailing ships had some advantages when attacking the early coast defences in that they could bring a whole broadside to bear. The service of the guns by their crews was, due to practice and experience, often quicker than that of the coast guns. The latters' advantage lay in the accuracy which came from firing from a fixed and stable platform protected by an earth parapet with embrasures. Though a ship could under favourable conditions of wind and water sail close inshore and deliver a reasonably accurate broadside before bearing away to reload, it was usual for a fleet, when attacking the defences of a port, to anchor off shore and attempt to reduce the coast defences by the weight of their combined broadsides. Even then it was seldom that coast guns received a direct hit though their crews were often wounded by showers of stone splin-

ters from shot striking the stone revetment of the gun embrasure.

On the other hand the coast gunners had a large target and one which was easy to hit when the ships were anchored. Red hot shot was particularly effective against wooden ships, as were the explosive shells which were developed in the nineteenth century.

The strength of the coast defences of Plymouth and Devonport lay initially in the number of batteries which ships had to pass at close range before they reached the Dockyard, combined with the narrow channel. The Citadel and Drake's Island were powerful and well armed fortresses and by the end of the eighteenth century there were permanent batteries at Western King, Devil's Point, Redding Point and Mount Wise. When there was a serious threat of invasion in 1779 additional temporary batteries were built and it was planned in emergency to anchor ships in the main channel at various points to act as floating batteries. These were too costly to man and maintain in peacetime.

Particular effectiveness was given to the Plymouth defences by the winding channel. An attacking ship had to turn through more than 90 degrees opposite the Royal Citadel and again at Devil's Point, which greatly reduced the speed of sailing ships. After that there were still bends in the channel opposite Mount Wise and South Yard. To obtain similar protection, when the French built a new dockyard on the relatively exposed Biscay coast - at the time when the Citadel was begun - they built it 15 kilometres up the relatively shallow river Charente at Rochefort so that it should be safe against English raids.

The existing coast defences at Plymouth were strong enough to deter attack by wooden sailing ships during the Napoleonic Wars, but later the mounting of shell guns on warships and the use of mortars on especially built, shallow-draft bombships designed to operate inshore made the open batteries of the day vulnerable. The steam-assisted sailing men-of-war which were being developed in the 1840s were less dependent on weather and more manoeuvrable, and the later propellor-driven steamships even more so. Many more guns, or more easily traversed guns, would be needed to bring sufficient weight of fire to bear on these faster moving targets.

By 1860 the first armoured warships were being launched, against which cast iron cannon balls were ineffective; new guns, new projectiles, more protection and, eventually, new methods of engagement were needed.

This requirement was met by the new rifled guns mounted in casemates and protected by iron shields.

References

[1] *Fortress Britain.* Andrew Saunders p. 136

[2] *Fortress.* Ian V. Hogg. p. 76.

[3] Lt-Gen. Robert Douglas, Lieutenant-General of the Ordnance, 1824, quoted in *The History of Coast Artillery in the British Army.* Col. K.W. Maurice-Jones. p. 138

3
THE THREAT FROM FRANCE

'neither England nor any other first rate power ever stood in such a condition of comparative military weakness, as that in which the United Kingdom (to say nothing of our foreign possessions) is now placed.

There is close to our shores a nation of 34 million people, the leading portion of which it cannot be denied, is animated with a feeling of deep hatred to England as a power.

...we ought to be on an equal footing, if not in our means of offence, at least in our means of defence; but this is not our condition.'

Lord Palmerston 17 December 1846

Three events in the year 1844 affected in different ways the development of the defences of Plymouth over the next thirty years. In May the Prince de Joinville, son of Louis Phillipe, King of France, published a pamphlet in which he discussed the weakness of the French fleet and how the building of new steam warships could reduce the superiority of British naval power. This pamphlet resulted in the first of a series of invasion scares which affected British policy over the next fifteen years, following a long period when the threat from France, though not forgotten, had been largely ignored. Secondly, more than thirty years' work on the building of the Plymouth Breakwater

was completed in 1844. Finally, in October an inter-service committee produced a report on the defences of Plymouth as they had stood since 1815 with its recommendations for their modernisation.[1]

British foreign policy in the nineteenth century was based on the maintenance of our naval supremacy and of the balance of power in Europe. Although there was no major war between 1815 and 1853 there was nevertheless a potential threat to our naval supremacy first from the Russian navy in the early years and later from the French. During this period British superiority was potential rather than actual, for reasons of economy. After 1815 most of our wooden line-of-battle ships were laid up for many years because they could be brought into commission again in a few months if a major conflict threatened. Even at the time when a British squadron fought at the Battle of Navarino in support of the Greek rebellion in 1827, only seventeen of the 95 British line-of-battle ships were actually in commission. In the 1830's developments began which would soon threaten the effectiveness of this huge reserve of wooden men-of-war. At the same time increasing commitments in the expanding Empire and in American waters had tended to drain our naval strength in the Channel.

Experiments with steam-driven ships - steamers - had been going on in Britain since 1792 and paddle steamers were developed commercially in the early years of the century. In 1822 the Navy took delivery of its first steam-er, the *Comet*. These paddle-driven ships, though indepen-dent of wind and tide, were in other respects less effective as warships. The paddles on either side limited the space for guns and so reduced the broadside the ship could mount. The paddles, the boiler and the engine room machinery were particularly vulnerable to damage in battle and the ships' narrow bow and stern were less suit-able for mounting guns. Also, the early steamers had heavy and inefficient engines which used vast quantities of coal so that their range of operation was limited.

By 1844 the Royal Navy had many small steamers, by then mainly screw-driven, but they were used primarily as tugs or for inshore work. The huge distances which the Navy had to patrol - from the China Seas to the Americas - made it essential that for fleet work ships should continue to rely on sail, conserving coal and using steam power as an auxilliary. Nevertheless the suggestion by the Prince de Joinville in 1844 that steamers might counterbalance the effect of British naval superiority in the restricted waters of the Channel caused alarm, and a heated debate developed in Britain over the design of ships, both steam and sail-powered, during the next five years. The result was that from the late 1840s onwards auxilliary steam power began to be fitted to line-of-battle ships and in 1852 the first British screw line-of-battle ship designed as such, the *Agamemnon*, was launched, a year after the French had launched the *Napoleon*. During the 1850s 'Screw-steam became the dominant instrument of sea power, offering a hitherto unimaginable combination of firepower, speed and manoeuvrability'.[2]

In 1837 the French navy took the decision, after many years of trials, to equip their fleet with shell guns, and Britain did the same the following year. The threat of shells in turn focused attention on the possible develop-ment of ships that were iron-hulled, and therefore less combustible. An early reaction to this idea was that it would be more difficult to plug holes in iron hulls than in wooden ones, an argument which led logically to the development of heavily armoured hulls immune to pene-tration by cannon fire.

The introduction of shell guns, and of larger guns generally, raised the possibility that close action would no longer be the dominant tactic of naval warfare in future. British naval gunnery was already being developed to a new state of efficiency following the establishment of a gunnery school at HMS *Excellent*, Portsmouth, in 1830. With shipbuilding also being considered in a more scien-tific light, the trends in the propulsion and construction of ships, and later in gunnery, reached fulfilment in the launching of HMS *Warrior* in 1859.   Such technological developments served to emphasise the importance of our naval dockyards in keeping the fleet at sea, and the need to defend them in the event of war.

Relations between Britain and France had been good since 1830, and especially since 1841 when Lord Aberdeen became Foreign Secretary. However, the rivalry and mutu-al suspicion between the two countries remained under the surface, for not only did France have the only navy then capable of challenging the Royal Navy but it possessed the largest army in Western Europe, supported by large reserves of former conscripts. Both countries felt that their long opposing coastlines were vulnerable to attack.

In Britain the Duke of Wellington became Commander-in-Chief of the army again in 1842. In the following years he used his immense prestige and experience to argue the need for additional land defences both to increase the effectiveness of the limited troops available in the UK and to reduce the burden of home defence on the Navy, so releasing ships for service elsewhere. His obsession with home defence, for such it became, irritated the Prime Minister. Peel was trying to reduce expenditure and abolish Income Tax and Wellington's expensive schemes were embarrassing. But 'the truth was that the British did not possess an army large enough to take the field and defend the country's fortified ports, especially if an enemy, using the rapidity of movement afforded by steamers, chose to launch a surprise attack on the country.'[3]

With the publication of the de Joinville letter other politicians began for the first time to share the Duke's concern. Had steam power tilted the balance in favour of the attack? Was our naval superiority, weakened by increasing world-wide commitments, no longer sufficient to protect our shores against invasion? Would there be time for our huge reserve fleet of sailing ships to be commissioned and assembled to resist a sudden invasion by steamers? However, in all this debate the defensive potential of our own steamers tended to be underestimated.

This was the background to the report on the defences of Plymouth by the Committee on Harbour Defences, established by the Inspector General of Fortifications, in September 1844. The recent completion of the Breakwater 3500 metres south of the Hoe had radically improved the defensive potential of the Sound in that it confined the approach to two channels, one 700 metres wide to the east and the principal channel 1300 metres wide on the western side. However there was only in existance one battery able to fire on the entrances. This was on Staddon Heights, 1250 metres from the east end of the Breakwater, and armed with only 12-pounder guns. No battery covered the main western channel.

The Committee proposed to build a battery of ten guns on traversing platforms opposite each end of the Breakwater - at Staddon Point and Picklecombe Point.

Each battery was to be protected at the gorge with a raised and loopholed guardhouse and equipped with a magazine and shot furnace. At Eastern King a third new battery in the form of a redoubt was to be built mounting 'six of the heaviest shell guns'.

The idea, which was to reappear in a memorandum by Jervois in 1858 (Appendix A) and again in 1860, of erecting batteries on either end of the Breakwater was rejected. These would have been of little use in onshore winds due to the spray, unless they were very high which would add to the danger of their being carried away in a storm. However the Committee proposed that there should instead be 'four heavily armed steam blockships, two to be 2-decked ships, two frigates, without masts and propelled by screws, and anchored near the ends of the Breakwater to co-operate with the batteries'. It also recommended that in view of the speed of enemy steamers, one of our own should always be in position at night beyond the Breakwater to prevent the defences being surprised.

The Committee found the coast defences to be armed with 18, 24 and 32-pounders left there since the Napoleonic Wars. They recommended that the existing batteries such as Western King should be re-armed with the latest 56-pounder cannon and 8-inch shell guns, with some 32-pounders remaining. Two additional 10-inch howitzers were to be mounted at Devil's Point where the range was short, due to the narrow channel, and mortars retained at Mount Wise for the same reason. By 1849, when the new batteries were completed, even more powerful guns were in production and some 68-pounder and 10-inch guns were to be mounted on the two new batteries at Picklecombe and Staddon Point covering the entrances to the Sound. These open barbette batteries appear vulnerable especially in view of the change to casemated batteries within a few years, but they were considered to be protected by their height above sea level. But an interesting development was the inclusion of two casemated emplacements in the face of the redoubt at Eastern King - Prince of Wales Redoubt (Plate 15).

Within the Breakwater the defences were to be considerably strengthened on Drake's Island and at the Citadel whose existing armament was impressive in number but largely obsolescent. Upon Maker Heights, Redoubts Nos. 5

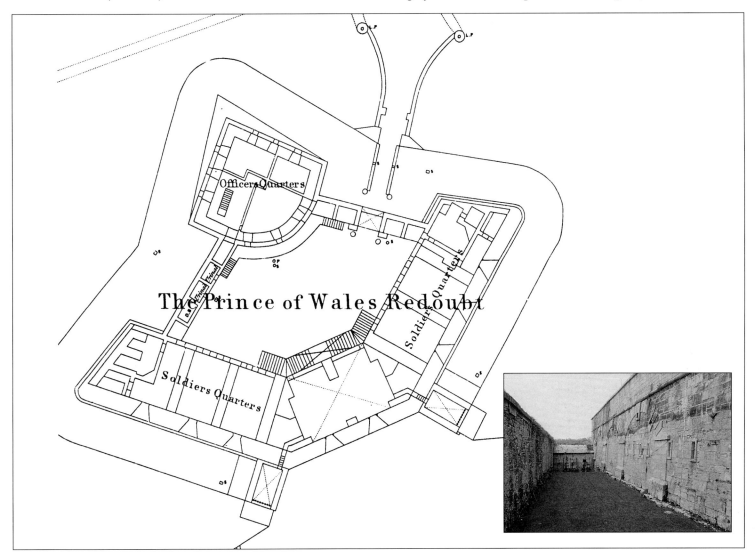

Plate 15: *Plan of the Prince of Wales Redoubt, Eastern King.* (PRO WO 78/4481, MPHH 629 Pt13).
Inset: *Rifle gallery in the ditch* (EXETER ARCHAEOLOGY ©).

and 6 were said to be in good repair and the dilapidated Nos.1, 2 and 3 Redoubts were to be 'immediately established in the event of war'. A significant development was that No. 4 Redoubt was to be armed as a coast defence battery, eventually with 68-pounder and 10-inch guns.

The Committee drew attention to Whitsand Bay from whose, admittedly exposed, beaches an enemy could advance on Maker Heights and then to Mount Edgcumbe, less than 2000 metres from the Dockyard, or alternatively on Torpoint. The Harbourmaster of Plymouth was asked to report on the feasibility of a landing in the area and he considered that Portwrinkle was the best point in a difficult coastline. The Committee recommended that a mobile force with field guns should be stationed in the area of Crafthole and Antony to contain such a landing: both the steep cliffs at Whitsand Bay and the country between there and Torpoint offer excellent defensive positions. From this time onwards all defensive schemes for Plymouth have paid particular attention to Whitsand Bay from whose beaches a surprise attack could be launched on the shortest route to the Dockyard.

The Committee's report was passed to General Sir Thomas Mulcaster, then Inspector General of Fortifications, for comment. In approving the general recommendations he made two points, the first of which seems routine these days but was novel then. The principal batteries 'should be always maintained in the state for immediate action, and occupied by an efficient force of the Royal Artillery. The mere construction of works exhibiting a formidable appearance, although doubtless producing a corresponding impression until their very efficiency for action be analysed, will soon lose that effect upon an enemy preparing for a coup de main...'. He commended to the Army the Navy's drill of assembling daily at quarters on board ship and for this reason was in favour of the use of movable floating batteries. Many years later there were trained coast gunners who manned the defences continuously, but then there were only men called to man the guns in emergency. Secondly, Sir Thomas recommended that the authorities should 'make good the enclosure of Devonport'. i.e. improve and complete the Lines.

This report might have been pigeonholed like an earlier one in 1839, but in December 1844 the Duke wrote a long memo for the Cabinet in which he emphasised that during wartime our fleets should act offensively and not be cramped by the need to defend the Dockyards. His memo must have impressed Peel at last for at the end of the year he wrote 'There are awful reports from a Commission on the state of defence of all the great naval arsenals and dockyards'.

The Duke emphasised the need for internal defence and pointed out the use made in Britain during the Napoleonic Wars of large numbers of militia and volunteers. The registration (recruiting) for the militia had been suspended since 1832 yet our small regular army was largely overseas, leaving only about 60 000 regulars in the British Isles. To relieve this small force from garrison duties, and so create a mobile reserve, he urged the formation of some form of local force.

It was at this time that Lord Palmerston (Plate 16), then out of office, first began to take an interest publicly in the question of national defence. His long term aim had always been to see Britain strong and so able to exert its influence abroad through the Navy. To do this effectively there must be no weakness at home which might be exploited by an enemy in a crisis. As he said, 'if your dockyards are destroyed your Navy is cut up by the roots'. He particularly appreciated the technological changes which were taking place and how they affected the country's security.

Plate 16: *Lord Palmerston 1844-45* (By courtesy of the National Portrait Gallery).

On 1 August 1845 he introduced a debate in the House of Commons on national defence, pointing out that with their new railway system the French could now assemble an army quickly in the Channel ports and then transport them across in steamers. However his suggestion that steam had 'bridged' the Channel and that at that time 30 000 French troops could be transported overnight to land unopposed in southern England the following morning, and perhaps occupy London three days later, seems now to be going too far. Yet at this time the Army at home had had no training in assembling a force of all arms and

manoeuvring it in the field. He was more to the point when he feared sudden damaging raids on Portsmouth and Plymouth in which the Dockyards would be destroyed and ships burnt.

Peel, then Prime Minister, dismissed Palmerston's conclusions as 'altogether erroneous', but the Duke followed up with a second memo on 10 September 1845 emphasising that due to the increased speed of steamers and the lack of dependence on wind and tide it was no longer necessary for an enemy to control the Channel before launching an invasion.

Palmerston and the Duke were advocating policies which were unpopular at the time with the mass of people whose feeling that Britain was safe from invasion under the protection of the navy was deeply ingrained. Many felt that the duty of the government was to save tax payers' money by cutting public expenditure and Palmerston's call to spend more on defence and to fortify the naval Dockyards against invasion had little effect initially.

In 1845, following the report of the Committee on Harbour Defences, a mere £34 000 was voted for new fortifications at Portsmouth and Devonport. But when a new government was formed in the following year with Palmerston as Foreign Secretary the climate began to change. Work had already begun in October 1845 on a battery at Staddon Point and by 1849 the three new batteries at Plymouth had almost been completed and the existing batteries began to be rearmed.

In the event the new batteries were more elaborate than required by the Report. Due to the steep slope on which it stands Staddon Point was built on three levels and protected in the rear by a narrow ditch and draw bridge. The lowest level had substantial towers at either end. In between them was the platform (terreplein) for the main battery with eight guns firing *en barbette* and one on each of the

Plate 17: *Staddon Point Battery, above Bovisand Battery.* (COURTESY R.C.F. SERPELL)

towers (Plate 17). The upper two levels were for the accommodation of the garrison.

The battery at Picklecombe was on a similar principle but no plan or illustration has come to light of its original form. The guns were sited *en barbette* on the terreplein in front of the elaborate barracks whose design it is said owes something to Warwick Castle. Because 'The Earl's Drive' along the coast from Mount Edgcumbe House to Penlee Point and back passed behind the barracks, the Earl apparently insisted that the barracks should be in keeping with the splendour of the drive and of his house (Plate 18).

The third new battery at Eastern King is in many ways the most interesting. It was originally to have been a battery of six of the largest guns. In the event a limestone redoubt capable of all round defence was completed in 1849 known as Prince of Wales Redoubt. With the two

central guns in casemates, the ditch covered by small rifle galleries in caponiers, the loopholed curtain walls from which riflemen standing on raised firing platforms could cover the glacis, and a small keep in the NW corner it foreshadowed some of the features of the forts built in the 1860s (see Plate 15).

In 1847 the Duke wrote in despair to General Sir John Burgoyne (Plate 19) who had been made Inspector General of Fortifications in 1845, pointing out that his attempts to awaken the attention of successive governments to the danger of invasion had been in vain. Burgoyne was well aware of the position. On taking office he had written a memo on 'The Application of Steam Power on Military and Naval Operations' and in the following year one on 'The Results of a War with France' pointing out that apart from troops required for the garrisons there were only 5-10 000

Plate 18: *Picklecombe, the 1849 battery.* (AUTHOR)

Plate 19: *Field Marshal Sir John Burgoyne.* (COURTESY OF THE DIRECTOR OF THE NATIONAL ARMY MUSEUM)

regular troops available in England as a field force and 'our Dockyards alone have a semblance of being fortified'. He had in fact prepared a report which Palmerston had submitted to the Cabinet in the previous month.

Burgoyne, appointed to this important post at the age of 63, was the third influential figure who pressed for improved defences during this period. To Wellington's prestige and Palmerston's political skills he added extensive practical experience of fortification and siege work during the Peninsular War, and later in an advisory role at the siege of Sebastopol. His approach was pragmatic; he did not support theoretical systems of fortification. In 1853 he wrote 'it is an object in all places, but especially in this country where it is difficult to obtain funds for any works of defence, to adjust the demand for them to the absolute necessity and not to take up a position with the design of giving the greatest possible strength'. As far as coast defences were concerned he had already advocated in a paper the dispersal of individual coast guns, a policy which

was not put into effect until the 1890s. It was unfortunate that in December 1847 a letter from the Duke to Burgoyne in the previous year, which had received wide circulation in political circles, was published in the *Times*. The gist of it is given in a single sentence 'We have no defence or hope or chance of defence except in our fleet'. But it resulted in the publicity and ill-informed discussion which Wellington had sought to avoid. A typical reaction in the popular press was 'Invasion! it is a joke!'. Cobden, an advocate of free trade and opposed to any further military expenditure (he had once described the Army as 'poor relief for the aristocracy') referred in a speech to the Duke's age (77) and declared 'that explains it all and excuses it'. The Duke was deeply hurt and his relationship with Burgoyne was temporarily soured.

Before long indirect support for those arguing for improved defences came from an unexpected quarter. When in 1848 Louis Phillipe abdicated following the Revolution in Paris, pressure for increased defence expenditure had been reduced. But when Louis Napoleon was elected President at the end of the year it put the government on their guard and national defence became a matter of concern. However the Manchester economists described the danger as 'moonshine', the Government's proposal to increase the Army Estimates was defeated in Parliament and they were in fact reduced. Although more was spent on armament that year, the proposed militia bill was shelved again. However in the winter of 1846-47, Dockyard brigades of volunteer dockyard workers had been formed with the object of training the men to handle the guns in the existing defences and to man the gunboats which were to be built.

When Louis Napoleon declared himself Emperor Napoleon III in December 1852 the possibility of war arose again. The new emperor's popularity was largely based on the fact that he was the nephew of Napoleon Bonaparte and there was always the possibility that he might try to increase that popularity by avenging his uncle's defeat. In the previous year the French navy had launched the first all-steam battleship *Napoleon* for use mainly in the Mediterranean. Although Britain probably exaggerated the threat from France at this time, the result was an increase in the naval estimates, with the emphasis on screw ships of the line, and the passing at last of a Militia Bill. This involved plans to raise 50 000 men in the first year and 30 000 more in the second. In 1853 a first attempt at 'autumn manoeuvres' was held at Chobham and much needed work

began on strengthening Devonport Lines, work which continued for the next ten years. Across the Channel, in the same year the breakwater for the new French naval base at Cherbourg was finally completed, after over seventy years of problems with its development.

Within a year of this scare the Crimean War had broken out and the British Army found itself fighting alongside the French in support of the Turks and against Russia. Even so, it was said that the British commander, Lord Raglan, spent more time worrying about the French and their attitude to the war than he did about the Russians. By the summer of 1854 the British fleet, its men-of-war still relying mainly on sail but with auxilliary steam power, was concentrated in the Black Sea. When it became necessary to transport the allied expeditionary force from Varna in Bulgaria to the shores of the Crimea the by now familiar, order 'Up funnel, down screw' was heard on the British ships, whereas the French still did not have enough steam tugs to tow those of their ships that were dependent on sail.

The long siege of Sebastopol by the Allies showed both that large stone artillery towers, such as the Malakoff, could still be effective at the key point of a defensive system, and the need for bomb-proof cover when the besiegers, particularly the French, used large numbers of mortars. But the main features of the defence of Sebastopol were the skill and ingenuity of the Russian commander, General Todleben, in organising improvised earthworks at key points such as the Redan to meet each threat as it developed, together with the stubborness of the Russian troops in defence of their homeland.

More important lessons were learnt from the Russian coast defences, lessons which were to be incorporated in the British defences of the 1860s. The initial attack on Sebastopol by the allied fleet on 16 October 1854 was driven off, and in this and other actions the Russian coast batteries proved their effectiveness against wooden ships-of-the-line. In particular the Anglo-French attack on Fort Constantine in the Crimea, which mounted over 100 heavy guns, resulted in substantial casualties to both ships and crews.

But a year later, in October 1855, an Allied fleet successfully attacked the old fort of Kinburn at the entrance to the Dnieper River. This time three French 'armoured floating batteries' protected by 4-inch iron plating on their sides anchored off the fort and engaged it with their 56-pounder shell guns. Although the Russian gunners, presented with a stationary target, scored some 200 hits with their 18 and 32-pounder guns, these did not penetrate the iron plating. After four hours the Russian commander surrendered, the French having suffered relatively few casualties. The result of this action was to confirm the French in their belief that shell guns and iron plating represented the way forward in naval architecture, lessons applied later in Britain to both ships and coast defences.

The Royal Navy was also involved in a long but ineffective campaign in the Baltic. The island of Kronstadt and its naval base were protected by a group of coastal forts armed with 300 of the latest large calibre guns. The Menchikoff battery for example had 44 guns in four tiers of granite casemates. In front of the fort there was also an extensive submarine minefield. Submarine mines, first referred to as torpedoes, had been developed by the Russians and were eventually of two types: either linked to the shore from where they could be set off by electrically or designed to explode on contact with the hull of a ship. The defences of Kronstadt were so formidable that they were never attacked by the Allies.

When in 1855 a powerful allied fleet bombarded Sveaborg, protected by five fortified islands and an almost continuous line of batteries, the bombardment failed to do serious damage and the fortress was not taken. Apart from the action at Kinburn, the effect of the Crimean War was to confirm the ability of coast defences to resist attack from the sea.

The greatest effect of the Crimean War however was on our strategic thinking. It had proved the vital importance of steam power, which now meant screw power, in open waters. Steamships survived the winter storms in the Black Sea better, and were able to remain on station in the Baltic longer than sailing ships could have done. Secondly, for the first time a large army had crossed the sea using steam power and invaded another country in spite of the fact that the enemy had a substantial fleet. The threat of a 'steam bridge' had become a reality.

The war highlighted weaknesses in the organisation of the army. In spite of the initial tactical errors and administrative failures it showed its customary stubborness in action and skill in improvisation. But for all the heroism extolled in the earlier actions of the War, it was the French who took their final objective, the Malakoff, when the British failed at the Redan. The peace was signed in Paris, emphasising the standing of Napoleon III on the European stage.

Like the navy, the army was severely stretched in meeting its commitments world-wide. At the outbreak of the war there were only about 65 000 troops at home, 40 000 in the colonies and 30 000 in India. By the end of the Crimean campaign the French, with their conscript army and correspondingly large reserves, had four times as many troops in the field as the British. This was in spite of our use of militia and volunteers at home to free regular troops, and even the recruiting of a mercenary force.

It was clear that there were insufficient regular troops at home to man the existing limited defences and to provide a large enough reserve army to meet the threat of invasion. To release regulars by making the militia and any local volunteers effective a modern system of fortifications was needed, which they could man. This was particularly true at Plymouth which was far from the probable main centre of operations in the south east and dependent on its own resources. The point was driven home when, within months of the signing of the Peace of Paris in 1856, the Indian Mutiny broke out and the British army there had to be rapidly reinforced by troops from England.

From the beginning of 1858 British suspicion of French intentions appeared to be justified. Early in the year the Paris press and some French generals took up a bellicose attitude to Britain following the Orsini Affair when an attempt was made to assassinate the Emperor with a bomb found to have been made in England. The Government had information that the French were secretly making preparations for war. It became known that the French had laid down the first iron-clad wooden warship, the frigate *La Gloire*. In April 1859 Napoleon III declared war on Austria in support of the movement for independence in Italy and after a successful campaign annexed Nice and Savoy in the following year. When the iron-clad *La Gloire* was launched in November 1859 it rendered our existing coast batteries armed with cannon obsolete overnight. In early 1860 the French Ambassador, Count Flahaut, discussed with Palmerston the anti-British feelings in France which he feared could lead to invasion.

During the Crimean War for the first time people became aware through the press of the suffering of the troops in the campaign, and the Indian Mutiny had raised the public profile of the services again. In the Duke's words

'the tide of commercial growth and pacifistic optimism had begun to turn and the public began to share the anxiety which had long troubled Palmerston and others'.

Palmerston became Prime Minister in June 1859. He had grown more and more distrustful of Napoleon III whose mind seemed to him to be 'as full of schemes as a warren is full of rabbits'. Already a secret committee had estimated that if the enemy obtained even for a short time command of the Channel a force of 100 000 effective troops would be needed to meet him in the field. In August he appointed a Royal Commission 'to consider the defences of the United Kingdom'. Following its report in February 1860 Parliament in August authorised a huge programme of expenditure on both coast and land defences. In November of that year the Royal Navy took delivery of HMS *Warrior* which combined steam screw propulsion, armoured protection on an iron hull and shell guns, some of them of a new and revolutionary design. It thus embodied much new technology which would influence the design of both the coast and land defences recommended by the Royal Commission.

References

[1] (PRO.ADM1/5543)
[2] *Steam, Steel and Shellfire. The Steam Warship 1815-1905.'* Ed. Robert Gardiner. p.38
[3] *Military Planning for the Defense of the United Kingdom, 1814-1870.* Partridge. p.66

4
PLYMOUTH'S PALMERSTON FORTS
- THE PLAN

'Most of the world's great systems of fortifications are known, not by the names of the men who designed them, but by those of the politicians who managed to manipulate the fears of their fellow countrymen in order to extract the money.'

Peter Kent. *Fort* 14

On 20 August 1859 the Royal Commission 'to Consider the Defences of the United Kingdom' was appointed. The Chairman of the Commission was Major General Sir Henry Jones, a Royal Engineer officer who had had experience during the Crimean War in the attacks on the Russian fortresses in the Baltic. The most influential members of the Commission were probably Captain Astley Cooper-Key RN - an active campaigner for technical reforms in naval armament - and Lt-Col. J.H. Lefroy one of the most forward-looking Royal Artillery officers of the time. The Commission was instructed to examine certain vulnerable points (including Plymouth) and to consider 'first, how they could best be made defensible in as short a time as possible and secondly, how they could be put in the most complete state of safety by permanent fortifications'.

The Commission began its report by pointing out that the navy provided 'the first and most obvious line of defence; but it is one which could not, in our opinion be relied upon at the present day...'. This represents a fundamental change from Lord St Vincent's trenchant statement fifty years before: 'I do not say they cannot come. I only say they cannot come by sea'.

Before making its recommendations for fortifications the Commission considered the alternative of increasing the strength of the regular army so as to have sufficient troops not only to oppose an invasion but also to defend the dockyards individually against attack. They calculated that in order to double the number of regular troops at home - at the time about 66 000 men exclusive of the men in depots for regiments in India - it would cost £8 million initially and nearly £4 million annually thereafter. They must also have born in mind that in some quarters the army was still seen as a threat to the liberty of the subject so that such a proposal would anyway be resisted in Parliament and in the country.

The same initial sum spent on fortification would be far more effective and would provide some barrack accommodation incidentally. The annual cost thereafter would be limited to a small sum for the maintenance of the fortifications and for three weeks training per year for the volunteers to man them - about 1/20th the cost of a similar regular force. The Commission concluded that 'By a judicial application of fortifications the means would be afforded of utilizing in the highest degree both our fleet and the regular army and the forces which would be brought in aid of it; and, further, that without fortification there is no mode of defence which can be proposed which would give the same amount of security to the country and at the same time be so economical both in money and in troops'.

The Commission quickly rejected the idea of fortifying the whole of the vulnerable coastline and proposed to concentrate on fortifying vital points: the dockyards at Portsmouth, Plymouth, Chatham and Pembroke, Woolwich Arsenal, and the harbours of refuge at Dover, Portland and Cork. They referred to the fact that in the last few years works costing £1.5 million had already been started at Portsmouth, Plymouth, Portland and Pembroke. Apart from the coast defences at the vulnerable points it would also be necessary to provide land defences to prevent bombardment of the dockyards following a landing.

Where the country allowed the enemy a full view of the dockyard within a practicable range (8000 yds.) of the new rifled guns the defences must command the ground within this range. Elsewhere, in the existing state of gunnery it was sufficient to deny the enemy immediate observation of the dockyard.

The Commission went on to say that 'the works should be so designed, as to be defended by a small body of men against a *coup de main*, but that they should at the same time have capabilities of resistance that would enable them to withstand any attack likely to be brought against them. With this in view they should be provided with redoubts at their gorge, by means of which an enemy would be prevented from holding the works should he obtain partial possession of it'. The ramparts should be capable of providing heavy fire from artillery and musketry, and bombproof cover should be provided for the garrison. Where the ditches could not be filled with water (as at Plymouth)

they should have revetted scarps and counterscarps and these should be flanked by artillery and musketry.

In view of the need for speed the Royal Commission recommended that the works should be 'so designed that the main ramparts and ditches could be formed without being delayed by the building of revetments or the construction of bombproof and permanent magazines, so that a certain degree of protection could be obtained in three or four months...' At each vulnerable point the position, strength of artillery and garrison for each fort was laid down, leaving the designs and detailed plans to be prepared later.

The cost of all the work recommended was £11.85 million and the Commission assumed that this expenditure would be spread over four years. As regards the cost of the armament, basing its figures on the cost of the 68-pounder smooth-bore gun and allowing for the fact that some of the guns would be the new rifled ones, the average cost of £200 per gun spread over at least 2500 guns would result in an expenditure of £500 000. (Within ten years the 10-inch RML gun was being mounted in the coast batteries at a cost of £2000 per gun).

Although the expenditure proposed by the Royal Commission was enormous, in his preliminary comments on the Report Burgoyne pointed out that this was because there were so few existing fortifications. He also warned that improvements in weapons and tactics were likely to render fortifications designed to resist present methods useless within a few years.

The resulting land forts and coast batteries which were completed in the next fifteen years are often referred to as 'Palmerston's Follies' as if they were the result of some sudden rash act by Britain's most experienced statesman of the time. In fact, Palmerston had himself been pressing the need for improved defences for fifteen years, and since 1856 two surveys of the coast defences had been carried out and a number of official memoranda on aspects of defence against invasion had been prepared. The government had already authorised a limited programme of construction of forts west of Plymouth and elsewhere in the U.K.

The appointment of the Royal Commission at this particular time must be seen as a reaction to the sudden pressure of public opinion which, after a long period of peace, had at last been made aware of military realities. In the event the pendulum probably swung too far in favour of fortification, and for financial reasons the Cabinet felt bound to make substantial reductions in the Royal Commission's eventual proposals. However, the results of the Commission's work was a system of fortifications such as Palmerston and others had been advocating for a number of years.

The two men who had the greatest influence on the implementation of the Commission's proposals were General Sir John Burgoyne and the Secretary of the Royal Commission, Major W.F.D. Jervois, Royal Engineers (Plate 20). He was shortly promoted to Lt. Colonel and became Deputy Director of Works for Fortifications under Sir John.

As Inspector General of Fortifications and Commandant Royal Engineers, Burgoyne was already responsible for the design and construction of fortifications in the United Kingdom. He received the plans for new works from his specialist officers, checked them and submitted them to the Board of Ordnance and Master General of the Ordnance for approval, often a formality. Particular questions on national defence were referred to the Defence Committee, a specialist standing committee of the War Office formed by the Secretary for War in 1856 and reporting to him. The chairman of this Committee was the Commander-in-Chief and it included a Lord of the Admiralty, and two artillery and two engineer officers.

Plate 20: *Major-General Sir William Jervois, GCMG, CB.* (NATIONAL LIBRARY OF AUSTRALIA).

The Royal Commission was superimposed on this system as far as its consideration of the defence of the dockyards and the arsenals was concerned and it tended to clash with the Defence Committee. Initially the latter would not accept the Royal Commission's assumption that naval superiority could not guarantee to protect the country against invasion, but after the two bodies were persuaded by Jervois to sit together the Royal Commission's report was agreed.

To oversee and carry out the plans of the Royal Commission, a Fortification Committee was established by the War Office on 29 August 1860, the day after the Defence Act was passed, under the chairmanship of Major-General Foster, formerly of the Royal Engineers, and including three members of the Royal Commission.

General Sir John Burgoyne was the illegitimate son of 'Gentleman Johnny' Burgoyne who surrendered to the Americans at Saratoga. He served in the Egyptian campaign in 1807 and under Sir John Moore at Corunna. Later he was involved in the building of the lines of Torres Vedras. He took part in many of the sieges in the Peninsular campaign, leading the 3rd Division's assaults on both Ciudad Rodrigo and Badajoz and being promoted brevet major and then brevet lieutenant colonel in recognition. In 1854 he was sent on a mission to Turkey before the beginning of the Crimea War to reconnoitre the probable area of the campaign including the Crimea itself. He was the senior British engineer during the early part of the war and later became in effect the principal military adviser to Lord Raglan. Afterwards he corresponded with the French General Canrobert about the lessons to be drawn from the Crimean campaigns.

Burgoyne has been described by Peter Kent as 'a pragmatist and a realist, more interested in what could be done with existing techniques and resources than wasting his time, and ultimately everybody else's, by devising ingenious hypothetical systems'.[1] In 1858 he wrote that 'works of fortification should be devised according to principles and not according to systems; the latter require the ground to be made to suit the works, while, by principles, the works are adapted to the circumstances of the ground'. For close defence, he considered the caponier better than the bastioned flank - 'it gains interior space, is more economical in construction and will, when effective, remain longer intact'. Finally, he quoted General Todleben's doctrine that 'le secret de la défense réside dans la force de l'Artillerie'.

In addition he appreciated that, apart from the shortage of money, the other principal factor was likely to be the shortage of trained troops. The charge to the Royal Commission emphasised the need to protect the royal arsenals and dockyards but at the same time indicated that there was to be no increase in the strength of the regular army, and particularly of the Royal Artillery, to man any defences which they recommended.

Burgoyne had a further influence through Jervois on the detailed design of the forts and batteries. As early as 1856 he had drawn up his own plans for the fortification of the dockyards and arsenals, had called for the improvement of the Plymouth defences and had proposed that trials be carried out with armoured shields. Having long been concerned about the possibility of a sudden raid or *coup de main*, he insisted on all batteries being wherever possible capable of all-round defence against a raiding party. As Peter Kent says, 'all the keeps and complicated entrances that were incorporated into forts of the period are the result of his obsession'[2] an influence which can be clearly seen at Plymouth and uniquely at Polhawn. Burgoyne was determined that every work must have its flanks covered either by its basic form or by the use of counterscarp galleries, caponiers or even machicolations. In this way the work would be secure even though manned by a small number of troops.

He continued to be interested in the development of ironclads and the corresponding iron shields for the protection of shore batteries and was writing to Lord Rosse as late as 1865. In the following year the successes of the

Prussians in the war of 1866 led him to suggest a shorter term of enlistment in the Army in order to build up a trained reserve. His views were not favoured at the time, but within four years Cardwell had introduced terms of twelve years with the colours followed by six in the reserve in the Army Enlistment Act.

Jervois' previous experience in fortification was during the period 1852-55 when as a captain he was sent to fortify the island of Alderney. He designed and personally supervised the building of a dozen forts and batteries of a remarkable variety[3]. In 1857 he was appointed secretary of the Defence Committee, and after the alarm in the following year over the Orsini plot was also employed in preparing plans for the defence of London in the event of invasion.

His influence on the defences built in the 1860s appears at an early stage and his memorandum giving an appreciation of the situation at Plymouth written on 26 February 1858 (Appendix A) was attached to the Commission's report and accepted as a basis for its detailed recommendations. The death of the Prince Consort in December 1861 was a loss to Jervois who had benefited from his interest in fortification and his support.

In his memorandum (above) Jervois pointed out that Devonport could be attacked either from the west or from the east. He considered first an attack from the west because, even though it could have no base of operation nearer than Fowey 20 miles away, such an attack represented the most direct threat to the Dockyard. The attack could develop in one of four ways: a landing in Cawsand Bay, a landing in Whitsand Bay, an advance along the peninsula between the St Germans River and the sea or a deliberate advance from Fowey resulting in due course in bombardment of the Dockyard from the ground around Saltash (Map II).

A landing in Cawsand Bay could be prevented first by building a battery on the knoll standing above the village and between it and Kingsand, and secondly by a battery at Hooe Lake Point flanking the beaches from 1500 metres to the north. To prevent a landing in Whitsand Bay with its exposed beach accessible only by gullies and cart tracks, he suggested four towers between the coastguard station below Rame village in the east and below Tregantle to the west.

An enemy landing further west at Looe or Fowey would be likely to advance along the peninsula between the St Germans River and the sea and this could be best resisted by the 'Antony Line' - from Scraesdon Hill (above Antony village and overlooking the St Germans River) to the north to the top of the ridge at Tregantle to the south. Between the two main forts on these hills there should be an intermediate work the same size as Scraesdon. Bomb-proof barracks were needed in the three forts for 1000 men altogether. To complete the defences of the western position there should be a defensible barracks for 1000 men, and a battery of field artillery, on Maker Heights. To cover the fourth line of attack from the west required forts on the high ground above Saltash and barracks for 600 men.

The existing defences on the east side of the Hamoaze were all relatively old, apart from the unfinished lines of Devonport which covered only the dockyard and the gun wharf; not the Steam Yard at Keyham. There was still the Citadel, and redoubts at Mount Pleasant and Stonehouse Hill, though the latter were considered insignificant.

The nearest harbour to the east of Plymouth large enough to sustain a prolonged operation by an enemy was Dartmouth, which might be seized directly or after a landing at Torbay, and as the advance proceeded the Yealm could be used as a subsidiary harbour or in a sudden raid. An advance on Plymouth from there would either be

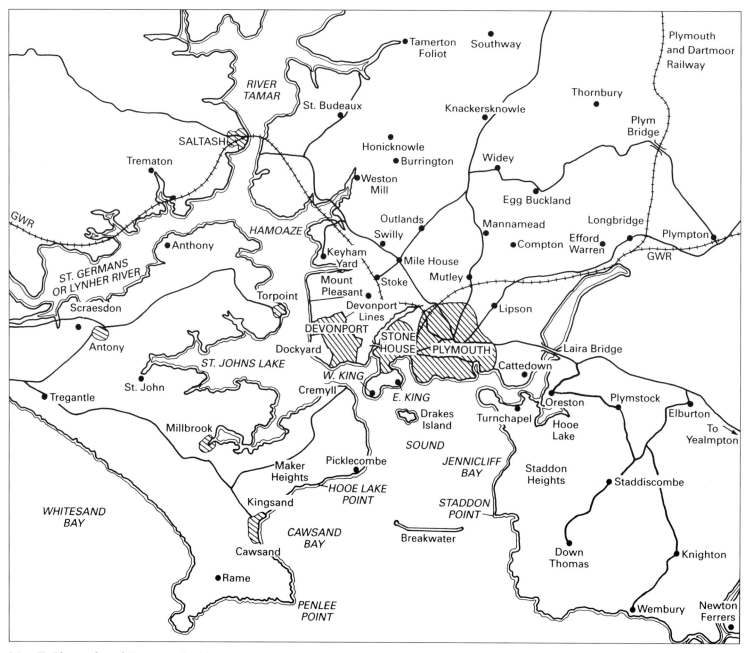

Map II: *Plymouth and Devonport in 1860.*

through Elburton across Laira Bridge or across Longbridge at Plympton - there were no fortifications to prevent them entering Plymouth on either road - and it would probably be accompanied by a bombardment of the Citadel from Staddon Heights or from the hill above Turnchapel.

Jervois concluded that the best defence of the Dockyard and of the Keyham Steam Yard beyond it was by creating a line from the heights above St Budeaux through a knoll above Burrington House at the head of Weston Mill Lake to Lipson and so down to Cattedown. This slightly curved line would be four miles long and about 4000 yards from the edge of any of the government establishments which, as they would not be under observation, it would therefore protect from bombardment. To the east of the Cattewater he recommended that three redoubts be built in a line on the heights above Hooe Lake and from there to Jennycliff Bay.

When discussing the main line of defence between St Budeaux and Cattedown he says that 'as regards the nature of the works generally, they will have straight faces, flanked by well covered caponiers, and will be provided with towers at their gorges, to enable a small number of men to secure them from a coup de main'. (The reference to towers probably reflects the earlier works which he had carried out in the Channel Islands.). These towers did not appear in the forts eventually but were replaced by defensible guardhouses at the gates.

He recommended building a new work at Mount Pleasant in spite of the fact that its surroundings were already obstructed by houses, because of its 'very influential position for preventing the actual capture of the arsenal'.

For the coast defences he recommended heavy batteries for about 60 guns at Picklecombe and Staddon Point each in three tiers, two of which would be in casemates and the third on top, with works of a similar description at each end of the Breakwater. Additional guns were recommended for Drake's Island and at Eastern and Western King.

He anticipated criticism of his proposals on two scores. On the question of expense he says that 'although their costs will no doubt be great, yet it will be comparatively trifling when compared with continental work having a similar object.'

As regards the lack of troops to man the defences, he pointed out that the works were divided into four positions separated by rivers and that it would be next to impossible to attack any two positions simultaneously, though he later admitted that half the defences would have to be manned in the event of an attack. Anyway, Plymouth whose population was then more than 100 000 would, with the surrounding districts, probably produce at least 10 000 fighting men 'capable of doing good service in the defence of the works'. This force, together with 6-8000 regular troops, militia and sailors, would be an adequate garrison. Significantly, in the final paragraph of his memorandum, he refers to the fact that on 17 November 1857 the cabinet had authorised the work on the position in front of Antony (Scraesdon) and that estimates for the current year included money to begin Tregantle Fort.

Jervois and Burgoyne continued to comment in memoranda on the position of Plymouth during 1858[4]. In May he wrote that Plymouth 'not possessing the same natural advantages for defence as Portsmouth, it will require the application of more works that are artificial, and which, if on a full scale, must be very costly.' In October writing on 'Protection of the Dockyards and Defence against Invasion'.[5] Jervois says of Plymouth 'this place is not strategically of the same importance as Portsmouth, although if it were fully fortified, it would form an entrenched camp which would be a main hold for the Western part of

England' and he goes on to refer to the superior natural advantages of Plymouth as a harbour, against Portsmouth, and the fact that it has a much better Steam Yard.

Once the Royal Commission's proposals had been approved after revision by the Cabinet and he had been in 1862 appointed Deputy Director of Works for Fortifications, Jervois was formally in a position to supervise the officers producing the detailed plans for the works. In 1860 he had written in the Professional Papers of the Royal Engineers his 'Observations relating to the Works in Progress and Proposed for the Defence of the Naval Ports, Arsenals and Dockyards'[6]. It sets out his principles for the design of fortificatons and is illustrated with ten specimen plans. It must have been compulsory reading for his staff.

This is not the place to discuss the development of his ideas in general as they affect all the works proposed by the Royal Commission but only in relation to the works at Plymouth. The following is a summary of his views on this basis:

For coast batteries, he again made clear his preference, where the nature and elevation of the site permitted, for open batteries with guns at considerable intervals, several such batteries dispersed being more effective than one big work. But he agreed that batteries must be casemated where sites were low or small in which case they might have to be in tiers to get the necessary height or volume of fire. Casemates were also desirable when the battery was backed against a rock or hill when the gunners needed the protection against shells bursting in their rear. Finally, casemates were needed where the battery could be approached by a large ship near enough for it to be able to fire grape effectively.

For these reasons all the new, as opposed to the modernised, coast batteries at Plymouth were casemated, apart from Cawsand where the site was high.

An attack on a Dockyard was likely to be in the form of a bombardment designed to put it quickly out of action, unless it was required as a base in support of an invasion. Any sites capable of observing the dockyard up to 8000 yards from it must therefore be denied to the enemy.

If defence in the form of continuous lines was not practicable, mutually supporting works would be needed to cover the front. The size of each of the works depended on the nature of the ground to be covered by fire and therefore the number of guns and men required, as well as the importance of an individual site in the general layout.

The design of a work would begin from the decision as to the lines of fire required from its guns to cover the ground to its front. This then indicated the layout of the ramparts on which the guns would be mounted. The ramparts in turn would be best protected by a ditch with straight faces covered by caponiers. The polygonal trace was the best form for the purpose and the angles should be sufficiently obtuse to the front so that the fire of one face took up that of the adjacent face and where possible converging fire resulted. The object was to cover all the ground in front of any work which could not be covered from another.

In certain circumstances bastions were acceptable but they had disadvantages since the usual size of a work would not permit of a fully developed bastion trace, its regular design would often not accommodate itself to the ground (where it was hilly) and the interior space of the work would be much reduced. At Plymouth there is only one small bastion at Cawsand, though bastionettes appear in some of the smaller works and the gate at Staddon Fort is covered by them.

The ramparts should be laid out so as to avoid the possibility of enfilade fire where possible, and where necessary guns should be protected on their flanks by solid or hollow traverses - the latter being used as magazines or side arms stores - or by building Haxo casemates. These casemates would enable the curtain of fire between forts to be maintained during an attack. They are not suitable for use on the faces of works because the masonry of their embrasures would be open to direct fire from enemy batteries.

The trace of the ditch should be considered irrespective of the line of the ramparts in some cases. It should not always be parallel to the ramparts if that means leaving ground which could not be seen from the works on either side. Also if following the rampart too closely resulted in the ditch having too many sides there might be problems flanking it.

Ditches flanked by bomb-proof caponiers well hidden by the counterscarp should be so placed and constructed that they could not be silenced by enemy batteries positioned in prolongation of the particular face. The alternative of galleries in the counterscarp to flank the ditch have the disadvantage that they can be destroyed by mining, though they are useful places from which to build countermines.

Caponiers should be built to house light guns or howitzers and not for musketry only: 'a few muskets would not prevent the success of a determined assaulting party on a long face of a work'.

On the other hand loopholes alongside the guns are needed to cover the ditch with fire during the intervals when the guns are reloading. There should be fireplaces in the caponiers to provide extra accommodation in wartime and to ensure the gunners are on the spot when needed.

Barracks should be bomb-proofed and suitable for accommodation in peacetime, but need only be for half the wartime garrison who could double up in emergency. Where the height of the rampart permits it, bomb-proof accommodation should be under the front face, the most secure place.

To protect the scarp from long range, i.e. descending, gunfire the ditch should be narrow - less than 45 feet - and the height of the scarp should usually be 30 feet. This can be increased by a further 7 feet by a loopholed wall on the top of the scarp (*chemin des rondes*) which should be 6 feet lower than the crest of the glacis on the front faces and 3 feet on the flanks.

The main advantage of a *chemin des rondes* is when opposing an escalade, since it gives greater height to the scarp, except where it has been demolished by bombardment, and it makes it easier to reform the parapet where it has been destroyed. However, in the event of a successful assault, the berm - the ledge at the foot of the ramparts - provides a footing for the assault party, though the effect of this can be minimised by providing flanking walls with rifle loops.

Jervois goes on to suggest that it is desirable 'for the economy of construction and to give a facility of constructing flanking galleries where required' to build both the scarp and counterscarp *en décharge* rather than with a solid revetment. This system is shown in Plate IV in his article and consists of a hollow arched revetment in front of the principal face of both the scarp and the counterscarp so that the earth piled on the arches can fall freely away into the ditch under bombardment allowing the scarp to be consolidated. This system was not used at Plymouth, except in one form at Tregantle.

Since the works must be defensible by a small number of men they should be provided with casemated keeps at their gorges, either circular or polygonal in plan, so as to give equal fire over the interior of the fort and projecting to the rear sufficiently to flank the ditches along the gorge. Jervois goes on to detail the various advantages of keeps and the important details of their construction. All can be seen at Tregantle (Plates 31 and 54):

1. Guns should be mounted in two tiers, the lower in casemates firing just above the scarp of the inner ditch and the upper tier commanding the ramparts of the fort and the ground to the rear of the keep.

2. It is important that the casemates of the keep should be built en décharge.

3. The inner ditch of the keep may be flanked by a counterscarp gallery from which underground tunnels may be made to the caponiers flanking the ditch of the fort.

4. In some cases keeps are designed to bring artillery fire on the ground to the rear so as to form the nucleus of a fresh position if one of the works is captured.

At Tregantle, although the keep does not project into the ditch at the gorge, the ditch is covered by musketry galleries linked by a system of tunnels to the keep and its counterscarp gallery, as well as to the rifle galleries in the ditch covering the gorge and a counterscarp gallery connecting them.

It is surprising at first sight that no other keeps were completed at Plymouth after Tregantle and the reasons for this will be discussed later. In 1863 the keeps planned for the line of forts on Portsdown Hill were revised and 'redans or casemated barrack blocks, with provision for rearward defence' were substituted.[7] This suggests that a decision to modify the keep at Staddon Fort was made at the same time; it had certainly been taken by 1864. Jervois completed his paper by discussing whether the detached works he had described should be connected by continuous lines of defence. Where the object was simply to prevent the bombardment of a dockyard it would be unnecessary.

In the event many of the elaborations in the specimen plans attached to his paper were never incorporated in the Plymouth works. Economy ruled, one suspects. But the, later, design of Crownhill Fort though relatively simple produced a most effective work.

It was not until 1862 that Jervois was made Director of Works for Fortifications and so was able to control, as well as to coordinate, the plans for the defences. This probably explains why the first plans for land forts at Plymouth, those for the Staddon Position dating from November 1860 onwards prepared by Captain Du Cane and initialled by Burgoyne and Jervois, included features which were later omitted. These include the elaborate design for the hexagonal keep at Staddon (see back cover). At Stamford there were to be 2 and 3-gun Haxos entirely faced with stone as well as a casemated mortar battery in the salient for 8 mortars.[8]

The detailed policy for the new coast batteries, based on the smooth-bore guns then available, was laid down in July 1860 in the report of a committee set up by the Commander-in-Chief. It emphasized that in view of the limited size of coast batteries the armament must be kept simple and that in place of the 23 varieties of guns found in batteries at the time they should be reduced to five:-

10-in gun of 86 cwt.
68-pdr of 95 cwt.
8-in gun of 65 cwt.
32-pdr of 56 cwt.
13-in sea service mortar.

Of these, the 68-pdr, 8-in gun and 32-pdr were the most effective as they were capable of firing both common (explosive) and the new Martin (liquid iron) shells which were the most effective way of setting fire to wooden ships.

Where practicable, all guns in a battery should be of the same calibre and all batteries should have shot furnaces. In earthwork batteries guns should be at least 35 feet apart and traverses provided between every two guns. Where batteries were close to a deep water channel or the site was small, they should be in casemates.

In spite of the attempt of the committee to simplify, five types of shell were recommended for the 68-pounder batteries: solid shot, common shell, shrapnel, case and grape, and in addition Martin's. Although the Martin liquid iron shells were considered a most important element the committee had no information about the furnace required to heat the molten iron with which they were filled. By 1862 trials were being carried out at Staddon Point Battery with Anderson's Cupola designed for this purpose. (The system was later abandoned.).

A most important development in gunnery occurred in 1858 when Sir William Armstrong's design for a Rifled Breech Loading (RBL) gun was approved after four years of trials (Plate 21). Manufacture began in 1859 after Armstrong had been appointed Superintendent of the Royal Gun Factory, Woolwich.

It had long been appreciated that a pointed projectile fired from a gun would, in theory, have many advantages. It would give greater range, because of its much improved aerodynamic shape as compared with a round shot, greater penetration and would hold a much larger explosive charge. It could achieve greater accuracy owing to its improved stability in the bore of the gun (round shot tended to wobble in the bore). But a pointed projectile when fired from a smooth bore gun turns end over end, and is hopelessly inaccurate and short ranged. The problem was to spin such a projectile in order to make it stable in flight.

The Lancaster gun which was tried in the Crimea achieved the object by having a slightly oval bore with a

Plate 21: *An Armstrong 7-inch RBL gun at Fort Nelson, Portsmouth.* (AUTHOR)

twist in it. In practice these guns proved too inaccurate and the idea was abandoned. However the Armstrong gun combined a number of original features and in particular it was rifled i.e. the barrel had a number of narrow spiral grooves. The projectile was coated with a sheet of lead alloy which bit into the grooves when the gun was fired. Not only was the projectile stabilised in flight in this way, but improved range, accuracy and consistency of performance was achieved.

The Armstrong gun was loaded from the breech through a hole which was closed for firing with a steel wedge dropped in and screwed into position against the face of the breech (Plate 21 above). More important for future development was the fact that the gun was built up of tubular hoops of wrought iron rather than being made of a single piece of cast iron. By shrinking successive tubes one on the other the gun was better able to withstand the force of the explosion of the charge in the chamber without increasing its weight unduly.

This gun was a great advance, not least because it achieved a range of over 9000 yards in trials, three times the practicable range of a smooth-bore gun. The new guns went first to the Royal Navy and HMS *Warrior*, launched in November 1860, was armed with a number of 7-inch RBL guns of this design. Although the Commission had to take into account the potential of the new rifled guns in the hands of an attacker it proposed that the new coast fortifications should be armed with a large number of 68-pounders and a corresponding number of 8-inch shell guns, all smooth bore, because it would be some time before the new guns would be available for coast defence, much less for land defence which was the lowest priority.

The first rifled breech-loading guns on the Armstrong principle proved unsatisfactory in naval service due to the relative inefficiency of the wedge system of sealing the breech on a large gun, and they were gradually abandoned by the navy in favour of a new type of gun - the rifled muzzle-loader (RML). This system was based on three deep spiral grooves cut in the barrel of the gun corresponding with three pairs of studs on the shell which was fitted into the grooves at the muzzle and rammed in the usual way.

The rifled muzzle-loading gun had many of the advantages of the rifled breach-loader. In addition it was more simple to make, more reliable and capable of rapid development in ever larger calibres using the built up system for the barrel developed by Armstrong (Plate 22). Its great disadvantage was the slowness of loading due to the problem of manoeuvring the increasingly heavy shells into the muzzle of the gun, and the shorter range as compared with the Armstrong gun, since the shell did not fit as tightly into the bore. However the development of RML guns did not occur until several years after the Royal Commission had made its report and only affected modifications to the coast batteries and land forts from 1866 onwards. The

Plate 22: *12-inch RML gun on Drake's Island, Plymouth.* (AUTHOR)

Commission's main concern was the fact that before long foreign armies which were working along the same lines would be armed with accurate field and siege artillery (RBL) with up to three times the range of existing cannon.

Just as Jervois provided the basis of the Royal Commission's layout of the Plymouth fortifications, so Burgoyne in a 'Memo on the probable effect of Rifled Cannon on the Attack and Defence of Fortifications'.[9] written on 7 February 1859 provided the background to the latest developments in artillery. He considered that the greatly increased power of guns in terms of range, accuracy and penetration would be of more advantage to the attack than to the defence. To reduce this potential advantage, the parapets on ramparts must be thickened and gun embrasures reduced to a minimum size. Bombproof overhead cover and screens of earth must cover magazines, stores and other vulnerable places since shells fired at such long ranges would descend almost vertically, not striking the defences nearly horizontally as previously. Guns would often have to be in casemates divided from each other by substantial partitions, and in the open would always be dispersed with earth traverses between them. The developments in artillery would result in 'the exposure of the great naval arsenals to a thoroughly effective fire from ranges that were before unobtainable'. This was another problem with which the Royal Commission had to grapple.

The Royal Commission published its report[10] on 7 February 1860, within six months of its being set up. It defined the object of fortifications as being:

(a) To enable a small body of troops to resist a superior force, or
(b) To enable partly trained bodies of men to contend successfully with those more perfectly disciplined than themselves.

It then went on to make the assumption that 'such troops as may be got together from the disembodied or less perfectly trained portion of the militia with local or other volunteers would, with an admixture of regular soldiers, be able to defend our dockyards against very superior numbers when fortified with due regard to these principles'. Even allowing for the relative simplicity of weapons and tactics at the time and the limited training required to make troops effective this seems an optimistic assumption to modern ears.

The Commission's report on Plymouth began by emphasising that 'of late years the construction of the Breakwater, which provides a safe anchorage for our ships of war, the erection of the fine victualling establishment at Stonehouse (Royal William Yard), and subsequently the great extension of our naval establishment by the Steam Yard at Keyham, have presented additional objects to be defended; whilst the extent of the ground which they occupy, and the great advances that have been made in the science of war, have rendered the defence more difficult'. Although Plymouth would not be involved in any invasion aimed at London 'on the other hand, its distance from the Metropolis, causes it to be almost entirely dependent on its own garrison for defence.'

The Commission discussed first the sea defences which had three objects:

1. The defence of the entrance to the Hamoaze.
2. The security of the Sound as an anchorage for our own ships and against its occupation by the enemy.
3. The adoption of means to prevent the bombardment of the dockyard by ships of the enemy at long range.

The Commission's recommendations for the defence of Plymouth are shown in Plate 23. They consisted of an outer and an inner line of sea defences, and the land defences. Starting with the inner line and Drake's Island, the Commission recommended strongly that its existing battery of 22 guns should be strengthened and the Island armed on every side to cover both the main channel between the Island and the Hoe and the shallow Bridge channel between the Island and Mount Edgcumbe. Additional guns should be placed on Eastern King and Western King on either flank of the existing redoubts and a new battery built at Mount Edgcumbe (Garden Battery).

When considering the outer line the Commission, whilst noting the existing forts at Picklecombe and Staddon Point and the work already begun on a fort at Cawsand, commented that the first two forts were 'from their construction entirely unfitted to resist concentrated horizontal fire of shells, that could be brought to bear on them by large ships of war'. More powerful casemated

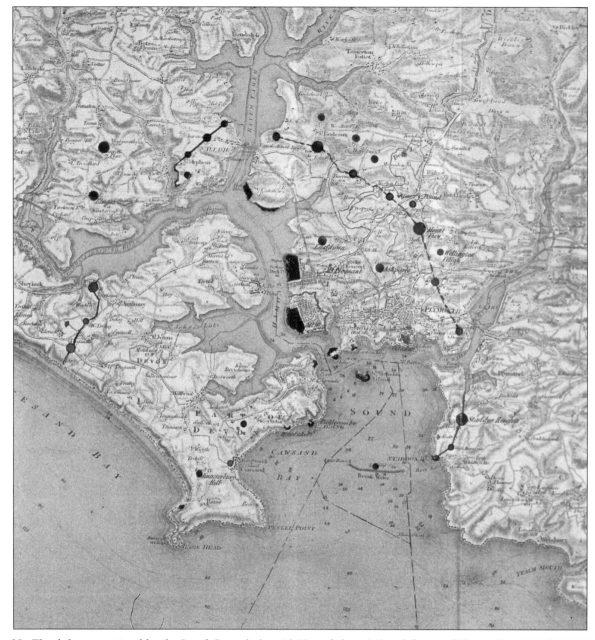

Plate 23: *The defences proposed by the Royal Commission, 1860, and the existing defences of Plymouth.* (PRO ZHC 1/2577)

batteries were recommended for these two positions, and there was to be an open battery at Hooe Lake Point.

Whilst these works would prevent the enemy from anchoring inside the breakwater, the main forts on either side of the Sound were nearly 4000 yards apart and it was therefore recommended that a powerful casemated work should be built immediately behind the Breakwater, and near its centre, to command the approach to both the entrances to the Sound from the seaward. The use of iron-sided steam-driven floating batteries were recommended in principle by the Commission, but never approved due to the drain on naval manpower and the cost of their maintenance in a state of readiness.

The land defences were considered under four headings:

1. The fortification of the peninsula between the St Germans River and the sea, to be called the 'Western Defences'.

2. That of the country between the St Germans River and the Tamar - the 'Saltash Defences'.

3. That of the country between the Tamar and the Cattewater - the 'North Eastern Defences'

4. That of the high ground between the Cattewater and the Sound - the 'Staddon Heights Defences'.

The Commission noted that work had already begun on the Western Defences in front of the village of Antony and 6000 yards from the Dockyard. It recommended that the main works and the intermediate redoubt should be linked by a permanent ditch and rampart. To cover Whitsand Bay a battery (Polhawn) should be built flanking the beach below Rame village and protected by a small work on Knatterbury Hill above. The existing old redoubts on Maker Heights were to be repaired and strengthened and a defensible barracks built in the rear (in the place of the existing barracks) to support the other works and provide garrisons for them. This in fact was never built and is probably the reason why the accommodation at Tregantle was increased to hold 2000 men.

The Saltash Defences were to be increased (from Jervois' proposals) to include four works on the high ground above the town connected by a ditch and rampart and, to prevent the bombardment of the dockyard at long range by rifled guns, the enemy was to be denied observation by redoubts above Burrell House and on a knoll near Elmgate.

Having reviewed the existing defences in and around the dockyard the Commission recommended that the North Eastern Defences should, following Jervois' general line, consist of seven works from St Budeaux through Kings Tamerton, Burrington House, Quarry Pound, Torr House, Mount View, Wallington Villas and in front of the Borough Gaol to Cattedown. The line would be covered by advanced works at Honicknowle, on a hill near Burrington Farm and on another hill north of St Budeaux. The main line of forts was to be connected by lines of ditch and rampart and supported by works within the line at Ash Park and East Down which together with the Citadel on the right of the line were to be the depots and principal barracks for the main line. Mount Pleasant Redoubt and the Citadel were to be improved, including casemated barracks in the latter and a deeper ditch.

The Staddon Heights Defences were to consist of two works connected by lines of ditch and rampart joining them to the sea at Staddon Point to the south and Hooe Lake to the north. The left flank of this position would be covered by the proposed fort at Cattedown. Finally, money was also included to cover the further cost of improving, and in some places realigning, Devonport Lines on which work had been resumed in 1853.

The total cost of the fortifications proposed by the

Commission was estimated at £11.85 million. After the Cabinet had carefully considered the report it made reductions in the number of forts and batteries which, after also deducting the estimates for the armament and the proposed floating defences, resulted in a revised cost of £6.57 million. This was to be covered by a special Defence Loan, to ensure that the works would be carried out quickly and would not be dependent on annual votes. The first part of the loan was authorised in an Act of 28 August 1860. The initial expenditure of £2 million was approved for the period to 1 August 1861 and consisted of £350 000 to cover the works in progress already sanctioned, the balance to be used for the works now approved. The money was to be paid initially from the Consolidated Fund and was to be repaid by 30 year terminable annuities.

It was only with difficulty that Palmerston had persuaded Gladstone, the Chancellor of the Exchequer, not to resign when faced by this huge new expenditure which had resulted in the addition of a penny on Income Tax in the previous April. But Palmerston was clear - 'Better to lose Mr Gladstone than to run the risk of losing Portsmouth'.

Also on 28 August a Defence Act was passed 'to make the better Provisions for acquiring land for the Defence of the Realm'. This Act authorised the acquisition of land for building the fortifications, and for the glacis surrounding them, and also for the purchase of clearance rights in front of and around the fortifications to enable an unobstructed field of fire to be created if an attack threatened.

The remainder of the money required to complete the programme of fortifications was authorised by subsequent acts providing for additional issues of annuities. The Fortifications Act of 31 May 1867 gives a schedule of revised estimates based on later decisions, such as the one to omit the proposed barracks at Maker, which saved

£20 000. Generally speaking, improvements to the fortifications authorised during the progress of building were charged to the Defence Loan. Alterations due to changes in the type of guns to be mounted were not charged to the loan, nor were later modifications such as the remodelling of the magazines on Drake's Island, which was subsequently recommended, both of which were covered under the Annual Votes.

The original cost of the works proposed at Plymouth was £2.67 million. They were to be armed in peacetime with 742 guns and manned by 7000 men. The garrison required for the defences in the event of an attack was estimated at 15 000 men of all arms. (When, in 1803, Major General Mercer had been asked to report on the defences of Plymouth as they then were, he said that they required a minimum of 9700 men - 700 of whom would man the Lines - plus a reserve of 3200 and 1200 artillerymen. A further 2000 would be needed to man Staddon Heights).

The Cabinet cut the Commission's proposals for Plymouth particularly sharply, reducing the total estimated expenditure to £1.55 million. Altogether some 15 works were removed from the original proposals. The central redoubt between Tregantle and Scraesdon and the linking rampart and ditch between the two forts was not built nor was the redoubt at Knatterbury or the battery at Hooe Lake Point. The three outlying redoubts of the North Eastern Defences and the two new fortified barracks inside the general line were also omitted.

The building of the whole of the Saltash position was deferred and in fact it was never started. This created what at first appears to be an alarming gap in the defences. But it was accepted on each occasion when the position was reviewed that it would take an enemy who had landed further west at least a week to reach this position due to the hilly country and the need to march round the estuary of the St Germans River. By this time the garrison would have dug strong field defences round Saltash and to the west, supported by the field guns held for the purpose at Saltash and at Ernesettle Battery.

In view of the limited reserve of regular troops in the Plymouth garrison and the predominance of militia and volunteer units, it remains uncertain whether such a force would have dug in and organised itself sufficiently to resist a determined attack in the time. There is in the Public Record Office[11] a map drawn in the spring of 1861 of the Saltash position showing five blocks of land corresponding with the positions in the Royal Commission's report with the glacis and clearance areas shown. Not only were these works not built but there is no sign that detailed plans for field defences covering Saltash were ever drawn up, though this was more than once recommended, and a specially prepared very large scale hand-drawn map of the Saltash position in the Public Record Office dated 1862[12] has no military dispositions marked on it.

The final account for the cost of the Plymouth defences was set out in a report on the fortifications in 1869 as follows:

Expenditure on land	£282 840
Expenditure under the loan	£1 315 891
Expenditure under annual votes	£80 816
Total	£1 679 547

Estimate of Defence Commissioners £2 670 000
Saving £990 453
Note: The total expenditure was 63 per cent of the Royal Commission's original estimate.

A detailed review of the financing of the construction of the fortifications is given in Appendix E.

References

[1] *Fort* 14. p. 40.
[2] Ibid. p.41
[3] *Fort* 8 Supplement. pp. 20-44.
[4] (PRO WO 33/5: 4.3.1858, 26.5.1858, June 1858, 29.10.1858, 10.11.1858).
[5] (PRO WO 33/5 p. 95)
[6] New Series IX. Paper XIX. 1860.
[7] *Solent Papers* No. 3. 'Fort Nelson and the Portsdown Forts'. p.4).
[8] (PRO WO78/4367/31).
[9] (PRO WO 33/7 p. 18).
[10] (PRO ZHC 1 2577)
[11] (PRO WO 78/ 4367 p. 11)
[12] (PRO WO 78/4428. Part I)

5
THE BUILDING OF THE FORTS - THE VIEW FROM WHITEHALL

'Many mistakes were undoubtedly made and much that was done in haste had to be re-modelled to suit later developments of artillery; but the untiring zeal and energy, the skill and engineering ability, shown from first to last by Col. Jervois, are above praise. His was the master spirit that crushed all opposition; that overcame all difficulties and that enthused into those around him, superiors as well as inferiors, a spirit and devotion to the works that have rarely been surpassed.

Whitworth Porter
History of the Corps of Royal Engineers

The revised Scheme of Defences passed by Parliament in August 1860 was the largest programme of fortification ever authorised in peacetime. The execution of the works was the responsibility of the Defence Committee to which plans were submitted by the Fortifications Committee, the successor to the Royal Commission. The Director of Artillery and the officer Commanding Royal Engineers also made recommendations when appropriate. Major decisions of the Defence Committee were submitted for approval to the Secretary for War.

The proposed designs of the individual forts and batteries were prepared in the first place by selected engineer officers, trained in fortification, under the control and general superintendence of Major Jervois who in 1862 was promoted Lieutenant Colonel and made Deputy Director of Works for Fortifications. It is significant that, though relatively junior at the time, all these officers achieved high rank and distinction later (Appendix F). Much that they achieved, and the fact that their detailed work was subsequently approved by the committee which reviewed it in 1869, must have been due to the inspiration, drive and supervision of Lt. Col. Jervois.

By October 1860 the designs of the main coast batteries at Picklecombe, Bovisand and Drake's Island had been approved and work begun. Plans for the Staddon Heights position had got far enough for the land to be purchased. On 23 November the first overall plan of the position, showing the fort with a hexagonal keep (Plate 24) was initialled by Du Cane and Jervois and marked 'Approved by Her Majesty' on 29 December.[1] Since the Prince Consort had for some years actively supported Palmerston's campaign to improve the country's defences, the approval was almost certainly his. Details of the subsequent development of the Plymouth defences over the next twenty five years are summarised chronologically in Appendix B. Here it is only appropriate to describe the main stages and the principal problems that arose during these years.

To see these developments in context it must be recalled that at this time Plymouth and Devonport extended as far North only as Keyham Lake, Stoke, Pennycomequick and North Hill. There were outlying villages at Outlands,

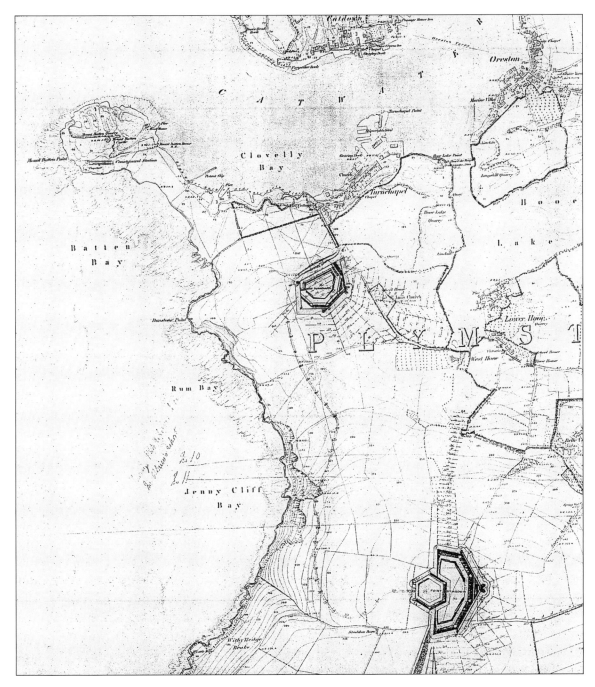

Plate 24: *Proposed layout of Staddon and Stamford Forts, 25 November 1860.* (PRO WO78/4367/3)

Mutley, Compton and Lipson, and further out at St Budeaux and Eggbuckland (see Map II). In view of this it is at first surprising that in July 1861 Lt.Col. Jervois reported that the purchase of land for the North Eastern Defences would cost £350 000 as against the £200 000 provided for this in the Defence Loan. The fact that some of the properties to be purchased or taken under control had recently been bought, or built upon, by leading citizens of Plymouth may have been responsible for the high prices asked. They included Mount View, the home of Mr. W.E. Rendle, Thornhill belonging to Mr. Whiteford, Town Clerk of Plymouth, and Compton Leigh recently built by Mr. Luscombe, the Mayor. After inspecting the ground the Fortification Committee recommended that the line of the defences should be advanced about a mile. Its left would then be to the north of St Budeaux village, and the line would run through Knackers Knowle (Crownhill) to Efford Warren on the right.

The Defence Committee approved this change which involved building nine forts and batteries in the main defensive line instead of the seven recommended by the Royal Commission. These works were eventually at: Ernesettle, Agaton, Knowle, Woodland, Bowden, Forder, Austin, Efford and Laira, and their design was finally approved in 1863.[†] The estimate for their construction was £350 000 - there were no figures for the specific works - and there was eventually a saving on this figure to meet the increased expenditure on Staddon Heights authorised in 1867.

It was proposed that these works should be supported by strong self-defensible keeps within the main line, serving as bombproof barracks and depots. These were to be at St Budeaux, Widey, Eggbuckland and Efford, but only Eggbuckland was eventually built. The batteries at Ernesettle, Agaton, Woodland, Austin and Efford were later turned into minor forts with bomb-proof accommodation in casemates for their garrisons. The accommodation at Efford was substantial so as to provide for the whole Efford-Laira position.

In addition a detached advanced fort was to be built at Crownhill, and military roads protected from fire on the enemy side by a bank and parapet were to be built linking all the forts and batteries. The main military road ran from Ernesettle Battery (Plate 25) roughly along the line of the modern Crownhill Road and Fort Austin Avenue. It can be seen in its original form south of Fort Austin and to the west of Efford Fort, as well as from there down to Plymouth Road at Crabtree. Where necessary spurs, banked on both sides, linked the military road to those forts and batteries which were in front of the general line of the road.

During the period from 1859 onwards there had been a lively controversy in military circles about the principles on which the fortifications should be based. Some argued for and against the incorporation of keeps in forts and there were some who doubted whether caponiers and counterscarp galleries would be effective in war. But the main dispute was between those who, like Col. Cunliffe Owen, recommended that in Plymouth the North Eastern Defences should be joined by a continuous ditch and rampart, and those who favoured detached forts and batteries. The argument covered the relative cost of the two systems, and which could in practice be defended by the smallest number of relatively untrained men. It was not until 1864 that Col. Cunliffe Owen made his final and unsuccessful representation in favour of continuous lines of defence.[2] In the same year Captain Du Cane who had by then completed the designs for most of the works in the North Eastern Defences was writing in favour of the use of iron shields in land forts in some circumstances and even of small iron blockhouses in the covered way.[3] The sug-

---

[†]'Fort' normally refers to a fortification entirely surrounded by a rampart or wall and including accommodation for its whole garrison. A 'battery' has accommodation only in a guardhouse and may sometimes be open to the rear. Due to changes in the layout of the defences and modificatons during construction the titles of the works varied from time to time.

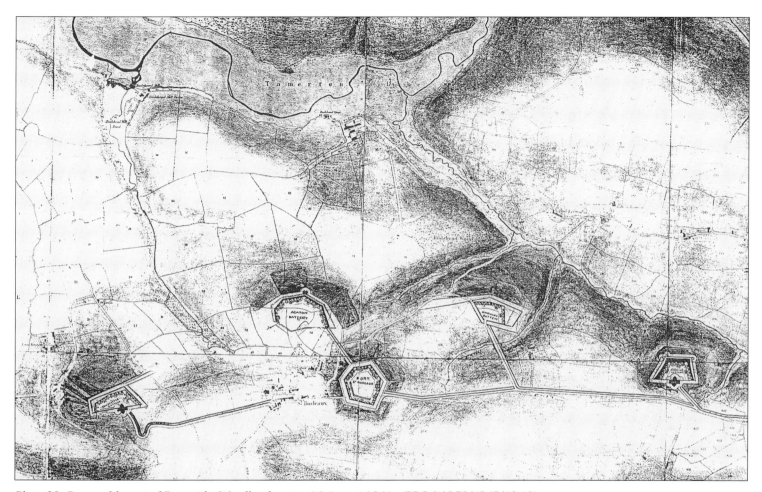

Plate 25: *Proposed layout of Ernesettle–Woodland sector, 16 August 1861.* (PRO WO78/4367/12-13)

gested use of iron, especially iron shields in front of embrasures, was aired at various times later.

In November 1864 General Todleben, the Russian General who had commanded with such skill and ingenuity the defence of Sebastopol in the Crimean War, visited England and with the approval of Burgoyne was shown the initial work on the defences of Portsmouth and Plymouth. This may seem strange at first sight but in those days secu-rity as we know it did not cover the construction of fortifications or even new naval developments such as the building of *La Gloire*.

Maps showing the layout of the forts built in the 1860s were soon available in France. Todleben's comments to the engineer officers who accompanied him were incorporated in a report, together with the later comments of Jervois who was unfortunately in Canada at the time.[4]

One of Gen. Todleben's first observations when seeing the extent of the land defences - from Tregantle through Crownhill to Staddon Heights - was to question how sufficient men could be found to garrison them. Later he modified this comment when he was shown the detailed dispositions and how difficult it would be for an enemy, in the case of Plymouth, to attack simultaneously and in strength more than one of the four positions, separated as they were by estuaries. It was also put to him that the tradition of volunteer units in this country, and the general instruction in rifle practice being given, would help to provide garrisons for such places.

In particular General Todleben praised the design of the 'large advanced fort' at Tregantle and was in favour of a keep for such a work, not as a refuge for the defenders of the fort itself but with its own commandant and garrison. Its object would be to hold out once the fort had been taken for up to two days, or at the least for several hours, until reinforcements arrived. When later he was shown the original plan of Fort Staddon which was also designed with a keep enclosed within a revetted ditch, he approved of this rather than the revised plan in which the area of the keep was not isolated from the rest of work other than by a parados. Jervois pointed out the huge additional cost - £52 000 - of building the keep in the original plan.

The principle of detached enclosed works rather than a continuous line was strongly approved by Todleben. In the North Eastern Defences he would have preferred to have seen four or five very strong forts at St Budeaux, Woodland (or the next spur to the east), Crownhill, Austin and Efford on commanding sites with a chain of open earthwork batteries in front of them. These batteries would have been able to cover the steeper forward slopes - sometimes out of view of the works which were built - with fire. The garrisons of these batteries would, when closely attacked,

retire into or behind the nearest fort leaving the enemy exposed to the fire of the latter. To the rear would be further earthwork batteries covering the gaps between the main forts. He could not imagine that an attacking general would dare to leave the principal forts untaken even if he did penetrate between them, and he emphasised the importance of the reserve army of 3000–4000 men without which any defence of the forts would be 'a simple impossibility'. This reserve would have the great advantage of a knowledge of the ground over which it would deploy.

The detached forts which he proposed would presumably have been built on the scale of Crownhill Fort. Jervois commented that the problem was to provide permanent defence for the whole of the North East of Plymouth at the least cost. He thought that this had been done more effectively and more cheaply than if General Todleben's system had been adopted. Five principal forts on the scale of Crownhill would have more than absorbed all the money available for the North Eastern Defences, without any batteries (see Appendix E).

General Todleben was high in praise of the line taken by the North Eastern Defences, declaring that 'the man who laid them out must have had an astute mind'. In his view 'the manner in which the valleys in front of the position were searched by the batteries of the different works was particularly well managed, and that the desired result of commanding the ground was obtained in a far higher degree than he would have thought possible from a first glance at the undulating character of the country'. In the end the North Eastern defences consisted of three mutually supporting groups of minor forts and batteries with a single powerful fort at Crownhill slightly in advance of the general line, capable of all round defence and prolonged resistance.

The position of Crownhill Fort Todleben described as 'magnificent' and he saw it as the keystone of the land defences of Devonport. Its building was still in the early stages and he emphasised that it should be made as strong to the rear, including a glacis and deep ditch, as to the front. (This principle he would have applied to all his main forts). Due to the importance of its position and to the fact that it was not completed until after the other principal forts, Crownhill represents a considerable advance in detailed fortification technique over, for example, Tregantle: the concealment of its ramparts from the north, the steep narrow ditch, the development of the caponiers, the *chemin des rondes* and the effective bomb-proofing of all accommodation. Yet its cost was only £76 409 as compared with a total cost for Tregantle of £198 999, including the earlier expenditure before the Defence Loan, due partly to the absence of a keep and the use of open rather than casemated mortar batteries.

At the Staddon Heights position, apart from his comment on the desirability of a keep at Staddon Fort, he approved of Brownhill Battery and the fact that in spite of the lack of a ditch it was secured from a *coup de main* by its south and east scarps. Its rear, as well as the whole plateau between Staddon and the sea, could be swept by case or grape shot from the fort. While inspecting the form of the embrasures at Bovisand (the report appears to refer to Staddon Fort but there are no such embrasures with shields there) he commented that the most vulnerable point was where on either side the shield joined the granite of the emplacement.

1864 was also the year by which the Scheme of Defences should have been completed. Much progress had been made with the granite casemated coast batteries but doubts had been raised about their final form as a result of the experience of the American Civil War, which had shown the relative effectiveness of earthwork emplacements, incorporating traverses, for coast batteries.

Earlier, in 1861, the Royal Commission had been reassembled to consider the results of trials carried out with armour plating at the artillery testing ground at Shoeburyness. Although its first conclusions were indecisive, by 1863 armour plating for casemates was being seriously considered. The experiments showed the effectiveness of wrought iron plate against even the fire of a pointed shell from a rifled gun. Later trials involved shields 2-3 feet thick built up of sandwiches of wrought iron plate separated by layers of iron concrete or teak which helped to absorb the impact of projectiles. It was eventually decided to build the granite casemates in their original form but to replace the recessed granite embrasures with iron shields covering the whole front of the casemate, which was meanwhile left open.

It is clear that Jervois had difficulty keeping the cost of the fortifications within the overall budget approved by Parliament, even after the new line of the North Eastern Defences had been agreed. Savings in the cost of the land were matched by the increased number of works to be built. Alterations and improvements to the individual fortifications made during the progress of the work had to come out of the Defence Loan. But alterations due to changes in the guns to be mounted, and particularly the cost of the iron shields, were not charged to the loan but financed separately. Subsequent modifications, such as those to the magazines at Drake's Island, were covered in the Annual Estimates.

In spite of the delays caused by these modifications and developments, and by the setback at Plymouth in 1866 due to the bankruptcy of the contractor for the North Eastern Defences, work had progressed sufficiently for General

Burgoyne to instruct Lt. Col. Jervois in 1867 to prepare a report on the progress of the defences as a whole.[5] In his covering letter to the Secretary for War, Burgoyne emphasised the need to provide iron shields for the embrasures of the coast batteries, now considered essential due to the launching of armour plated warships with much more powerful guns.

At Plymouth, Jervois looked first at the coast defences and found that whereas the battery at Cawsand had been finished, those at Bovisand and Picklecombe were half complete and only the foundations and basement of Breakwater Fort had been built. He commented that the sea defences were likely to be completed under cost apart from the iron shields which would increase the original figure by 20–25 per cent. The earthworks at Eastern and Western King were finished and so was Garden Battery apart from the iron shields. The much larger casemated battery at Drake's Island was only three-quarters finished and again had no iron shields. Here it was intended now to mount in addition five 23-ton RML (12-inch) guns *en barbette* on the upper battery on top of the island.

Of the Western Defences, Tregantle and Polhawn were finished and Scraesdon was 5/6th complete, but no work had been done at Maker Barracks. He noted that the Saltash Defences had never been sanctioned. On the Eastern side the forts at Staddon and Stamford were complete and the scarp wall joining Staddon to Bovisand had been finished and was covered by a battery (Brownhill). The North Eastern Defences were being finished by day labour under the War Department using methods which must have been similar to those used at Nothe Fort, Portland (Plate 26). He calculated that the Staddon and North Eastern Defences would be completed within the scheduled cost, including a work to cover the bridge at Laira - not then begun and in fact never built.

In the following year (1868) the Fortification Committee considered the possible use of guns mounted on disappearing carriages, an idea originally put forward by Captain Moncrieff in 1865 and at that time rejected. A 7-inch RML gun on this type of carriage had been tested earlier in the year, and its success resulted in the enthusiastic adoption of the system. In the main Plymouth Forts one or two of the characteristic deep concrete pits were eventually built at salients in the ramparts. However, in the following years the demand by the Navy and the coast defences for increasingly large, and heavy, RML guns which it proved impracticable to put on Moncrieff mountings, other than the 9-inch, 12-ton RML, resulted in the system being abandoned in the 1880s after a number of 7-inch RBL guns on this type of mounting had already been installed both at Plymouth and elsewhere.

In 1868 in response to questions raised in the House of Commons a Committee was appointed by the Secretary for War under the chairmanship of Admiral the Hon. Sir F.W. Grey, GCB, to enquire into 'the construction, condition and cost of the fortifications erected or in course of erection, under the Defence and other Acts of 1860'.[6] The Committee visited all the works, questioning at length Colonel Spencer Westmacott, Commanding Royal Engineers Plymouth and Colonel Jervois about the works at Plymouth, and reported in detail in 1869.

In its general report the Committee pointed out that 'as the reductions made at Plymouth were very large and have materially affected the defensive strength of that important position, and the resisting power of its various works' it was necessary to set out both the original recommendations and what was actually being built. All the sea defences had been built apart from the batteries at Hooe Lake Point 'but the character of the works has been materially altered, and a much smaller number of heavy rifled

Plate 26a-d: *Construction methods used by the Royal Engineers at Fort Nothe, Portland.* (ROYAL ENGINEERS LIBRARY, CHATHAM)

guns substituted for the numerous 68-pounders and 8-inch guns then contemplated'.

In the Western Defences the intermediate work between Tregantle and Scraesdon and the connecting ditch and rampart had not been built - it was again recommended by the Committee - and no works had been carried out at Maker Heights or at Knatterbury Hill. Instead a military road had been constructed along the cliffs from Tregantle

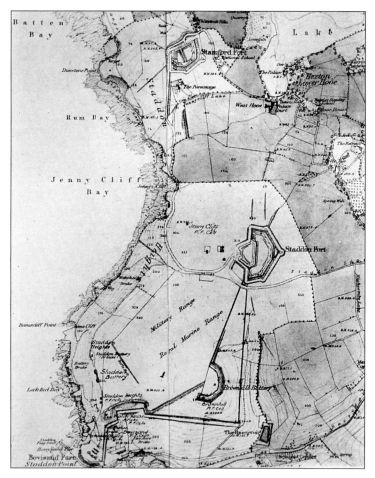

Plate 27: *Staddon Heights Defences c. 1870.* (PLYMOUTH PROPRIETORY LIBRARY).

to Knatterbury, which would enable the large garrison at Tregantle to move under cover from direct fire from the sea to oppose a landing in Whitsand Bay. Noting the absence of the Saltash Defences, the Committee agreed that there was no pressing need for the heavy expense which permanent fortifications here would involve but recommended a careful study of the ground and the preparation of detailed plans for providing a quick defensive position there.

They noted that considerable changes had been made in the layout of the Staddon Defences (Plate 27). The powerful Staddon Fort was connected by a ditch and rampart to Brownhill Battery and then on to Bovisand. Between Brownhill and Bovisand were two small earthwork batteries at Twelve Acre Brake and Watch House Brake flanking the ditch above Bovisand. The line had not been extended north to Hooe Lake as recommended but instead a further fort at Stamford had been built in rear of the proposed line to replace it (and the fort originally to have been at Cattedown across the estuary). A military road linked Stamford and Staddon and ended at Watch House Brake above Bovisand.

The inner line of the North Eastern Defences had been abandoned and the outer line thrown forward. The omission of three of the proposed keeps on the inner line had considerably reduced the defensive power of the position which now had little depth. The report went on to emphasise the importance of Crownhill Fort as the key to the position. 'Much care and skill had been bestowed upon its construction' which was considered necessary since it would 'from its advanced position and the nature of the ground in front of the line, receive but little support from the adjoining works...'. It was particularly noted that Whitleigh Hill overlooks the forts west of Crownhill from 1000–1500 yards away and is over 100 feet higher.

The Efford/Laira position (Plate 28) was one of considerable strength, improved by the building of earthworks both between the fort and the battery and on the high ground behind them, but there were no plans to fill the gap between Laira and the Staddon position.

The sea defences except for Breakwater Fort were almost complete but in the opinion of the committee Cawsand Fort and Eastern and Western King had been constructed for lighter guns than was required and they needed to be remodelled.

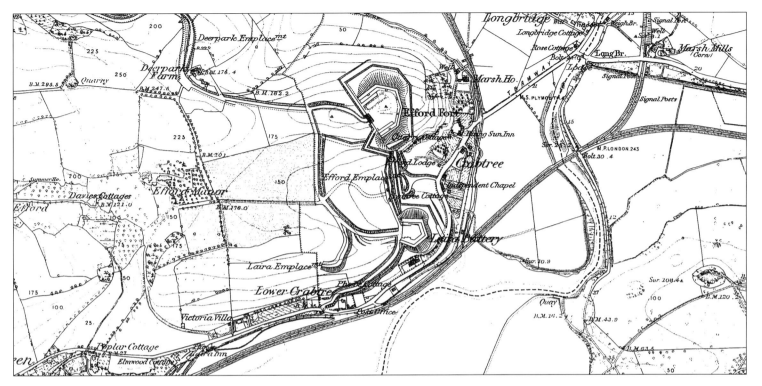

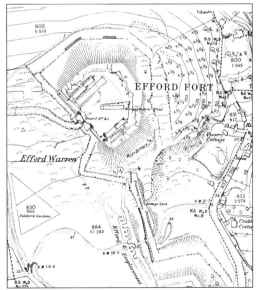

Plate 28a-c: (top) *The Efford–Laira Defences in 1882.* (PRO WO78/2314/9); (left) *The layout of Efford Fort, 1896*; (above) *Efford Fort and its casemates from the south* (COURTESY R.C.F. SERPELL)

Plate 29: *Casemates with wrought iron shields at Bovisand Battery.*
(AUTHOR)

Amongst the appendices attached to the report was one on experiments at Shoeburyness on the accuracy and rapidity of fire from heavy guns against moving targets, which illustrated the limitations of heavy RML guns in a coast defence role. Although the moving targets were judged to have been hit, the rate of fire of a 9-inch RML gun firing a 250 lb shell was just under one round a minute, and a 22-ton (12-inch?) gun firing a 600 lb shell only got off a round in just under 2.5 minutes.

The second appendix was a memorandum on the modifications required in the design of casemates and magazines in recent years when 'the progress in artillery had been rapid and continuous'. This summarises the results of the trials of armour plate at Shoeburyness from 1865 onwards and the conclusion that shields made up of sandwiches of 5-inch wrought iron plate and iron concrete or teak were more effective than solid plates (Plate 29). To keep the embrasure in the shield as small as possible it was

desirable not only to have carriages on which the guns pivoted horizontally about the muzzle but to develop carriages which also pivoted vertically about the muzzle, referred to later as 'small port' or 'muzzle-pivoting' carriages.

Detailed recommendations were also made for the design of magazines. Many of these had been built by contractors to no standard pattern in important respects. They needed further protection against heavier shells and the effects of plunging fire, both in the coast and the land batteries. In this connection the Committee criticised the expense magazines on Drake's Island and recommended modifications.

In particular the Committee was concerned about the design of the embrasures at Tregantle and the need for a large traverse across the middle of the fort to cover the accommodation on the south side from horizontal gunfire. Also, large coast guns were needed to cover the west end of Whitsand Bay and as a result six casemates for 64-pdr guns were built on the south-west face of the fort, which was re-designed. The Committee still considered that a battery at Knatterbury was important, as without it Polhawn was vulnerable to bombardment from ships lying off to the south, whose fire it was unable to return.

In the years immediately following this report, RML guns were produced in large numbers: first the 32-pdrs converted to 64-pdr RML, then the purpose built and heavier 64-pdr RMLs of 64-cwt , and guns of ever-increasing calibre. They were much more costly than the smoothbore guns on which the Royal Commission had based its estimates. But when the Defence Committee was invited to review the armaments in Plymouth with a view to reducing them, it only recommended the reduction of two guns on Drake's Island so that casemates 20 and 21 were turned into an artillery store. Anyway, in 1867 it had already recommended that a further three 10-inch RMLs should be mounted on No. 4 Redoubt at Maker, overlooking Cawsand Bay.

A decision was eventually taken by the Defence Committee in 1872 to recommend the replacement of all obsolete smooth bore guns in the defences with the 64-pounder (converted) RML gun. This was a 32-pounder smooth-bore converted to RML by inserting into the bore a specially designed tube with three deep grooves by way of rifling (known as the Palliser tube after its inventor). These guns were later superceded by the purpose-built, and more powerful, 64-pdr RML. At the same time the Committee added the comment, at first sight astonishing, that 'the armament of the new land defences, which have not yet received any guns, was left for future consideration'.

1872 was also the year in which all the land forts at Plymouth were completed (see Map III). The coast batteries were receiving their iron shields and even the huge shields covering two tiers of embrasures at Picklecombe were in position by the following year (Plate 30). The armament at Breakwater Fort, whose upper tier had been built entirely of iron, was still under consideration.

Jervois made a further report on the progress of the construction of the fortifications in 1874, commenting favourably on the two lines of sea defences, the outer line based on the Breakwater and the inner line on Drake's Island. The latter was now reinforced by the heavy guns mounted at Fort Stamford and by medium RML guns mounted at the Citadel.

The strength of the Western and Eastern Defences Jervois considered satisfactory. On the North Eastern Defences 'the upper portions of the parapets have only been finished in block, and the ramparts have not been fully prepared for the reception of their guns, pending the

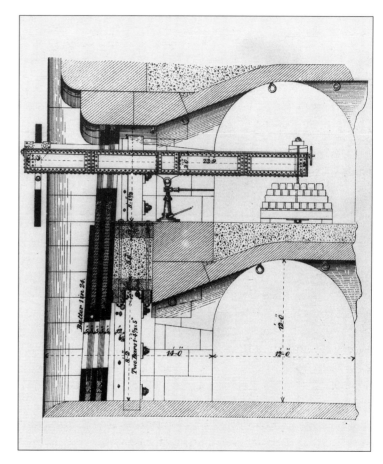

Plate 30: *Installing the gun shields at Picklecombe Battery, Plymouth.*
(COURTESY IAN V. HOGG)

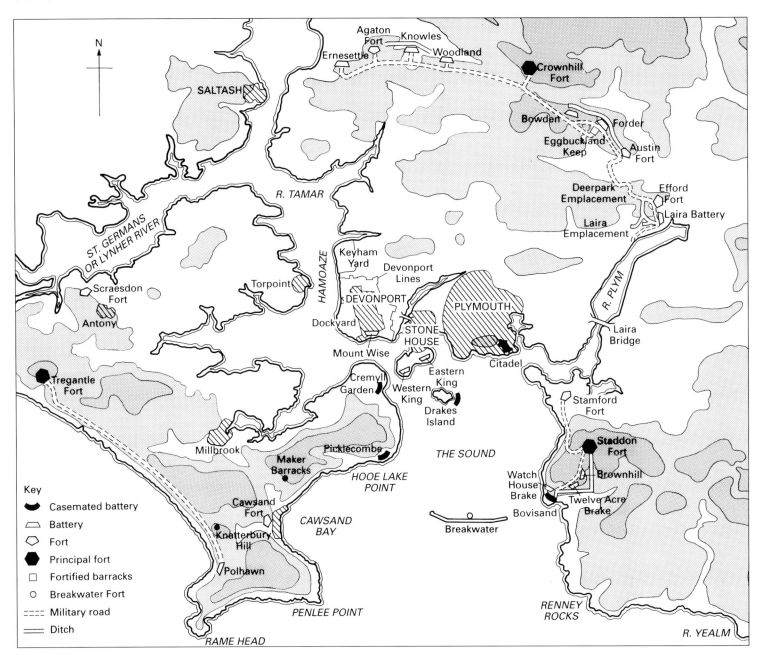

Map III: *Plymouth's Palmerston Forts in 1872.*

Key
- 🌙 Casemated battery
- ⬣ Battery
- ⬠ Fort
- ⬢ Principal fort
- ☐ Fortified barracks
- ○ Breakwater Fort
- ---- Military road
- —— Ditch

final decision on the subject of the armament'. On the other hand in the sea defences 'a considerable portion of the heavy guns (9-inch and 10-inch RMLs) required for their armament have been supplied and mounted'.

Following this report the Defence Committee at last in 1875 made detailed recommendations for the armament of the land works. These were to have 7-inch RBLs, 64-pounder RML guns, 8-inch rifled Howitzers (to replace the mortars originally recommended) and smooth-bore flank guns (these were eventually to be 32-pounder SB.BL guns).

Finally, in 1880, twenty years after the Royal Commission had made its original recommendations, the Inspector General of Fortifications made a report[7] that 'the works are on the whole in a satisfactory state'. He referred to the progress in artillery science since 1860 and the constant modification of the design of the works which this caused. 'Although a large margin of safety was allowed in all vital parts in the original design to provide for such a contingency, this margin has been outstripped, and magazines in many cases require further protection and additional traverses are required.' He considered the sea defences satisfactory as soon as their armament was completed but the small battery at Polhawn required improvement and heavier guns.

The Inspector went on to comment that the omission of the Saltash Defences left a serious gap and neutralised to some extent the remainder. He noted that Breakwater Fort was receiving its guns but that some of the shields on Drake's Island had not yet been fitted; this should be done at once. Submarine mines had been laid at the entrances to the Sound. The Staddon position was complete and a fixed armament on the land fronts of Fort Staddon and Stamford was being mounted. In the North Eastern Defences 'the parapets have been prepared for part of the standing portion of the armanents, magazines are being strengthened, and extra bomb-proof cover and traverses erected.' Finally, the development of siege artillery made the occupation of the high ground between the river Tamar and the St Germans River west of Saltash more necessary than ever and the central work there should be constructed at once (this was never done). Consequent upon this, the gap between the Laira and Staddon positions, resulting from pushing forward the North Eastern Defences, needed attention.

The Royal Commission's timetable in 1860 for the construction of the forts seems to have been hopelessly optimistic even in the short term. In mitigation it can be pleaded that the task was enormous and the times exceptional, due to the rapid development of new types of artillery and the appreciation that coast batteries now needed armoured protection. The result of these two factors on the effectiveness of the coast batteries which were first priority and were finished relatively early, is shown by the fact that by 1867 not only were there few if any armoured shields in position but there were only four RML guns in the whole of the Plymouth Defences.

The design and construction of the land fortifications went forward reasonably quickly apart from the delays in completing the North Eastern Defences. But except for the Western Defences which had been begun previously, there is nothing to suggest that the ditches and ramparts were sufficiently advanced to form a basis for defence within three or four months as envisaged by the Commission. In 1870 when the land defences were almost complete the Franco-Prussian War and the utter defeat of the French army removed at once the main threat of invasion. In these circumstances the further delays in completing the armament of the land forts can be understood.

References

[1] (PRO WO78/4367 MR1849 p.3).
[2] *Duties of the Corps of RE.* New Series Vol 13, 1864 p. 102
[3] 'Fortification in Iron'. RE Papers. Vol III. 1863
[4] (PRO WO 55/1548/23)
[5] (PRO ZHL 1/1747)
[6] (PRO. ZHL 1/1884).
[7] (PRO WO33/2772 p.10)

Drake's Island c. 1870. (COURTESY PAT MOLYNEAUX)

6
THE BUILDING OF THE FORTS - THE PLYMOUTH SCENE

'Much activity has been recently exhibited by the Government engineers in the vicinity of Plymouth and Devonport, and through the advertisements which they have issued some indication has at length been given of the direction of the fortifications.'

Plymouth & Devonport Weekly Journal.

Whatever the delays in Whitehall, there was great activity around Plymouth from the autumn of 1860 onwards. The work on the Western Defences was well under way and soon surveyors began to swarm over Staddon Heights and the proposed line of the North Eastern Defences. The coast batteries were first priority and plans for Picklecombe, Bovisand and Drake's Island batteries were approved in October of that year. The first design for Breakwater Fort was approved shortly afterwards, followed by the plans for the extensions to Eastern and Western King redoubts together with the first plans for the Staddon Position and preliminary ideas for the layout of the North Eastern Defences. Plans for the two small batteries at Polhawn and Mount Edgcumbe Garden were approved in the spring of 1861.

However, these great building projects had apparently little effect on life in Plymouth at the time to judge from the shortage of references in diaries and in the local papers. In the first place most of the men who worked on the pro-ject must have been itinerant 'navvies' who, having helped to complete the Great Western line to Penzance - with its thirty viaducts - in the previous year, were attracted to the work on the fortifications at Plymouth. Assuming the recommendations of the Royal Commission were carried out, these men were housed in tents or temporary hutted camps near the sites of the forts.

Any local men involved in the works were anyway far from home, even those working on the North Eastern Defences which were out of sight of even the outskirts of the town. At that time there were some cottages at the top of what is now Mutley Plain and between there and the centre of the town were only a few big houses with spacious grounds (see Map II). St Judes was virgin soil and Beaumont House was at the edge of the town. The first villas at Mannamead had been built and to the north of these were a handful of big houses and their estates - Thornhill, Burleigh, Montpellier. Old Town Street and Ebrington Street had been named but were both very narrow. Alexandra Road did not exist and to get to Laira one had to go down through Fuzzy Lane, now Furzehill Road. Only from the Hoe, then an open space apart from the Royal Citadel, was it possible to see the activity at Garden Battery, on Drake's Island and, later, out near the Breakwater.

Some local interest in the fortifications was aroused in 1861 by the visit of the Commander-in-Chief, HRH the

Duke of Cambridge. He visited Staddon Heights and Bovisand and then crossed by steamer to survey Cawsand Bay and Picklecombe before landing at Stonehouse Point. This visit prompted an article in one local paper, quoted above, describing the activity over the fortifications, some of it accurate and some less so. The comment that 'many of the original plans have been abandoned. Some of them were given up in consequence of the heavy claims by the owners of land lying in the line of the proposed chain of forts' was correct. The writer went on to say that 'the present difference between the value of this land for building and for pasture purposes will be paid to the owners...', in which case the main beneficiary appears to have been Mr G.W. Soltau who owned the estate known as Little Efford.

Though the land acquired eventually for the North Eastern Defences was mainly pasture, the building of the military road from Pomphlett to Staddon Heights caused considerable disturbance at Hooe - 'this retired village' - according to the article. It appears that the principal farmstead in the village was to be razed, the small church of St Anne probably destroyed and notice served on the vicar to give up the parsonage house and school. The fact that similar notices were served on other local landowners, including Lady Rogers, Lord Morley, Col. Harris and Rev. H. Bulteel indicates the widespread effect of the acquisition of land for the defences around Plymouth.

Jervois' letters show that he was continually on the move during the years after 1860 supervising the work of his officers at Plymouth and elsewhere. The Plymouth coast batteries, apart from Breakwater Fort, were designed by Major Porter who also planned most of the batteries at Milford Haven. Captain Siborne, whose main work was in the Thames and Medway defences, was responsible for Breakwater Fort as well as for the sea forts at Portsmouth.. The design of Fort Scraesdon and the early part of the work

at Tregantle was done by Captain Crossman, but after the Royal Commission had reported he was moved to Portsmouth where he designed a series of forts in the Gosport Line which are in many respects similar to Tregantle.

The most important figure in design of the Plymouth defences was Captain du Cane (later Major General Sir Edmund du Cane KCB, see Appendix F). He designed the whole of the North Eastern Defences, as well as the Staddon Defences. In addition he finished the building of Tregantle and designed Polhawn. His skill was demonstrated in the way he adapted the designs of the forts and batteries in the North Eastern Defences to cover the hilly country, and particularly the steep valleys, with the fire of both guns and mortars.

Although he was given another appointment in 1863 he had by then written a paper on 'Fortification in Iron'[1] in which he pointed out that the penetration of a pointed shell into masonry was three times that of a smooth bore, that about 95 per cent of musket and canister balls striking the flared cheeks of a masonry embrasure would be deflected into it and therefore that iron shields were desirable in land defences which were any way subject to more accurate fire than from ships. His arguments do not appear to have been accepted, at least at Plymouth, though there was a reference by Jervois in response to Todleben's criticism of the stone embrasures at Tregantle that iron shields would be provided in the event of attack.

Subsequent record plans made over the next twenty years of all the casemated coast batteries are in the Public Record Office. There is an early plan of Scraesdon Fort (1859) signed by Queen Victoria herself and early plans of Staddon and Stamford Forts (November 1860) marked 'Approved by HM'. Unfortunately no detailed contemporary plan of Tregantle has come to light nor are there plans of any of the forts and batteries in the North Eastern Defences or final plans for the forts in the Staddon Position. It is possible that this is because the North Eastern Defences were completed by the Royal Engineers, many of whose local records were destroyed in World War II. However there are several maps in the PRO on which early ideas for the layout of the North Eastern Defences are sketched in, including in two cases the position of the proposed fortified barracks at St Budeaux and Widey (see Plate 25 and front cover). Owing to the absence of detailed plans one is left to refer to the special War Department Survey of 1896 on the scale of 1:2500 which does indicate how the forts were eventually built, some after modification following the Report of the Committee of 1869.

Civilian contractors were employed in the first place for the building of the fortifications. All the details are not available, but we do know that F. Roach of Plymouth built Scraesdon and Messrs Kirk and Parry built Tregantle. Roach moved on in 1861 to build Staddon, and presumably Stamford and the rest of the Staddon Defences.

Hubbard & Co. built Picklecombe. The granite work of Breakwater Fort, which was a novel project and under a different designer, was built by Henry Lea & Sons, London. The ironwork was carried out by the Millwall Iron Company from London. The North Eastern Defences were in the hands of Messrs George Baker & Co. of London, who had earlier built Bovisand. The former was a huge project spread over six miles of hilly country. It was the last to be completed and was for financial reasons subject to a large number of modifications, so it is not entirely surprising that in 1866 George Baker & Co were declared bankrupt. A strike of building workers in Plymouth in May 1865 may have contributed to the company's failure. The work was completed, albeit slowly over six years, by the Royal Engineers using direct labour.

Although the two forts in the Western Defences had been started before 1860 Tregantle was not completed until 1865 and Scraesdon until 1868 (Plate 31). The delay over the latter was due to the extensive and steeply sloping galleries built into the north section of the fort. The

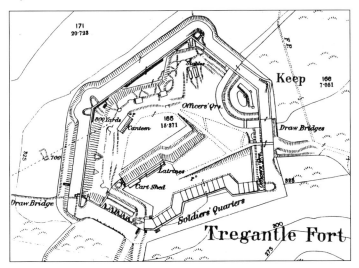

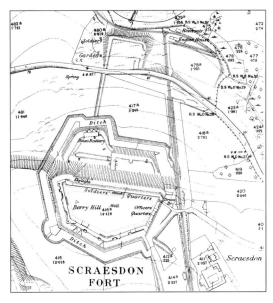

Plate 31: *Tregantle and Scraesdon Forts in 1896.* (PRO. WO78/2314/19-20)

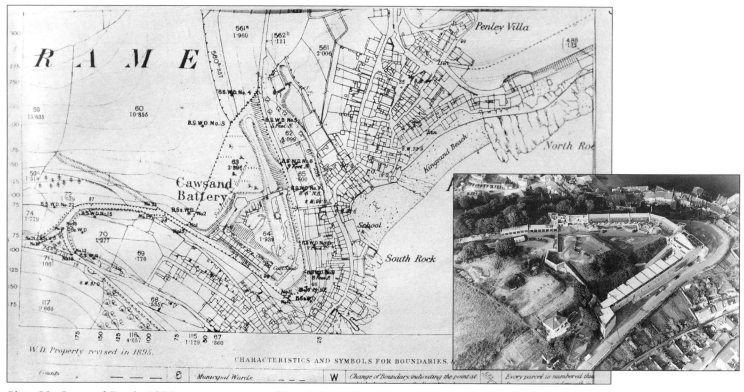

Plate 32: *Cawsand Fort in 1896* (PRO WO78/2314) *and* (inset) *in 1993.* (CORNWALL ARCHAEOLOGICAL UNIT © ABP/F25/93 ©).

traverse across the parade in the south section recommended in the 1869 report was never built, leaving the main magazine in the centre of the existing traverse exposed to fire from the south. At Tregantle five new Haxo casemates were later built, and a sixth from the modification of a basement room, on the SW flank firing out to sea as a result of General Todleben's comments and those in the 1869 report which pointed out that the exterior of the large barracks, 45 feet high, was open to the fire of ships at a range of 1200 yards and at 'elevations that are not difficult of attainment'.

The first of the works to be completed were the two small coast batteries at Cawsand and Polhawn which were

finished in 1863. The larger of the two works, at Cawsand, had been begun before 1860 as part of the Western Defences but it was later considerably extended (Plate 32). It stands on the outcrop between the villages of Cawsand and Kingsand and the battery of six 68-pounders originally proposed would have covered the sheltered anchorage in Cawsand Bay. Because of the danger of a raid following a landing in Whitsand Bay the fort was eventually adapted for all-round defence with projections at the salients to cover the faces with musketry fire. In the rear a ditch with a small bastion in the middle was built covering the North and NW faces (Plate 32). By 1869 it mounted 9 guns behind earth parapets on its sea face and 4 guns on the

Plate 33: *Polhawn Fort from the air (above left) and the gun embrasures and drop ditch (above right).* (CORNWALL ARCHAEOLOGICAL UNIT © ACS 1309 © AND EXETER ARCHAEOLOGY ©)

land side. These included 68-pounders, 8-inch shell guns and 7-inch RBL guns.

Polhawn (Plate 33) was an isolated battery for 7 guns firing west along Whitsand Bay from a position below the steep slope of Rame Head. Because of its isolation it was built like a keep with its own accommodation and protected on the land side by a narrow ditch with a small caponier in the middle. The battery is approached from the steep slope of Rame Head which is covered with undergrowth and brushwood.

To counter the threat of a surprise attack from this direction or from landings in one of the coves nearby, the short bridge which enters the fort at roof level is provided with an unusual drawbridge with a quick release mechanism (Plate 34 and see Plate 52). By pulling on a lanyard to release a pin and throwing up a lever the drawbridge could be partially raised in a moment, and then quickly pulled up into the fully closed position.

Plate 34: *Drawbridge at Polhawn Fort.* (AUTHOR)

The proposed coast defences of the Sound were based on an Outer line, consisting of the batteries at Bovisand, Breakwater and Picklecombe, supported by Cawsand, and an Inner line based on Drake's Island and Garden Battery, supported by the improved armament to be mounted on the south faces of the Citadel and additional guns on the redoubts at Eastern and Western King. Apart from Breakwater Fort whose guns covered all round it, the other coast batteries were built with their casemates in a wide arc - nearly 180° at Bovisand and Picklecombe and some 220° on Drake's Island. This was to compensate for the limited traverse which the design of the casemates allowed and the slow rate of fire of the guns. In this way it was possible for a ship crossing the front of a battery to be engaged continuously by several guns at any one point. At Picklecombe the two tiers of guns could produce a particularly heavy fire on ships entering the main entrance to the Sound.

The effective range of the smooth-bore cannon which were originally proposed for the batteries was 1,000–1500 yards according to Burgoyne and a relatively high site, 80–100 feet above the water, was considered desirable so as to attack the decks of the vessels. When the batteries were to be fitted with RML guns whose pointed shells were designed to pierce the sides of the new ironclads, height was no longer important and the maximum range increased to about 4500 yards at an elevation of 10°.

The casemated batteries were first designed to have a single large detached magazine to the rear but with the development of RBL, and later heavy RML, guns firing at them from longer ranges, better protection was needed and the magazines were normally built under the casemates and below ground level. Originally the embrasures through which the guns fired were to have been recessed in granite but this idea was abandoned quite early in the construction and an opening left for an armoured shield.

The rifled guns mounted on HMS *Warrior* proved capable of piercing the armour-plating available in the early 1860s, so a Special Committee on Iron Plate was established to carry out trials at the Gunnery Establishment at Shoeburyness in 1863 with various types of iron shield. By 1867 the decision was taken that every casemate should have a shield giving protection against gunfire at least equal to that of its own gun. By then the casemates were being armed with 9-inch and 10-inch RML guns. The shields found in Plymouth, which are of more than one type and thickness, generally consist of three (Garden Battery) or five wrought iron plates, each 5–6 inches thick, separated by 3–4 inches of iron concrete or similar material to help absorb the energy of a shell striking it. Their total thickness varies from 2 feet 2 inches to 3 feet. The results of the trials at Shoeburyness were published in May 1868 and the modifications to the casemates were carried out in the following years.

The horizontal width of the embrasure in the iron shield was kept to the minimum by designing the racers on which the platforms traversed so that the gun pivoted about a point a foot in front of the muzzle. Only space in the embrasure for limited elevation was required for the guns then in use and in this way the embrasures were only about 2 feet wide and 3 feet 4 inches high.

Even with an iron shield further protection was required for the detachment from the shower of splinters which would be struck from the inside of the shield by a direct hit. This threat and the need to keep the working space in the casemate free from the acrid smoke of the gunpowder resulted in the development of mantlets. These were adjustable curtains made of heavy rope - double thickness 6-inch rope in some cases - capable of absorbing the metal fragments struck from the inside of the shield. They also offered some protection from case shot and rifle fire from

Plate 35: *Picklecombe Battery completed.* (COURTESY DENNIS W. QUARMBY)

ships - at longer ranges. They were of various designs but all hung so that they could be drawn close around the gun on whatever bearing it was laid. In action they had to be regularly drenched with calcium chloride to prevent them catching fire.

Ammunition was supplied to the guns from the magazines below and was raised by davits operating over vertical circular shafts in the casemate floor. One cartridge hoist was in each casemate towards the right front and one shell hoist between each pair of casemates towards the rear. Shell were raised in a rack to the level of the casemate floor, moved to the gun on a shell trolley and then raised to the muzzle by block and tackle from a ring in the casemate roof or a bar across the top of the shield. The layout of a typical magazine is given in Plate 72. It indicates how the passage of cartridge and shell from the respective magazines was kept separate, and shows the system of lighting for the magazine.

It was not until 1873 that the huge shields at Picklecombe covering both the upper and lower casemates were in position (Plate 30). Trials with live ammunition were carried out there to test the effectiveness of casemated batteries in action. The object was 'to ascertain practically the effect produced by the firing of several heavy guns when mounted in casemated works of modern construction protected by iron shields'.[2] This shows that the whole concept of casemated batteries was largely unproved.

The Picklecombe trials involved the firing of three 10-inch guns on the lower tier and three 9-inch guns on the upper tier. The arrangement of the battery and the working of the guns was declared to be satisfactory although there were many detailed recommendations about the service of ammunition and of the casemates in action.

There were also a number of recommendations for improving the sighting system and the laying of guns, but the main problem which arose was that of fire control. A single officer should in the opinion of the Committee direct the fire of the whole battery. He needed to be far enough away from 'the smoke and confusion in the casemates' yet he needed to be in touch with each gun crew. A method was required of observing the target which the battery was to engage, calculating the range and bearing and passing the orders of the battery commander to his guns. From these requirements was born the system of range finding and fire control developed over the next thirty years. But at this time control was still in the hands of the No. 1 in charge of each gun, once the battery commander had pointed out the target and given the order to fire - when the target came within each gun's arc. The resultant noise and smoke can be imagined. There was much to be done to make these large casemated batteries more effective in action beginning with the development of communication by telephone.

New standards were laid down in the late 1860s. The 68-pounder SB gun was declared obsolete as a coast defence weapon and no gun less powerful than the 9-inch RML of 12 tons was to be mounted in future. Granite casemates were always to be covered in front by an iron shield not less than 2 feet thick and these were later modified to give the protection needed against the 12-inch RML gun of 25 tons. New standards for magazines were introduced and incorporated at Bovisand and Picklecombe. Where it was not practicable to build a magazine storey under the guns, magazines were placed in rear of the casemates, but separate from them, with expense magazines as close as practicable to the gun to be served and on the same level. A variation of this can be seen at Garden Battery.

On Drake's Island where it was not practicable to excavate below the casemates a wide open passageway was formed between them and the high wall cut in the rock face of the island (Plate 36). Within this rock wall were the expense magazines with hatches on to the passageway so

Plate 36: *Passageway behind the casemates, Drake's Island.* (EXETER ARCHAEOLOGY ©)

that shell and cartridge could be passed out and ferried on trolleys to the guns. These expense magazines are connected to a tunnel running behind them and are lit from a separate lighting passage behind and above them. The tunnel is connected at either end to tunnels running to the main magazine (Plate 37).

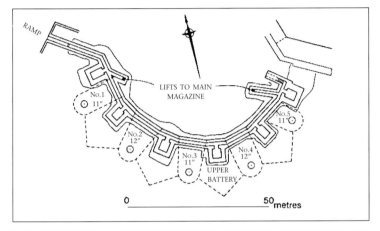

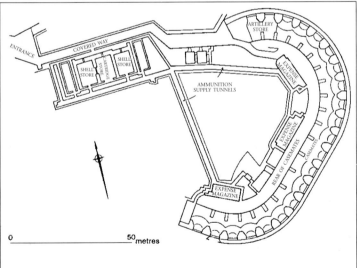

Plate 37: *Upper and Lower Magazines, Drake's Island.* (DEVON ARCHAEOLOGICAL SOCIETY ©)

The 1869 Committee was critical of these arrangements which had already been modified to give more protection to the expense magazines from plunging fire by thickening the wall in front of them. New racers were being laid for the heavier RML guns being installed. The Committee reported that a fourth expense magazine was planned as three were not enough to supply 21 guns in action. The Committee was critical too of the narrowness of the tunnels from the main magazine deep in the rock to the expense magazines, since this would limit the speed at which the latter could be supplied.

A decision had already been taken to redesign the upper battery on the island to mount five of the heaviest rifled guns *en barbette* with magazines below this battery connected by hoists to the existing main magazine system supplying the casemates. The proposal that the emplacements should be designed to enable them to be adapted later to the Moncrieff system of disappearing guns may never have been carried out as the Moncrieff system proved unsatisfactory when applied to heavy guns.

All the casemated coast batteries were eventually equipped with 9-inch, 12-ton, and 10-inch, 18-ton, RML guns which fired shells weighing 250 and 400 lbs respectively and were capable of penetrating eleven and fourteen inches of iron plate. Their disadvantage remained that even a 9-inch gun could only get off six rounds in just over five minutes at a target moving across its front and the heavier guns were correspondingly slower. The need to have a large number of guns in casemates arranged in an arc remained, as long as heavy guns were muzzle loaded.

It took twelve years after the original plans for the coast batteries for them to be modified and fitted with iron shields, and nearly twenty years for the full armament of RML guns to be emplaced. If this seems extraordinarily slow it was due to the delays in the development of the iron shields, the increase in the size of the guns with which the batteries were eventually armed, and the problem of manufacturing sufficient of the larger guns to equip both the navy and the coast batteries. In the meanwhile to prevent the defences being penetrated at night or in bad visiblilty, it was proposed in 1869 that 'torpedoes' (as the first submarine mines were called) should be laid at the entrances to the Sound opposite Bovisand and Picklecombe, and they were certainly in position by 1880 if not earlier.

The last of all the coast forts to be finished was Breakwater. Provisional approval for the design was given early in October 1860. This was for a fort with two tiers of casemates of granite with iron shields. There were to be 33 guns in casemates and 7 on the roof. The whole position was reconsidered in May 1862 when the Royal Commission reconvened to review the question of the sea forts at Spithead and Plymouth. After reviewing the alternatives of a fort on each end, in the centre or inside the Breakwater, the latter option was confirmed. This would

reduce costs, remove the danger of subsidence, protect the lower tier of guns from the sea and enable communication with the fort to be maintained in all weathers.

Preliminary work began in June 1862 on the design with two tiers of casemates, but the initial structure was swept away by a gale in the following August. The first stone of the foundations was not officially laid until March 1863. Work proceeded slowly and in April 1866 a revised plan was considered by the Defence Committee. They were concerned about the developments in the design of artillery and the probability of a hostile squadron bringing heavy and concentrated fire to bear on the fort. In place of the original two tiers of casemates, one tier for 17 guns, faced wholly with iron, was approved and arrangements were to be made for two turrets each with two of the most powerful guns to be mounted on top.

When in February 1870 Sir L. Simmons raised objections to the turrets on top of the forts, the Defence Committee noted that funds had not in fact been provided for them (Plate 38).

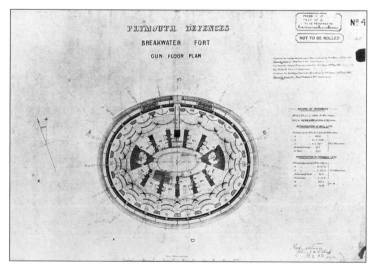

Plate 38: *Breakwater Fort - from the breakwater (left) and upper floor plan (right).* (AUTHOR AND RCHME. CROWN © PLM/494).

By April 1873 the Defence Committee was concerned about the increasing size of the guns which could be brought against the sea defences generally, whose heaviest armament was 10-inch, 18-ton guns. The Secretary for War confirmed in November 1874 that the turrets on the latest plan for Breakwater Fort should be omitted and it was recommended that the fort should be armed with fourteen 12.5-inch, 38 ton RML, guns and four 10-inch, 18 ton, RMLs, the latter facing the inner waters of the Sound. By this time the special 'small port' carriages had been developed, which is why the embrasures are smaller than in the shields of the coast batteries and almost square. But it was not until July 1880 that the Inspector General of Fortifications in his report noted that Breakwater Fort was 'now receiving its guns'.

It comes as no surprise to anybody who has been on the fort that in 1885 orders were given for seven of the 12.5-inch guns to be withdrawn as these huge guns were considered too crowded (Plate 39).

Plate 39: *12.5-inch RML gun at Hurst Castle, Solent.* (AUTHOR)

When work began on the North Eastern Defences in 1863 the construction of the Staddon Defences was already well advanced and they had been strengthened by the addition of the substantial fort at Stamford, originally called after Turnchapel which it overlooked. This partly covered the gap which had opened between Staddon and the Citadel because the fort originally planned at Cattedown had been moved forward to Laira. The cost of this in addition to Staddon Fort itself (even without its original keep) and of the works linking Staddon with Bovisand resulted in the expenditure on Staddon Heights exceeding the estimates.

In the revised estimates of 1867 the cost of the North Eastern Defences and the Staddon Defences were combined and it is clear that from then on the authorities were looking for corresponding economies in the North Eastern Defences, which they eventually achieved, to the tune of £27 419. This is one reason why the defensible keeps at St Budeaux, Widey and Efford Warren were never built, although the Efford position was strengthened by earthwork emplacements at Deer Park and on the high ground overlooking Laira Battery, where the keep would have been.

The Fortification Committee, and Du Cane in particular, faced special problems at Plymouth. At Portsmouth the land defences to the north consist primarily of five large forts, with a further one in front, forming the Portsdown Hill Line. Portsdown Hill itself is a long, fairly regular ridge of chalk, so the digging of ditches, revetted with brick, and the brick-faced fortifications created no special problems. To the west of Portsmouth the three new forts in the Gosport Line were similar to one another in general design. They are on level ground and have wet ditches.

The problems of defending Plymouth from the north and east in particular are very different. The defences had to cover in detail the broken country. Most of the ditches

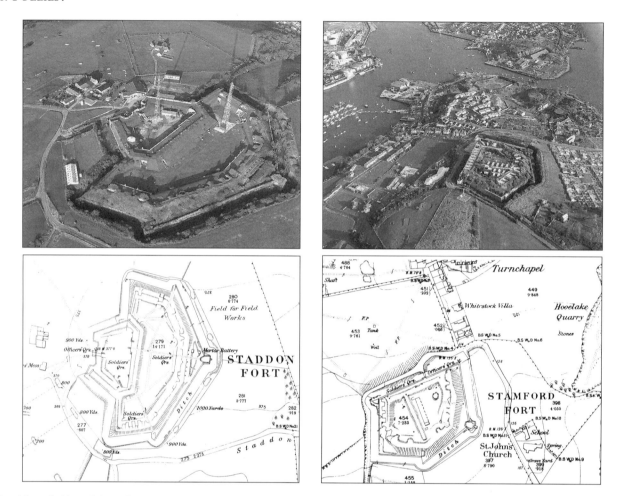

Plate 40: Staddon (left) and Stamford (right) Forts showing plans in 1896 and aerial photographs as they appear today. (PRO WO78/2314/29 (plans) AND (photos) F.M. GRIFFITH, DEVON COUNTY COUNCIL. 10.1.92 ©)

had to be dug out of slatey rock and the walls and buildings were faced in cut stone with dressed stone detail. The building of the forts and batteries which were often on uneven sites and overlooking steep slopes created its own problems, and it is not surprising that none of the Plymouth forts are similar in trace, i.e. in outline, although they do have many common features. These are described in detail in Appendix.C.

There were a number of modifications made to the forts as the work progressed - the elimination of the keep at Staddon Fort (Plate 40) is the most notable - and there were further changes made as the result of the recommendations of the 1869 Committee. The heavy guns required to fire seaward from Fort Tregantle were mounted in six casemates on the south west face. The recommendation for heavy guns at Cawsand Battery and at Eastern and Western

Plate 41: *Crownhill Fort. Double Haxo casemate (left) exterior and single Haxo casemate (right) interior.* (AUTHOR)

King resulted in the mounting there of 64-pounder RMLs in place of the 68 pounder SB guns recommended originally. However the recommendation for a small additional battery of heavy guns at Knatterbury to support Polhawn was never authorised.

At Scraesdon the Committee in 1869 noted that three Haxo casemates on the lower level of the fort, which were not in the original design, had been added and a scarp gallery built round the lower work. The creation of a massive traverse by bomb-proofing the casemates already built between the upper and lower works was 'absolutely necessary' and was later done.

Relatively few changes were recommended in the North Eastern Defences by the 1869 Committee other than the addition of an artillery store at Ernesettle and improvements to the magazine. No modifications were recommended in the Staddon position which the Committee noted was 'well and skilfully constructed with reference to stability and permanancy, and possesses great powers of resistance'. Later Moncrieff emplacements were built at Tregantle, Scraesdon, Crownhill, Staddon and Stamford.

By the end of 1872 the land forts and coast batteries, with the exception of Breakwater Fort, appear to have been complete (Map III) and the modifications recommended in the 1869 Report incorporated. In the following years developments continued in a number of directions. The first addition to the coast defences was the approval in that year for the mounting of three 10-inch RML guns on No.4 Redoubt on Maker Heights. In 1872 it was also decided that the 64-pounder RML converted gun should be substituted for any remaining smooth bore guns. Surprisingly, at the same time the armament of the new land defences which had not yet received any guns was left 'for future consideration'.

It was not until 1875 that the first armament table for the land defences (see Appendix B) was finally approved, consisting altogether of :

Plate 42: *64-pdr RML (blocked up) at Fort Nelson, Portsmouth.*
(AUTHOR)

209 7-inch RBL
49 64-pounder RML
45 8-inch rifled howitzers
132 SB flank guns

The 7-inch RBL, by then rejected by the Royal Navy, was to be the principal armament and these guns were mainly mounted in Haxo casemates (Plate 41). The 64-pounder RMLs were generally mounted in barbette emplacements with 360 degrees traverse but there were many variations in the platforms, carriages and emplacements. Many of the 64-pdrs mounted later were on 'blocked up' platforms to enable them to fire over a parapet 6 feet high which, gave protection to the detachment (Plate 42). The 8-inch rifled howitzers were a new pattern of gun first produced in 1872. An improved design was produced in 1876 but the gun did not go into full production until 1880 (Plate 43). They appear in the1885 armament table in the moveable armament, and at Efford Emplacement for example.

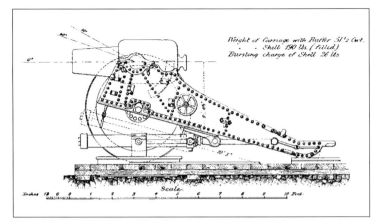

Plate 43: *8-inch, 46-cwt howitzer.* (OFFICIAL TREATISE)

At no stage is there any mention of the mortars, for which positions were built in many of the forts and batteries, either in the 1875 armament table or subsequent ones. Possibly they were originally held centrally at the Gun Wharf or were in the forts but not recorded. They were going out of favour anyway and in a lecture in 1868 Jervois had referred to the fact that the Royal Artillery were considering 'a rifled howitzer which will afford vertical fire with accuracy'.[3] In due course the 8-inch, and later the 6.6-inch, RML howitzers were to perform their role. There appears to have been a further gap in the armament of the forts in the 1870s and early 1880s until the howitzers were available in quantity.

The SB flank guns referred to in the 1875 table were to be mounted in the floors of the caponiers and those that were mounted at this time must have been old 32-pounder muzzle-loading guns. This gun was later modified for breech-loading (SB.BL) and gun drill trials were carried out on this new weapon in a caponier at Crownhill Fort in the late 1870s. It was issued from 1880 onwards in large numbers and firing trials were carried out at Tregantle at this time (Plate 44).

Plate 44: *32-pdr SB.BL gun and detachment of Portsdown Artillery Volunteers at Crownhill Fort.* (Author)

In 1877 the Defence Committee revised the armament at Fort Stamford since it was realised that the 9-inch RML guns mounted on the west face could not fire into Jennycliff Bay satisfactorily. It was recommended that instead two 10-inch RML guns should be emplaced on the south-west face. In order to give them an effective field of fire the top of the cliff had to be cut away in front of them and it is said that several hundred navvies were employed to do this.

In the same year the Committee revised its approval in 1872 that three 10-inch RML guns should be mounted on No.4 Redoubt on Maker Heights and recommended instead two of the latest 12.5-inch 38-ton RML guns, though they were not emplaced until ten years later. This represented the first move in the rearmament of the coast defences with heavier RML guns, which was not completed until the early 1890s. Not only were the coast defences then extended southwards to Penlee and Whitsand Bay but these batteries incorporated developments in optical rangefinding and telephonic communications which revolutionised both the direction and the control of fire of coast artillery.

In 1885 appeared the first detailed armament table entitled 'Revision of the Armaments of Plymouth'[4] and recording both the existing armament and that which was proposed. As far as the land defences were concerned this is the only table which indicates the exact position of each gun or group of guns in all the land forts.

By then the casemated coast batteries were almost fully armed with their 9-inch and 10-inch RML guns. Cawsand Battery and Polhawn were armed on their sea faces with converted 64-pounder RMLs and Cawsand had some old 8-inch SB guns on its land face.

Of the land forts, Tregantle had relatively few guns mounted, other than on its vulnerable north and west faces, although there were 26 guns of various types in the fort unmounted. Much the same applied to Scraesdon where even fewer guns were actually in position but 21 were lying in the fort.

Most of the North Eastern Defences apart from Crownhill Fort, had up to half-a-dozen 7-inch RBL guns mounted and more guns, in some cases including the new 8-inch RML howitzers, lying in the fort. Crownhill was by then almost fully armed according to the table then approved for it, including the new 32-pounder SB.BL guns in the caponiers.

The armament proposed in 1885 showed little change as far as the casemated coast batteries were concerned since by then they were fully armed, but the new 12.5-inch RML guns were proposed for positions at Twelve Acre Brake (renamed Frobisher Battery) and Staddon Heights Battery, and on the opposite side of the Sound at Maker and Whitsand Bay. There were already three 11-inch and two 12-inch RMLs in position on the Upper Battery of Drake's Island. Other recommendations at this time included the introduction of quick-firing (QF) guns to cover the submarine minefields off Picklecombe, Bovisand and Devil's

Point. A new generation of BL (breech-loading) long range guns was in development and these were to be mounted at Penlee and Rame.

The proposed armament for the land forts did not mean that all their emplacements would have guns mounted in them even at this stage; Crownhill alone was to be fully armed. The other forts and batteries were mainly to be armed on their more exposed faces and according to their importance in the scheme of defence. The guns were still 7-inch RBLs and 64-pounder RMLs, with 32-pounder SB.BLs in the caponiers. Some 5-inch BL guns were also to be introduced, two of them in Moncrieff emplacements at Efford. The other Moncrieff emplacements at Tregantle, Scraesdon, Crownhill, Stamford and Staddon were to be armed with 7-in RBLs.

There were substantial reserves of moveable armament to cover the unfortified Saltash position, the front from Ernesettle to Crownhill and the front from Crownhill to Laira, held respectively at Saltash station, Crownhill Fort and Efford Fort, as well as guns at Watch House Brake and Brownhill for the Staddon position. There was also a small number of guns held in the Citadel for use on Cattedown .

The final armament table for the land forts was published in 1893,[5] which details the guns for which we can in most cases still identify positions on the ramparts of the forts. Crownhill had its complete approved armament and so had the rest of the land forts apart from a shortage of 32-pounder SB.BL guns in some cases. Even the pools of moveable armament appear to have been made up to strength apart from some 6.6-inch RML howitzers outstanding. There were no recommendations made for changes, which tends to confirm that this represents the ultimate armament of the land forts. (For the detailed armament of each fort see Appendix D.).

The guns of the casemated coast batteries were progressively removed from the 1890s onwards when the complete coast defence layout was modernised and the outer defences were moved further south. The casemates remained structurally unchanged apart from the mounting later of modern QF guns and BL guns in the casemates or on the roofs of the batteries. The last of the armament of the land forts and batteries was not finally removed until after World War I.

References

[1] *Duties of the Corps of Royal Engineers*. New Series. Vol 12. 1863

[2] *Proceedings of the Department of the Director of Artillery*. Vol.XI.Part II. 37. 30/4/1873

[3] *RUSI Journal*. Vol. XII. 1868. p. 558

[4] RA & RE Works Committee. Report 11 3.12.1885

[5] Ibid. (PRO WO33/2772) Report 12. April 1893

7

THE DEFENDERS

'Defences were short or long, contemptible or brilliant, in accordance with the spirit of the troops, the genius and readiness of the thought of their commanders, the available supply of food and ammunition and not because the fortress is laid out on simple or complex lines.'

Sir George Sydenham Clarke - *Fortification*

In the main body of its report of 1860 the Royal Commission sets out the assumptions on which the call for stronger defences was based. Whilst the navy was 'the first and most obvious line of defence', in view of the need to protect the colonial empire it could no longer be relied upon to maintain at all times a fleet in the Channel, which could equal any which might be sent against it. On land, the army had for many years been kept relatively small, due to the distrust of a standing army dating from the Commonwealth reinforced by fear of the influence of large conscript armies such as were common on the continent. In practice the army at home was dispersed in garrisons throughout the British Isles for internal security duties, though the other aspect of this was reflected by the general who once said 'it is only by keeping the troops scattered and out of sight that we are enabled to keep up any army at all in this country'.

A volunteer army, such as the British army of this time, was man for man much more costly than a conscript one,

so that sheer lack of money tended to keep its strength to a minimum. As the empire expanded during the mid-nineteenth century the army became increasingly stretched to maintain the garrisons required in India and in the colonies. Further, there was not the reserve of trained men at home which a conscript army could have called upon in the event of a threat of invasion. The effect of the growing overseas commitment was shown at the outbreak of the Crimean war when out of a strength of 135 000 men, only about 65 000 were at home. This figure covered the substantial garrison in Ireland, a smaller one in Scotland and those required both to protect London and the dockyards and to man the other fortresses.

Even when those units of the militia sufficiently trained to act with regular units were added, the force capable of manoeuvring in the field in defence of London would never compare with the numbers available to the French. Whilst recognising that a large number of volunteers had come forward in the previous year, the Royal Commission was of the opinion that these troops would not be capable at the beginning of any war of meeting regular disciplined soldiers on the field of battle.

In its brief the Royal Commission was particularly instructed to bear in mind the limited number of men of the Royal Artillery who were likely to be available for the defence of any fortification. No increase in their strength was to be allowed for, though in the event the number of gunners in this country was increased to help meet the demand of the new coast defences by bringing units home from overseas. After pointing out that less than a quarter of the course of training laid down for men of the Royal Artillery referred to the duties of garrison artillery, the Commission came to the conclusion that 'previously untrained men of average capacity could be taught the ordinary duties required for such service, in about a month'. Within three months such men should be capable of performing most of the duties for the efficient manning of garrison artillery in the fortifications proposed, when supported by a proportion of fully trained men and commanded by properly qualified officers.

On this basis the Royal Commission did not consider that the strength of the gunners available was a limitation on the number of batteries and guns to be recommended, and referred to the importance of the training of Local Militia Artillery and Volunteer Artillery Corps in the neighbourhood of the fortifications. They did however note that where coast defence batteries were likely to fire time fuses one or two skilled men per gun would be required. It is difficult without knowing a great deal more about the manpower and training position at the time to judge whether, as seems to be the case at first sight, the Commission was being over optimistic.

Even after the Cabinet had made considerable reductions in the fortifications which the Royal Commission had recommended, and therefore in the number of guns to be manned, in broad terms there were according to the 1869 Report the following guns to be emplaced at Plymouth or, in the case of Devonport Lines, to be manned:

1. Three large casemated batteries - 104 guns (Picklecombe, Bovisand, Drake's Island) together with Breakwater Fort.

2. Five smaller coast forts/batteries - 58 guns (Polhawn, Cawsand, Garden, Eastern and Western King).

3. Twenty land forts/batteries/emplacements - 318 guns

4. Devonport Lines - 31 guns*

Total - 511 guns

In the original report of 1860 the total of guns under 1 and 2 above was originally 262 and the total of 3, including Tregantle and Scraesdon, 412. The figure for section 3 shown above reflects not only the amended layout of the North Eastern and Staddon defences, but also the effect of the introduction of more powerful rifled guns and the revised principles of their deployment.

Allowing for the additional men required to man the magazines and the ammunition supply system in the casemated coast batteries, these would have required a garrison of 1200–1500 men, assuming that all the casemates were armed with smooth-bore guns, and of those a minimum of a third would need to be trained men. But already the batteries were being re-equipped with 9-inch and 10-inch RML guns which had crews of 12–15 men thereby increasing the total of men required to nearer 2000.

Even assuming that only one sector of the land defences would be attacked at one time, the gunners required for the land defences with their smaller and older guns would be of the order of 700–1200 depending on which sector was attacked. Yet if the attack came from the east, both Staddon Heights and the North Eastern Defences as far west as Crownhill Fort would have to be manned, increasing the total to around 2000. These figures assume that all the guns were in position and ready for action, whereas this was never the case except in the coast batteries.

* 28 guns and 3 mortars mounted in 1850 - considered of little importance by the Royal Commission.

Of the total of 2500–3500 gunners required, 800–1000 would have to be fully trained artillerymen and as many as possible of the others would have to have done drill on the guns they were to fire in action if they were to be effective. This seems a minimum requirement. How were these men to be found and from where would come the infantry and other arms - some 12 000 men - to make up the wartime garrison to 15 000 as recommended by the Royal Commission? As the layout of the land defences in their final form consisted of a single line of fortifications it was all the more important to provide a mobile reserve of regular troops to give depth to the defences to the west and the north east, and also to build and man the Saltash defences should they be threatened.

The 'garrison' at Plymouth between 1860 and the early 1870s was a hotchpotch of units varying from regular regiments of foot with experience of active service in India or the colonies, to ill-organised and ill-trained volunteer units whose main strength in action would be their determination to defend their home town. How the militia and volunteer units, which were independent and under no single commander in peacetime, would have been moulded into an effective force in time of war was fortunately never tested.

There were normally two regiments of foot in the garrison during this period, though in 1861 for example there were three. If they were fortunate they were stationed in the recently completed Raglan Barracks in Devonport but there was normally one regiment in the seventeenth century buildings, and damp casemates, of the Royal Citadel. There had been some modernisation of the accommodation there in 1845 but it was still second best. For short periods, especially in the 1870s there was only one regiment of foot in Plymouth due to delays in the passage from India or from the colonies.

During the 1860s, 3rd Brigade Royal Artillery, consisting of 5–7 batteries, was based on Plymouth with its headquarters in Granby Barracks, Devonport. Batteries or detachments were stationed at Maker Barracks, Drake's Island, and Bovisand. (After 1874, under the Cardwell Reforms, the formation at Plymouth became 10th Brigade of seven batteries, and in 1877 Plymouth became the base for a garrison brigade of artillery and the coast fortress became a district under a Lt-Colonel.) The total strength of the regular gunners in the 1860s varied between 600–700 all ranks. The batteries, as long as they were part of a garrison such as Plymouth, would have been trained on both coast defence guns and moveable field guns. They formed the backbone of the artillery of the defences with the emphasis on manning the coast batteries rather than the land forts.

Although the strength of the regular artillery batteries in Plymouth appears adequate their effectiveness was limited in practice by the developments which followed the Royal Commission's report. The period after 1860 is referred to in the official history of the Royal Artillery as 'the dark ages' in coast artillery, because of the effect that the enormous increase in the coast defences and the corresponding time taken to move and emplace the new guns had on training. Not only did the new coast batteries have to be armed with guns 'they had to be re-armed with each change in gun construction, so that for nearly a quarter of a century the energies of the artillery were absorbed in this gigantic task'.[1]

The movement of the guns and carriages was based on the repository system, using wooden blocks and tackle and the power of men and horses, often a large number of cach. All officers had to be skilled in repository work. With the increase in the size and weight of guns - the smallest coast gun being emplaced was the 9-inch RML of 12 tons - the

Plate 45: *Transporting heavy gun barrels by water.* (COURTESY A.L. CLAMP)

effort involved in Plymouth can be imagined. Guns were delivered by sea to the dockyard or to one of the railway stations and had then to be moved by land or sea (Plate 45) to Bovisand, Picklecombe or Drake's Island, each with its particular difficulties due to its topography. A contemporary photograph shows a ramp at Drake's Island from the shore to the level of the casemates up which guns and carriages were hauled.

Further, the gunners had not only to mount but to look after the guns and their stores. 'Officers instead of training their men to fight their guns were absorbed in looking after the immense mass of stores connected with them' says the official history.[2] There were further complaints that the men were dispersed on fatigues of all kinds even when the officers had time to spare from their ledgers. Anyway, practice firing was limited by the small amount of ammunition allowed and the target was an anchored barrel in the sea - nothing like service conditions.

The 'dark ages' covered a period when new and revolutionary types of guns were being introduced and the first armoured ships built. Yet it was not until about 1885 that technical developments effecting fire control and new methods of firing practice against a moving target produced a corresponding revolution in the effectiveness of coast artillery fire.

The militia had been reconstituted by an act of 1852. They were to form trained units for home defence who could take over garrison duties and so free regular units for service elsewhere at home and overseas in time of war. They could be embodied (called to the colours) in the event of rebellion or insurrection, or in the event of invasion or 'imminent danger thereof'. Control of the militia was at first largely in the hands of the Lord Lieutenant until 1870 when, as part of Cardwell's plans to integrate the regular army, the militia and the volunteers into a single force, their officers were appointed by the War Office. At the same time a series of military districts were introduced, each containing a depot for the local regiment of foot and acting as a base for the local militia and volunteers - the beginning of a territorial system.

The organisation of militia units and their training was in the hands of their permanent staff. One of the two infantry militia regiments in the county was the 2nd (South) Devon Militia based on the barracks built at Mutley in 1840. The battalion had been embodied during the Crimean War and in 1854-56 served in Ireland. So this was a trained body of men with experience of service outside its home base.

In 1852 the 3rd. (North) Devon Militia were converted into the Devon Militia Artillery. The C.O. and most of the officers and men accepted conversion, though they cannot have remained in the unit long because the training in garrison artillery duties was shortly transferred to Plymouth. It was obvious that militia artillery units must live near enough to the guns they were to man if they were to be mobilised quickly and at the same time they must be familiar with, and train on, these guns. Initially the Devon Militia Artillery had a strength of 367 men, all picked for the fact that they were over 5ft. 6in. tall. By 1860 the number had risen to 454, though this compared with an establishment of 1000.

The annual training period for the militia was not less than 21 days and not more that 28 days, although later training could be extended to 56 days if necessary. The permanent staff of a militia artillery regiment was substantial and usually consisted of:

Adjutant (a captain)
Quartermaster
Sergeant-Major
Quartermaster Sergeant
Paymaster Sergeant
Sergeant Instructor-in-Gunnery
Orderly Room Sergeant
Sergeants
Trumpeters

Most of these would have been voluntarily transferred from the Royal Artillery. If the permanent staff for the artillery militia seems large it is partly due to concern at the time that 'many Lord Lieutenants were more concerned with appointing influential members of the local gentry to the position of field officers than finding applicants with the appropriate service qualifications and experience'.[3] It took two years to make an artillery officer at the Royal Military Academy, Woolwich, yet artillery units in the militia were being placed in the hands of country gentlemen, many of whom had never served in the army let alone in the Royal Artillery.

As early as 1848 Dockyard Volunteer Battalions had been formed for the protection of the main dockyards. The men were volunteers in theory though there must have been considerable pressure to volunteer since every trade was represented amongst the other ranks and they were officered by Principal and Subordinate officers of the various departments. They formed a body of all arms; there were not only infantry but also artillery, engineer, boat (manning ship's boats with light guns) and recruit sections together with a band. In 1853 the total strength of the Devonport Brigade, Royal Dockyard Corps, was 1598.

The Devonport Brigade included the Devonport Battalion based on the dockyard itself and also the Royal William Battalion based on the Royal William Victualling Yard, and another unit referred to as the Breakwater Battalion, drawing its men from other establishments in the port. However, during the Crimean War when we were allied to the French, due to pressure of work in the dockyards, the corps were run down, ceasing to exist by 1857.

In response to popular alarm - the same alarm which contributed to the appointment of the Royal Commission - on 12 May 1859 the War Office in a circular to Lords Lieutanant authorised the formation of volunteer corps. There was a tremendous response - 130 000 had been enlisted by June 1860 - and over the next few years the whole volunteer movement came to represent 'the rejection of the dominant liberal pacifism for militant patriotism of the most sabre-rattling kind.'[4]

Volunteers received no pay or uniform except when called out on service. The unit was paid an annual capitation fee of 35 shillings. Drill and training was carried out in the evenings and there was to be one week (later two weeks) in camp each year. In practice, volunteers were limited to those who could afford to buy their own uniform. This was what the Government wanted - 'to get the middle classes imbued with an interest in our own means of defence'.[5]

Exeter had earlier shown the way when in January 1853 the Queen had specially commissioned the first officers into the Exeter and South Devon Rifle Corps which became in 1859 the 1st Exeter and South Devon Rifle Volunteers, the senior volunteer unit in the country whose establishment later reached a total of eleven companies.

Elsewhere, from the summer of 1859 onwards, volunteer corps were established wherever there was a demand. They might consist of thirty, or up to several hundred, men. In the countryside in Devon the response was slow at first as compared with the cities and the richer parts of the country. But when the Government agreed to bear a larger share of the costs of arming the volunteers and early in 1860 began to issue them with Enfield rifles, recruiting picked up. Within a year there were rifle corps spread all over Devon, from those in Plymouth and Exeter, through towns like Totnes and Ilfracombe to the villages of Buckrell, Hatherleigh and Ottery St Mary. By April 1861 there were 25 corps of rifle volunteers. More important in the view of the government, since their main object was to raise volunteers to man the coast defence batteries, there were 13 corps of artillery volunteers.

The men of Plymouth were quick to volunteer and within a month or two the 2nd Devon (Plymouth) Volunteer Rifle Corps was formed, initially of about 150 men but growing in the following years eventually to battalion strength. Early in 1861 they marched from Raglan Barracks to the Guildhall to take the oath of allegiance. Later the corps formed part of the 2nd Devon Administrative Brigade which included both the corps at Plymouth and those at Devonport, Stonehouse and Tavistock.

Their uniform which they bought themselves consisted of 'shako, black leather cross and waist belt, and dark green tunic and trousers, with black kid gloves'[6] The first drills were carried out in the Cornmarket and threepence was paid each drill to the Sergeant Instructor from the militia. The first headquarters of the unit was at Corporation Grammar School in Finewell Street and a parade ground was formed there.

The fact that the headquarters was in the centre of the town helped considerably with recruitment and by 1860 there were six companies in Plymouth.

When the site of their headquarters was required for the new Guildhall the volunteers moved to Millbay where the Volunteer Drill Hall, completed in 1871, was built. This huge hall 260 feet long, 86 feet wide and 45 feet high was later used for concerts and election meetings. In 1879 the Battalion adopted the additional title of 'Prince of Wales Own' from the old 2nd Plymouth Volunteers of the Napoleonic Wars and the former battalion's colours were presented to it.

With corps of volunteers springing up all over this part of England in particular, a local co-ordinating body was required and administrative battalions with a regular officer as adjutant were formed in the countryside from March 1860 onwards to take over control of the various small volunteer corps.

Similarly the 1st Admin. Brigade of the Devonshire Artillery Volunteers was formed with headquarters in Teignmouth in August 1860 and controlled the first 12 artillery corps to be formed in Devon. In June 1861 the county's 2nd Admin Brigade was formed with its headquarters in Devonport and by the following year the corps at Devonport Dockyard and Keyham and those at Dartmouth and Salcombe constituted the brigade. For some reason its headquarters was moved to Dartmouth in 1874 but returned to Devonport in 1877. To give an idea of the numbers involved, on their inspection on 8 January 1863 the Royal Dockyard Corps had 207 men on parade and the Keyham Corps 114. But the various corps were never properly organised as part of the field or coast artillery available for the defence of Plymouth for example.

Although the 1st Royal Devon Yeomanry based on Exeter cannot be counted as part of the forces available in Plymouth there were in the area three units of light horse volunteers known as Mounted Rifle Volunteers. These were the 1st, 2nd and 3rd units based on Berry Pomeroy, Yealmpton and Modbury. They must have been at about squadron strength to judge from the fact that the C.O.s were in 1865 captains, although the 3rd Modbury Unit had no officers apart from a cornet of horse. These units were disbanded in 1874-7.

The troops immediately available for the defence of Plymouth in an emergency appear to have been in the early 1860s:

	Infantry	Artillery etc.
2 Regiments of Foot	1600	
6-7 companys Royal Artillery		700
2nd (South) Devon Militia	500	
Devon Militia Artillery		400
2nd Devon (Plymouth) Volunteer Rifle Bn	600	
2nd Admin Brigade Volunteer Artillery		600
Total	2700	1700

This must be compared with the Royal Commission's initial estimate of the garrison required for Plymouth in the event of attack of 15 000 men. To achieve this, units from the rest of the country would have had to be made available and posted in rapidly in an emergency. More realistically, no more than half of the land defences would have to be manned at one time and for this Jervois in 1868 suggested that only 6000–7000 men would be needed. There would still be the need for reinforcements unless the coast defences were to be denuded.

Much depends on an estimate of the effectiveness of the various types of units in the event of attack. Apart from the infantry and artillery units of the regular army, the militia units and the volunteer artillery appear to have been regularly trained and would have been effective in the static roles they were required to fulfill. The South Devon Militia in particular, having been embodied during the Crimean War, enjoyed a common experience and presumably a strong *esprit de corps*. It is significant that for three years in the 1860s they spent their annual training period in the Royal Citadel. The militia and volunteer artillery trained on the type of guns, and along the south coast of Devon on the actual batteries, they would man in wartime.

As far as the rifle volunteers are concerned the Duke of Cambridge, Commander in Chief, reported to a select committee in August 1860 that the volunteers represented 'a very dangerous way of meeting an invasion'[7] and there were many others who shared his view that they would be 'quite as much in the way'. General Burgoyne too doubted whether they would have been effective in war.

The rifle volunteer units attracted a good deal of publicity in peacetime and in the early 1860s the *Western Daily Mercury* contains notices of their drill nights and their firing practices, apart from their other activities. The nature of the organisation of these corps is perhaps better indicated by reports of their Annual Meetings.

On 23 January 1863 at the Annual General Meeting of the Stonehouse Rifle Corps at Millbay Barracks the Earl of Mount Edgcumbe, Captain Commandant, was in the chair. It was reported that of the corps only 67 had attended any drills at all and 14 had attended no drills. Many had not attended the 24 drills required to make them effective. Altogether 47 had fired on the range and the average was better than that of the previous year, but there was only one marksman and four first class shots in the corps. Fines were proposed for non-attendance at drills in future. It was announced at the same time that the Battalion would attend the theatre on the following night and as many as possible were urged to be in uniform.

The same edition of the paper reported that there was an inspection of the 9th Duke of Cornwall's Own Volunteer Rifle Company at St Austell. Reference was made to the fact that at formation this corps was considered second to none in the county but it had now lost so much of its spirit that it might be reduced to a sub-division. These extracts, which could be multiplied, give an impression of the varied military value of these corps (the fact that on the following day 400 people attended a temperance meeting at the Royal Marine Barracks is a reflection of the spirit of the time). There is the impression that the enthusiasm tended to wear off especially where the training was limited almost entirely to drill parades. The salvation of many corps was the emphasis on rifle shooting and the success of the monthly and annual competitions and meetings organised by the Devon Volunteer Association.

The efficiency of the Volunteer Artillery appears to have been higher. There are a number of contemporary photographs of volunteers doing gun drill (Plate 46) and the local battery, often of old smooth bore guns, formed a focus for the units in the coast towns of South Devon. There is a press report in 1863 of the 11th Devon Volunteer Artillery Corps at Brixham practising at Fishcombe Battery, hitting the target (stationary) and destroying it with the

Plate 46: *A Devon Volunteer Artillery Corps on parade, c. 1870.*

last shot. Their officers and 60–70 rank and file were on parade.

There must have been similar enthusiasm among the artillery volunteers in Plymouth where they were along-side, but never apparently co-ordinated with, the regular units. The batteries and guns on which they did drill were more up-to-date and their unit's importance to the defence of Plymouth was obvious. Bovisand Practice Battery must have played an important part in the training of all the artillery units. Whereas the coast batteries could in some cases safely practice firing out to sea, Bovisand was the only place where the types of guns allotted to the land defences could be fired. Its armament was progressively upgraded during the 1870s and 1880s and in 1873 one of the first twenty Pattern 1 Moncrieff mountings to be manufactured was emplaced there.

If the Plymouth defences were to be effective in the event of war, the garrison needed rapid reinforcement.

Although the defences spread into south-east Cornwall, at no stage is there any reference to militia or volunteer units from that county sharing in the defence of Plymouth. To bring the reserve force up to brigade strength one or possibly two regiments of foot and 3–4 companies Royal Artillery would be required. In this way the existing artillery companies in the garrison could be used entirely to man the coast batteries on which they had been trained and the land forts manned by the new companies. But to man the coast defences adequately would have required the support not only of the volunteer artillery but also of a further 700–1000 dockyard men and sailors to complete the detachments.

The 2nd (South) Devon Militia Battalion and the rifle volunteers, as well as some of the militia and volunteer artillery, would have manned the land fortifications in that sector which was threatened at the time. There would have been a shortage of infantry in view of the size and extent of the fortifications to the North East in particular, and at least another militia regiment would have been required. This might have been the 1st Devon Militia from Exeter, or more likely a regiment from another county. More trained artillerymen, whether regular or militia, would have been needed, and in general the volunteer units of both infantry and artillery would have been the better for a stiffening of regular reservists on embodiment.

It was only in 1876 that specific units were designated to form 'Garrison Armies' in the event of an emergency. From this time onwards militia, volunteer and also pensioner (reservist) units of infantry, artillery and engineers were designated as part of the Plymouth garrison in the event of war. These would have been moved down by rail following the recall of reservists to the colours and the embodiment of the militia. The volunteer units were not liable to service until an invasion took place. What would have happened by way of reinforcement in the event of invasion before this plan was drawn up must be a matter of conjecture.

The situation seems extraordinarily vague to modern soldiers to whom mobilisation plans are routine and the staffs plan for all likely contingencies. It was only in 1855 following the administrative weaknesses revealed in the Crimean War, that the War Office was set up with a Secretary for War at its head. There was still no general staff, though there were a small number of trained staff officers. At least, in the next ten years military problems were being studied by committees so that when Edward Cardwell was appointed Secretary for War in 1868 he was able to begin a programme of reform based on their work. His first object was to reduce the garrisons in the colonies and in 1869-70 he brought home 25 000 men. But even after this, when in 1870 the government was considering a force to ensure Belgian neutrality in the impending Franco-Prussian War it was found that only a force of 20 000 men in under-strength battalions could be put together.

Cardwell succeeded in localising the military system in territorial areas so that regular regiments of the line could be linked to local militia regiments, and the country was divided into districts which formed an administrative brigade. In this way for the first time the regular army, militia and volunteers were welded into one system and regiments of the line were given permanent depots. It was not until 1890 that a Royal Commission recommended the establishment of a general staff responsible for preparing plans for military operations and the abolition of the post of commander-in-chief, which had been held since 1856 by the Duke of Cambridge.

Before 1876 the defence of Plymouth was under the command of the General Officer Commanding, Western District assisted by a Commander Royal Artillery and a Commander Royal Engineers. The GOC commanded the regular units in his district but the assorted militia and volunteer units in the Plymouth area were not under his command and there was no combined training or apparently any joint planning for war. The reaction of the local forces on the outbreak of war, at least as far as the land defences were concerned, was likely at first to be fragmented if not confused.

References

[1] *The History of the Royal Artillery.* Vol.I. 1860-1899. Callwell & Headlam. p. 294)
[2] Ibid.p.295.
[3] *The Militia Artillery.* 1852-1909 Litchfield. p.2
[4] *JSAHR.* Vol.37.1959.Barrie Rose. p.99
[5] Ibid p. 102
[6] *History of Plymouth.* Jewett. p. 603
[7] *JSAHR* Vol. 37 1859. Barrie Rose p. 101

8

THE BATTLE AT BOWDEN BATTERY

*'Some 20,000 troops and an ample provision of artillery...
could be rapidly conveyed to and landed in the neighbourhood of any of these arsenals, and a very few days would
be sufficient to master and destroy them...'*

General Sir John Burgoyne
to Secretary of State for War - 5 March 1860

This 'eyewitness account' is designed to show how the
North Eastern Defences of Plymouth might have reacted to a large scale raid designed to put Devonport
Dockyard quickly out of action. Simultaneously the main
invasion would have been on the Sussex coast aimed at
seizing, or at least masking, Portsmouth and marching on
London.

To make such a scenario credible one only has to imagine that the defeat which the French suffered in the
Franco-Prussian War in 1870 left their army beaten but not
destroyed, and that this defeat was followed by a negotiat-
ed, though humiliating, peace settlement. As a result
Napoleon III would have looked for an opportunity to
restore his fortunes by a successful military venture. He
had earlier sent groups of French officers over to England
to study the landing places and invasion routes used by
Julius Caesar, nominally to provide the detail for his life of
Caesar which was published in 1865. French maps of the
British defences were available in the late 1860s, including
one of the Plymouth defences.

In the following years he would have found no difficulty in fanning his people's hatred of England, their
traditional enemy. With our small standing army mainly
deployed overseas and the navy stretched to cover our
expanding Empire where he could easily foment trouble, it
would have been practicable for a French fleet, based on
Cherbourg and Brest and carrying the latest heavy guns, to
achieve dominance of the Channel for long enough to
land a large force at any time in the 1870s, especially if a
diversion had been engineered in the Mediterranean to
prevent the Channel fleet being reinforced.

Tension between the two countries would have built up
in the preceding months and the possibility of an impending invasion would have become apparent several weeks
beforehand. It is assumed that:

1. Strenuous efforts had been made since 1870 to speed up
the completion and the armament of the land forts and
batteries, and Major-General Smyth had been appointed
commander of the whole garrison at Plymouth. The scale
of armament recommended by the Defence Committee on
5 January 1875 had been confirmed earlier and largely
achieved by the time of the invasion. The development of
the 8-in howitzer had been completed and production
begun. The armament would therefore have consisted of
7-inch RBL (Armstrong) guns, 64-pounder RMLs and some
8-inch rifled Howitzers. 32-pounder smooth-bore, muzzle-

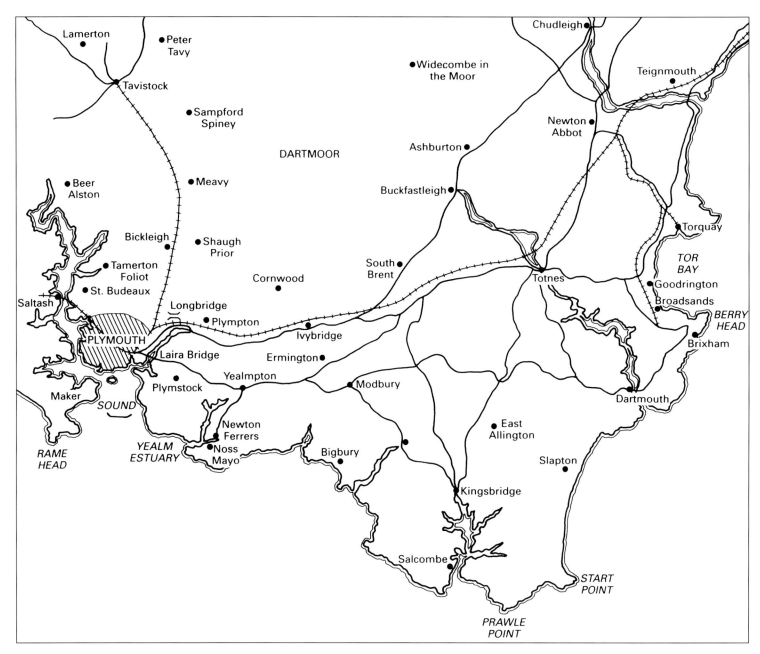

Map IVa: *South Devon.*

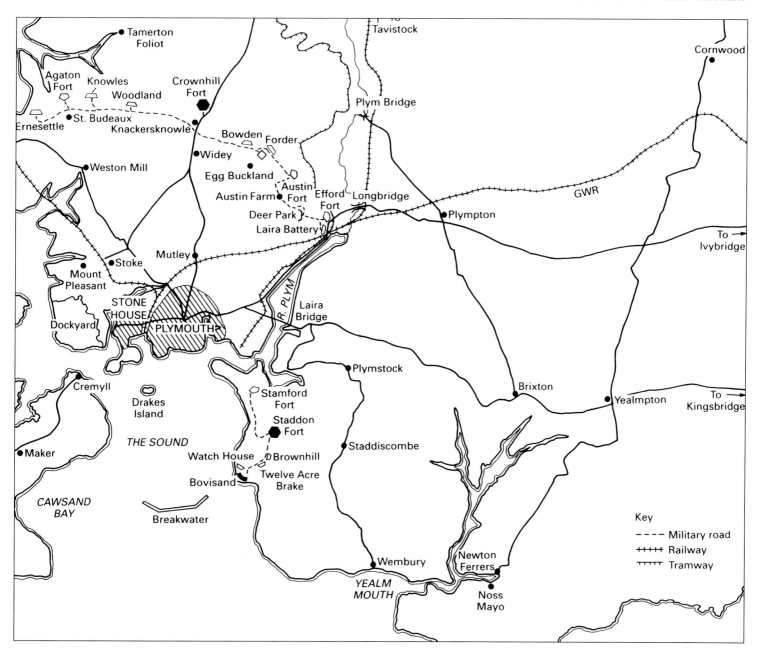

Map IVb: *The eastern approaches to Plymouth.*

Key
- - - - Military road
+++++ Railway
⊤⊤⊤⊤ Tramway

loading flank guns would have been mounted as a temporary measure in the caponiers and there would have been some of the obsolescent 10-inch and 13-inch mortars still available for the mortar batteries.

2. The militia would have been embodied a few days before the actual invasion and regular reservists recalled to the colours at the same time. The volunteer units could not be called up until the invasion took place.

3. On the day of the invasion there would also have been a call by the Lord Lieutenant for volunteers from the civilian population and these would have been drafted to the existing units.

4. In order to prevent the Channel Fleet being reinforced before the invasion the French would have created a diversion in the Mediterranean designed to tie down our fleet there.

On the French side, the commander of the raid on Plymouth, General Lafond, had been given his objective by the Emperor in person in true Napoleonic style three months before: 'To destroy Devonport Dockyard with all speed and at all costs'.

The General, a hero of the Franco-Prussian War, had made his outline plan. He would land at Torbay (Map IVa) take Dartmouth from the land side, make it his base and later use the Yealm estuary as an advanced base. He started with an outline plan of the Plymouth defences which he supplemented with intelligence from a number of 'travellers' whom he had arranged to pass through Plymouth in the following weeks.

Whilst aware of the strengths of the defences, he intended to exploit certain weaknesses: their lack of depth, the economies made in some of the later works and the shortage of trained troops. He planned to attack the gap between Crownhill Fort and Bowden Battery (Map IVb),

seizing the latter and penetrating as far as the main road from Crownhill to Stoke in the first phase of the attack, with the eventual objective of seizing the high ground at Mount Pleasant and bombarding the Dockyard and the Steam Yard at Keyham. The initial attack would be under cover of darkness unless the speed of his advance and favourable weather conditions made a daylight attack practicable.

To reach the forming up area for the attack north of Coleridge Hill (Map IVc), it would be desirable to move his leading brigade over Plym Bridge under cover of darkness. Once Bowden was taken he would be in a position, if it became necessary, to roll up the line of defences to the east of it as far as Austin Fort, by attacking them from the rear, and later take the Efford position. This would enable him to move up reinforcements in daylight and progressively shorten his lines of communication. He arranged to land siege artillery at Dartmouth in case his first attack was held up and he had to besiege Crownhill or one of the other forts.

To stretch the defences to the limit he would initially threaten the line all the way from Staddon to Crownhill and draw off part of the reserve - there were only two regiments in Devonport according to his intelligence - by an attack towards Laira Bridge, which would have to be resisted to protect the town and Sutton Harbour.

Crownhill Fort represented a threat to the initial attack from the north since its guns covered at a distance the valley across which his troops would have to advance. He had no intention of attacking the fort itself unless the initial attack failed and he planned to neutralise it in two ways, one of which involved the use of specially trained gunners using the latest French equipment.

*   *   *   *

'The story of the battle in September 1874 was written down for me by Miss Northmore, my former school mistress at Cornwood. I talked about it to her over many evenings, adding much that was out of my sight at the time but was told to me by my comrades afterwards.'

John Wilcocks.
Sergeant, 2nd South Devon Militia Regiment.

(See Maps IVc and IVd)

The first time I realised how bad things were for us on that Sunday evening in September was when Captain Deane, our company commander, ordered me to mount double sentries from 6pm - two at the gate and two patrolling the ramparts - and to raise the drawbridge at sunset. After that things happened fast.

The rumour that the French had landed had reached us late that afternoon and on Monday morning it was all in the *Western Daily Mercury*. They had landed at Goodrington and Broadsands in Torbay (Map IVa) early on Sunday morning and were in Brixham when people there were still in church. They overran the batteries covering the bay at Brixham and attacked the fort at Berry Head in the afternoon. But the main news was of a big landing on the Sussex coast and of a naval battle in the Channel off the Isle of Wight, in which our ships were worsted by the French fleet and were driven back into Spithead.

I had been put in charge of the guard house and magazine at Bowden Battery soon after we were embodied. There was talk of the French Emperor threatening to have revenge on us for some fighting between our fishermen and theirs. They kept cutting our nets and eventually our men rammed one of their boats and some of the crew drowned before they could be rescued. The French came back later and fired on our boats until a frigate of ours came up and sank a couple of the Frenchmen... .

On embodiment three companies of the South Devon Militia were sent to Eggbuckland Keep which was the barracks for Bowden, Forder and Austin Batteries. We spent the first couple of days drawing our kit and drilling on the square behind the keep. Then each of the companies was posted to one of the three batteries and the men spent their days learning their way around and their positions in action. Most of our company, No. 3, returned to the keep at night because the only accommodation in Bowden Battery was in the guard house.

Our company commander, Captain Deane, had been an officer in the 31st (Huntingdonshire) Foot for fifteen years and had served in South Africa and in the Kaffir Wars. He was a fine rifle shot and had trained us well on the ranges. For the last three years we had won the shooting cup in the battalion.

In the battery we had three 7-inch Armstrong guns, five 64-pdr RMLs, a couple of the new 8-inch rifled howitzers and four old mortars, two 13-inch in the NE salient and two 10-inch in the west salient. There were also two 32-pounder cannon in the guardhouse which had been brought up from the Gun Wharf with the mortars. In the last few months the battery had been looked after by an old gunner and a storeman so the guns and ammunition were in good shape.

The day after I took over the guardhouse ten more gunners were posted to the battery - regular reservists who knew their way around the guns. A day or two later they were joined by a dozen more artillerymen from the Militia Artillery, so we had two or three gunners for each gun and mortar. Some of our riflemen were at first told off to learn the gun drill but this left us very short for manning the rifle galleries since the company was not up to strength.

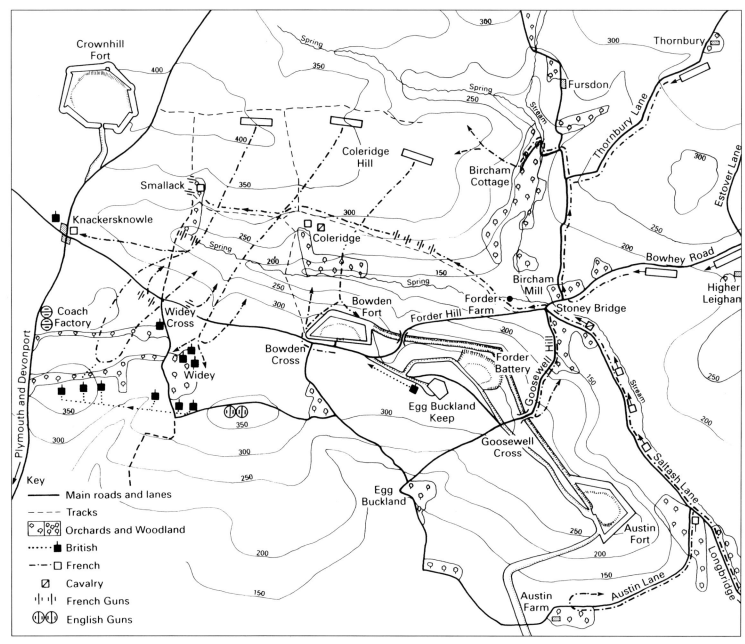

Map IVc: *The attack at Bowden Battery.*

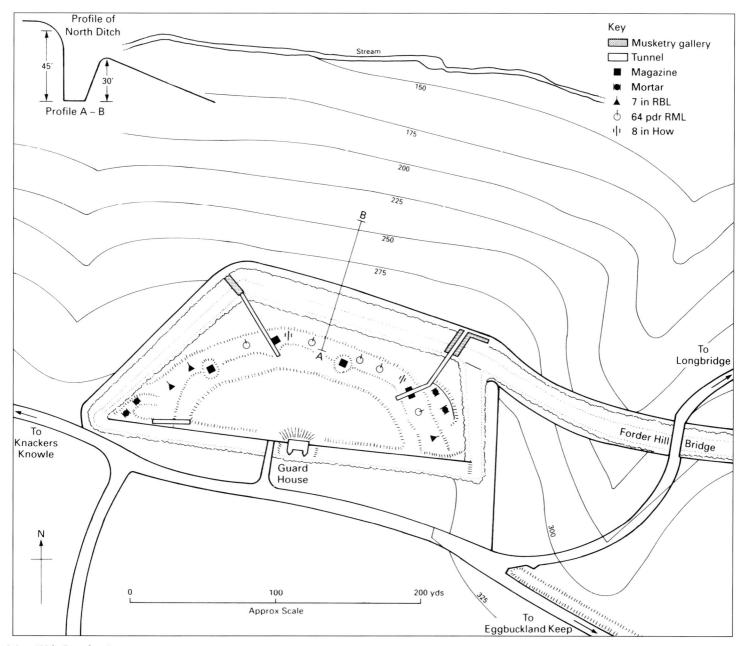

Map IVd: *Bowden Battery.*

Profile of
North Ditch

45′

30′

Profile A – B

Stream

150

175

200

225

250

275

B

A

300

325

To
Longbridge

Forder Hill

Bridge

To
Knackers
Knowle

Guard
House

To
Eggbuckland Keep

N

0   100   200 yds
Approx Scale

Key

Musketry gallery
Tunnel
Magazine
Mortar
7 in RBL
64 pdr RML
8 in How

We were very pleased when on Sunday afternoon the number of gunners was nearly doubled by the arrival of a party of volunteer artillerymen. Later that evening thirty volunteer riflemen marched in in their smart uniforms, keen as mustard to do their bit. They were only armed with the old Enfield rifles whilst we had the improved Snider-Enfields and a few of the latest Martini-Henry rifles, but they made up our numbers. On Monday small parties of civilian volunteers from Plymouth began to turn up in response to the Lord Lieutenant's call. Some of them were townies and not much use except in the cookhouse, but amongst them were fishermen and retired Dockyard men who were useful in humping ammunition for the guns and could turn their hands to any work.

On Monday morning we had a visit from the Master-Gunner from Crownhill Fort, a fine figure of a man in a splendid uniform. He brought with him a grey headed old sergeant called Horton who had fought in the Crimea. He was to be in charge of all the gunners and to advise Lieutenant Westcott who was put in command of the guns and the supply of ammunition. The Master-Gunner drilled the regular gunners on each type of gun while our men watched. It was splendid to see how it should be done. Then with one of the howitzers they dropped a shell in front of Coleridge Farm using a small charge, showing that these guns could fire into the steep valley in front of the battery (Map IVd).

All this gave our men confidence but upset the farmer at Coleridge! A couple of hours later we saw him driving his sheep towards Crownhill with his wife following behind with a cart loaded up with all they could carry. We reckoned he would finish up on Roborough Down. He had already had all his trees cut down two days before when the army sent gangs of men round to clear the land in front of the forts, as we were told they were allowed to do under

Act of Parliament. He heard that they were coming back later to pull the buildings down as well.

On Monday afternoon, by which time things had shaken down in the battery, Captain Deane, at the suggestion of the old gunner sergeant, sent a large party of men down to the stream at the bottom of the valley in front to dam it in places so as to make the land boggy. Then they dragged the felled trees and branches lying around down to make a barricade along the stream as well.

By Monday evening there were rumours that Berry Head Fort had fallen that morning. Our yeomanry and volunteers covering Totnes had been driven back and the railway to Plymouth cut. When Captain Deane came to mount the double guard at six he told us that Dartmouth had been taken by an attack from the land and from the sea and that French cavalry were on the Exeter road near Ivybridge. It showed how serious things were that Lt. Westcott rode over from Eggbuckland at 3.00am to turn out the guard, instead of his usual time of 10 or 11pm.

Next morning early on there was heavy firing from the Sound for over an hour. We later heard that a French squadron from Brest was driven off by the heavy guns at Picklecombe and Cawsand Forts when they approached the western entrance. Two of their ships had been badly damaged and a frigate which tried to slip round by the lighthouse on the Breakwater was sunk by a mine. At the same time, under cover of fire from some of their warships, the French had landed at Newton and Noss and were moving inland. The French squadron withdrew later but could still be seen off the Eddystone.

Soon after, we heard that the *Mercury* had reported that French cavalry had been in Ivybridge the evening before. About 3 o'clock that afternoon we heard guns firing from over to Efford. Soon after our signallers on the guardhouse got a message from the Keep to 'stand to' and later an orderly came galloping along the military road from the Keep with orders to open fire if the enemy approached our ditch or Coleridge Farm.

Fresh troops were advancing from Newton Ferrers on Yealmpton and cavalry were reported to have rushed Longbridge. Soon after Captain Deane rode over and inspected our men at their action stations. His batman came over with him to make up a bed for him in a shelter on the top of the guard house.

The firing we had heard was when some cavalry had tried to charge up the valley to take Austin Farm (Map IVc). They had been fired on by the guns at Deer Park, but what had stopped them in the end was some field guns firing from the bank of the military road at the foot of the valley. They were from the moveable armament at Efford and had been dragged into position that morning by gunners and volunteers. The French lost a number of men and horses.

The Captain said that our pickets were out on the approaches to our position. Forder Battery semaphored 'enemy in sight' and soon after we heard a bang from our right. We guessed this was the wooden bridge over the ditch on Goosewell Hill (Map IVc) going up, for we had already seen some engineers putting charges under the bridge on Forder Hill below us that morning. There was rifle fire from time to time and some of it seemed to come from our right rear. Later we heard that a French patrol moving towards Eggbuckland village had been driven off by a strong picket covering Goosewell Cross.

The next we heard was a bang when the wooden bridge over the ditch on Forder Hill went up. Soon after we saw a small party of French cavalry moving at a fast trot up the lane towards Coleridge Farm. Most of them were on splendid horses but those in the rear looked as if they were on nags picked up on the way through. Lieutenant Westcott ordered two of our guns to open up and when the shells landed behind them the calvary broke into a gallop and made for the farm.

We had hardly finished cheering this, our first engagement, when the sentry on the right of the battery reported men approaching the ditch up Forder Hill. They were in blue uniforms and were moving in open order - in rushes from one bit of cover to the next - and were obviously skirmishers. We were glad we had cleared away all the gorse bushes which gave cover on the glacis. When they came close in to the edge of the ditch our men opened fire from the ramparts. The French were too scattered to make much of a target but they fired back and one of our men got his head blown off by a Frenchman 150 metres away. After that we took more care.

Before long some of the skirmishers moved across our front towards Knackers Knowle covered by the others. A mortar on the west face of our battery fired two or three shells at them when they looked like trying to cross the military road. But the light was going and we couldn't be sure how far they had gone or whether they were still in the gully five hundred yards west of us which leads towards Widey. We set double sentries on each salient that night and the men slept by their guns.

After dark Captain Deane sent me with six men on patrol towards Knackers Knowle. I was to find out if there were any enemy still on the road or in Widey but to keep out of trouble. I was able to pick my men and set off under the light of a harvest moon - too bright for my liking. We kept on the south side of the main road mainly but checked down the gully and found it clear. We then turned south at Widey Cross and approached the first cottage with some care. I knew the place and the people because we had been there several times to buy eggs and potatoes. No one seemed to be about until we heard a slight noise from a shed. In there were the woman, her mother and two children cowering in great distress. The French had come down at dusk and carried away her husband, leaving her with orders to make no noise or the sentry they were leaving would shoot them.

The cottagers were very glad to find it was us and that the story of the sentry was untrue. After checking there were no enemy in Widey Court or the lodge I hurried back along the military road. Leaving the men at the battery, after we had had some trouble in getting the guard to lower the drawbridge on the password, I was sent by Captain Deane to the Keep to report to Major Seale-Hayne who was in command there. He was pleased with what I had done and what we had found out. He told an orderly to prepare to take a message to General Smyth at Devonport and another to try and get through to Crownhill Fort.

At first light we could see that there were troops around Coleridge Farm and some were still marching up the sunken lane from Forder Farm. When Forder Battery dropped some shells amongst them they turned into the fields and used the cover of the banks. Later I heard that large numbers of infantry and some guns had moved up during the night over Plym Bridge, along Plymbridge Lane and Thornbury Lane to Bircham Cottage, and so onto Coleridge Hill. There was the smoke of many fires beyond the hill to our front and we reckoned there must be a large body of men up there where they were out of sight of Crownhill Fort. There seemed to be a lot going on around Smallack Farm too.

From time to time we could see troops on the crest of Coleridge Hill and they appeared to be forming up in large numbers under cover of the banks. We were told to save our ammunition for the attack which we knew would come, except for lobbing a howitzer shell from time to time into Coleridge Farm. We saw a couple of batteries of guns towed up the lane to Coleridge as fast as they could

go. Some of them managed to get along the farm track to Smallack. The rest went into position on either side of Coleridge facing us. They took cover behind the banks and made gaps in them for the guns. Later we were surprised to see that the farmhouse was alight and soon there were fires in the orchard below where the trees had been cut down. The smoke drifted away up the valley.

Just after 10am all the guns around Coleridge opened up on us. Their first volley of ball shot did little harm, bouncing off the glacis if they were short or ploughing into the ramparts. Some of the overs hit the bank in front of the guardhouse and we learned to keep our heads down. When they switched to shell they cut their fuzes too long at first but soon they began to get rounds into the battery and there were casualties amongst our men. Soon after the bombardment began the French infantry appeared over the skyline, moving down the hill in two directions.

On our left we could see a long column - about 2000 men - keeping just east of Smallack from where there was a lot of smoke coming. They were burning the buildings it seemed. Anyway, the wind being from the east after the long hot spell it blew the smoke up the valley and made it hard for the gunners at Crownhill to see their target as the column got into the open, and soon they were in dead ground again. When the head of the column was opposite Knackers Knowle the leading companies halted, faced right and moved forward in line towards the village. The rest of the column carried on towards Widey.

On the right facing us a strong line of skirmishers came first, followed by two columns of companies which kept east of Coleridge Farm and headed for our battery. In this way the French got cover for part of the way from the fire of Crownhill Fort and most of the time we could not signal to the Fort because of the smoke. About the time the leading troops reached the valley in front of us, a large body of infantry - a couple of regiments - began to move in column down between the other two, heading for the gully to our West and towards Widey. From time to time, when the smoke cleared, we saw shells bursting among them.

Lt. Westcott had ordered our guns to open fire on the right hand column as soon as it began moving down the hill. It took a few rounds for our men to get the range and the fuze but once the gunners warmed to the job they did great execution on both columns as they passed the farm and came on to the bottom of the valley. There they were held up by the flooding and the barricade we had made which made them an easy target and our howitzers and mortars were able to drop shells amongst them. Due to the steepness of the glacis our other guns could no longer shoot down on them. Meanwhile their skirmishers pushed up the hill and kept up a lively fire on our ramparts.

It took some time for Forder to respond to our signals but once they were sure they were not going to be attacked themselves two or three of their guns joined in the firing at Coleridge Farm and into the valley in front of us. This probably prevented the French reinforcing their attack on our north face and later they concentrated on the NW face.

Captain Deane had ordered 2nd Lt. Stephens to pick 30 of the best rifle shots in the company and line them along the top of the rampart facing the attack. They held their fire until the main body of the French who had to break ranks to get through the barricade had begun to re-form in line on our side of it, about 200 yards away. They opened with a volley and then continued firing with great effect as the French line advanced slowly up the steep slope.

I heard that about this time Sergeant Horton had a word with Lieutenant Westcott who ordered two of the guns on the left of the our battery, which could no longer engage, to switch their fire to the centre column, while the Sergeant went over to the west mortar battery to switch their fire to that column as it approached the gully.

In front of us the French, who found the glacis steep, checked about half way up, closed ranks as their officers rallied them, and as soon as they re-formed came on in a rush. We could see that behind the centre of their line men were carrying ladders and grappling irons and in a moment they were attacking the ditch on the north and NW faces.

All this time I was watching the centre column over to our left through the smoke and dust of the battle, whenever it blew away. My heart was in my mouth when I saw the head of the column disappearing into the gulley leading to Widey and I knew there was nothing between them and the main Tavistock Road leading down to Stoke and the Dockyard. But our mortars were getting the range and I saw smoke from several of their bursting shells coming up from the gully.

Over on the far left, the front of the column which had turned on Knackers Knowle must have had a surprise as they were met with heavy fire from Redcoats who had occupied the cottages and the orchards. I heard that there was a stiff fight that went on for several hours. Again, the French were quick to fire any buildings they took. The main part of this column had continued its advance to the south and had disappeared in the smoke, presumably over the military road. There was not much firing from the guns at Crownhill Fort now due partly to the smoke and dust. I heard later that the French guns around Smallack - the new 75-mm - had fired back very accurately against the casemates on the ramparts when they first opened up and knocked two of the guns out. For a time they kept the others quiet using some new 'machine guns' as we called them (*maitrailleuses*).

All the time I could hear the noise of the fighting in and around the ditch and I was called down from time to time when more wounded came in. They were treated in the guardhouse by an apothecary who had joined us as a volunteer. I heard later that when the French came to the counterscarp of the north face many of them shinned down the ropes they had brought with them into the ditch while others kept up a fire from the edge of the glacis on the ramparts so our men had to keep their heads down.

The men manning the flanking gallery at the north east salient picked off the first of the French as they landed in the north ditch but as more and more came some of them got up to the face of the gallery and pushed grenades through the loophloes. Before long almost all our men were casualties and the gallery was abandoned. As more French pressed on into the ditch they tried to throw up grapnels and put up any ladders which were still in one piece. Though our battery had no *chemin des rondes* like at Crownhill, their ladders could not nearly reach the top of the scarp which, owing to the fall of the land towards the valley, is 35-40 feet high here. As it was, it was touch and go when small groups of Frenchmen climbed up on to the ramparts and sometimes had to be driven off with the bayonet. But by throwing grenades down from time to time the French were prevented from mounting a real attack. 2nd Lieut. Stephens was in charge on the rampart and led the men gallantly.

A runner came to me from Captain Deane ordering me to lower the drawbridge. As I did so our company orderly galloped off down the military road towards Forder. Later, half a company of the Warwickshire Militia came marching down the military road to join us, after which we pulled up the drawbridge again. The Warwickshires, who had been stationed in the Citadel during the Crimean War, had been sent down by train to Plymouth a few days before.

The sentry I had left on the roof called me up again. We were surprised to see that the head of the centre column as it came out of the gulley was held up by a line of Redcoats spread out along the bank of the military road. I heard much later that the 11th Foot, our own Devonshire Regiment, had marched up from Raglan Barracks during the night with orders to fill the gap between us and Crownhill Fort by holding Widey. As I watched, the head of the French column drove the riflemen back and after extending into line under the cover of the bank of the military road they began to advance over it towards Widey 200 yards away. No sooner had they come out into the open than they were met by a volley of rifle fire from the woods and buildings around the house and they checked after a second volley. More troops came on from the gully, the line reformed and they advanced again. I could see that part of the line had swung left towards us and it looked as if they were trying to get round Widey on our side. Through the smoke I had just seen the head of the left column of the attack reaching the rise between Widey and Knackers Knowle and it looked as if whoever was in Widey would soon be surrounded.

Meanwhile the French were concentrating their attack on the NW ditch and helped to silence the rifle gallery at the NW salient. Soon they were round the rear of our battery and firing on the guard house and the line of the gorge. Captain Deane ordered men of the Warwickshire Militia to man the loopholes in the gorge wall and to help us in the guard house. Heavy firing developed all along the line of the gorge as the French tried to establish themselves along the counterscarp and in the ditch. Our 32-pounders swept most of them away in the ditch but some tried to close the guardhouse where fire from the flanking rifle galleries in the scarp saw them off. About this time our whole battery came under fire from heavier guns - Napoleons firing a 12lb shell I was told later - which the French had moved up onto Coleridge Hill during the morning.

A stalemate seemed to have developed in the NW ditch where 100 or more French soldiers were in possession after silencing the rifle gallery. We couldn't see what was going on there because of the marksmen firing at the top of our rampart from the edge of the glacis. Suddenly there was a loud explosion followed shortly by another one. They had mined the scarp in two places in front and to the north of the mortar battery. With a cheer two parties of the French scaled the scarp.

Fortunately the solid rock which formed most of the scarp had prevented the explosion bringing down much of it so their men did not come up together and had to rely on their grapnels. But those that did get up rushed the mortar battery and tried to break into the fort by the tunnel behind it. Confused hand to hand fighting developed with the gunners laying about them with their handspikes. They would have been overcome but for some men of the Warwickshires who rushed down the tunnel from their position at the gorge led by their officer. He was shot as he came out but the rest poured on to the mortar battery. The men at the rear, not being able to get through the narrow tunnel quickly enough, charged over the top of the rampart with a cheer. This turned the tide in the mortar battery and any Frenchmen left were pushed back into the ditch.

Many of the gunners in the mortar battery, including the bombardier in charge, were killed or wounded in the attack, so Sgt. Horton came down with any men who could be spared from the guns on the east side of our battery to get the mortars in action again. He sent men to the magazine to get more ammunition and selecting half a dozen bombs he began to fire them from one of the mortars with a low charge on to the glacis as close as he could get to the edge of the counter scarp. This silenced some of the French riflemen but he could not get the rounds as close as

he wanted so he next traversed the mortar to the North and put a bomb in the ditch near the flanking gallery. But he could hear that the French were working on the breaches they had made in the scarp below the battery so after loading a very small charge and setting the shortest fuze he ordered all the other men into the tunnel and fired the mortar himself. The bomb hit the counterscarp, fell back into the ditch and a moment later exploded with terrible effect on the scaling parties, as we saw later. They never tried again.

While this was going on the situation had changed on our left. On the far left as the French reached the rise overlooking Widey they were fired on at close range by guns from the main road near the coach factory. Taken in the flank - in enfilade as the gunners call it - they were raked with terrible effect. The line wavered and broke for the shelter of the line of trees in front of them and began to reform on the far side where they were out of view of the guns. Clear in a pause in the firing came three loud 'huzzas' from over there. I later heard that as the French line re-formed and prepared to sweep down upon Widey men of the 11th, who had been moved up from their position in reserve south of Widey House, rose from the wood running west from Widey House, fired a volley into the French line and charged them with the bayonet. They broke and were pushed back towards the military road.

Soon after, that part of the centre column which was moving round Widey on our side came under fire from the far side of the valley in which Widey lies from guns on the high ground to the south east of it. The guns had taken up a position to cover the open country between our battery and Widey. The leading company wheeled to face the guns but they were hit by a volley of cannister. The remainder turned back towards the military road or ran for the Widey woods where there was already confused fighting with our men there.

The French who had got round the back of our battery were making it difficult for us on top of the guard room to watch what was going on. I was just going down the stairs when there was a loud crack and the parapet near me disappeared in a shower of flying splinters several of which cut the sentry up there around the face and arms. Looking towards Knackers Knowle I saw that some guns which I had seen moving in rear of the centre column had wheeled into action just north of the military road and were now facing us only four hundred yards away. Several more shots hit the wall of the guard room and I knew we were in for a pounding. That we did not come off worse was due to the fire of one of the Armstrong guns on the NW face which now engaged the battery and drew its fire.

About this time the Frenchmen in the NW ditch turned their attention to the counterscarp gallery which our men had abandoned. Their sappers blew in the wall and when they had cleared away the rubble they began to come along the tunnel into the fort. But Captain Deane had already put a picket there, who had built a barricade near the magazine and now their fire made advance up the tunnel impossible. The French gave up.

What happened next I discovered was due to the way the battle had gone over to the left. Blasted in their right flank by the guns at the coach factory and then charged by the 11th from the front the remains of their left column fell back in confusion towards the military road where it mixed with those men who were still fighting round Knackers Knowle. Soon they were all streaming back towards the shelter of Smallack followed by the fire of the Redcoats who were now lining the bank of the military road. Before long the officers of the 11th had re-formed the companies which had made the attack and began to

lead them along the military road towards our battery taking in the flank the remainder of the centre column who were still fighting around Widey. Confused and bitter fighting continued between Widey and the military road.

The battery firing on the guardroom suddenly stopped, limbered up, and headed back towards Smallack leaving one of its guns disabled and many of its men and horses on the field. Before long the remains of the centre column was streaming back towards Coleridge, followed by the men who had attacked our battery, and the rest of the French were being rounded up by the defenders of Widey. Any thought of pursuit beyond the military road went when some French cavalry appeared in the valley to cover the retreat. That retreat was hastened by the gunners from the coach factory who had limbered up and moved to Knackers Knowle and then along the military road to Widey Cross where they came into action again. As the smoke began to clear we saw that there were some field guns on the rampart over the gate at Crownhill which were speeding the French on their way.

About this time our sergeant-major told the cooks to get a meal going and take a brew of tea to the men on the guns and in the galleries. Captain Deane who had faced shot and shell all day on the ramparts came in for a cup of tea as well. Sadly Lt. Westcott had been picked off by a sharpshooter. More than thirty other men were dead and many more wounded.

Soon after, Major Seale-Hayne galloped over from the Keep and we gladly lowered the drawbridge for him. He went round praising all the men for the gallant fight they had put up, but telling them to make ready and then get what sleep they could as the French were likely to try again. He had been watching from Forder and men and heavy guns were moving up along Thornbury Lane all the time.

He told me that as a result of the information from my patrol last night the 11th Foot had been ordered up by General Smyth to stop the gap between Crownhill and Bowden. They had been on their way home from India after a campaign there and had been diverted into Plymouth a few days before whilst on their way to Ireland. It was lucky that several of their officers and many of their men came from Plymouth and knew the country round about. Parties from the 11th had been sent to Eggbuckland and Widey to look for possible positions the evening before.

Before first light the 11th had put their Grenadier Company into Knackers Knowle and skirmishers had manned the line of the military road. Four more companies went into Widey and the other three were held in reserve in the park to the south of the manor. It was these companies who had made the decisive attack on the left and then wheeled right to dislodge the centre column. A battery of artillery with 9-pounders had been sent with the 11th They had put three guns into position on the high ground South East of Widey and the other three in the coach factory south of Knackers Knowle.

After he had given orders and seen that the wounded were being cared for Captain Deane ordered me to take a party of twelve men along the military road to report if it was clear of the enemy, to contact the infantry at Widey and to bring back any stragglers or lightly wounded.

I set off in daylight this time with a lighter heart, but not for long. There were dozens of dead and badly wounded French soldiers in the gully. We were able to round up some who were either dazed or not too badly off and I was giving water to a few who were calling for it when I realised that our men were stripping the dead and even the wounded. It took me some time to get them under orders again. I told three men to escort those Frenchman who could still walk back to the battery. I was about to move on with the remainder when there was a shot from down the gulley and I felt my right arm go numb. It was shattered above the elbow. After they had strapped me up I sent the corporal on to Widey with the patrol and was helped back to Bowden with the others.

This was the end of the war for me as I finished up next day in the military hospital on the shore of Stonehouse Creek where they cut off what was left of my arm leaving a stump. I also lost my gold watch while I was there.

It was the end of the war for all of us luckily, as it turned out. The French who had landed at Newton and Noss had been held up after stiff fight with the 45th Foot at Pomphlett on the other side of Laira Bridge. But though the enemy were moving up all the time the big attack never came. The French squadron off Plymouth was surprised that same evening by a powerful squadron of ours which had slipped out of the Mediterranean some days earlier unknown to the them. Some of the French ships were sunk and the others dispersed. Our squadron, after destroying some small shipping in the Yealm river, went on to join with the rest of the Portsmouth squadron and later defeated the main French fleet off the Sussex coast.

The following day the French began a general retreat. We were not strong enough at Plymouth to do more than harry them. Many of them were taken off from Newton and Noss by night and the remainder withdrew to Dartmouth where they re-embarked. Several of their ships were rounded up or sunk by our frigates as they tried to escape.

So ended the great invasion. For me it meant I could no longer think of working on my father's farm at Cornwood. Two years later I married my childhood sweetheart Emma Barons whose family had owned Wisdome Mill for many years. We had both been pupils at the National School at

Cornwood when it opened in 1859. When her father had to give up the mill and I could not carry on on my own we set up shop in Fore Street, Cornwood as bakers and general provision merchants. Fortunately we prospered for in all we had nine children. The loss of my arm was not such a misfortune after all. They gave us a medal a year later to remind us of the day when we all - regulars, militia, volunteers and townies - fought together to save Plymouth and the Dockyard.

9
FORTS OR FOLLIES?

The vast cost of any system of land fortification sooner or later prompts the question as to whether it was justified, especially if it was never challenged. Yet the object of such a system is to deter. It cannot claim to be impregnable in all circumstances but it achieves its object if it convinces an attacker that it will impose losses and delays in achieving his objective, which are unacceptable.

A direct attack from the sea, though often launched, has seldom silenced the coast defences of a port, even when these were not up-to-date, since until the development of long range guns an attacker had to close the coast batteries and 'slog it out' with them. They were well protected and had the advantage of their stable platform and a large target, whereas ships had difficulty in maintaining a prolonged and accurate enough bombardment to disable the individual guns. Coast defences have almost always been silenced following a landing on the coast nearby and an attack from the rear, hence the need for defended gorges and land defences in support.

Though the land defences eventually built at Plymouth in the 1860s were successful in deterring attack, even after being greatly reduced in cost by the Cabinet, they are still referred to as 'Palmerston's Follies', partly on the basis that they were politically unnecessary. This charge must be faced. Were they in response to a real threat of invasion or merely to a scare? Fortification can be 'less the consideration of concise military needs and more the expression of

vague political fears.'[1] There can be no doubt about the underlying rivalry and suspicion between Britain and France at this time after more than 150 years of intermittent conflict. Invasion had not merely been threatened by Napoleon in 1803-5 but invasion fleets or substantial raids had been launched by the French against the British Isles on eight occasions since 1692. By the beginning of 1858, a resurgent France under the rule of an Emperor Napoleon had created alarm in the minds of politicians and military men in Britain but not yet in the popular imagination. Amongst politicians confidence had been shaken by the military setbacks of the Crimean War, when the army lost much prestige, and by the distraction of the Indian Mutiny. The Victorian vision of indefinite peace, progress and prosperity had been shattered.

Tension between Britain and France began to rise in 1858. In January an attempt was made to assassinate the French emperor by an Italian, Count Orsini, with a bomb proved to have been made in England and this incensed the Parisian press and many of the French generals. In August the enlarged naval base at Cherbourg was opened by the Emperor with much ceremony, and in the presence of Queen Victoria and many distinguished British guests. The huge new basin which made it the most modern naval base in the world was called after Napoleon, and the Emperor unveiled an equestrian statue of Napoleon I. The base was connected to Paris by a new railway line. All this was within 200kms of Portsmouth, Portland and Plymouth. As the *Times* wrote tartly on the occasion '...we see no subject of rejoicing in the erection of Cherbourg with the sole view of rendering easy and successful operations against this country', and it pointed out that the heavy guns mounted in the numerous forts and batteries there were considerably larger than those to be found at Plymouth or Portsmouth. In the autumn it was reported that the keel had been laid of *La Gloire*, the French ironclad warship - the first of its kind.

1859 was a turning point. Early in the year the report of an internal committee pointed out that the Royal Navy's considerable superiority in numbers over the French consisted largely of gunboats and other small vessels and a pamphlet by 'a Naval Peer' quoted a French naval officer's opinion that the French could obtain command of the Channel at any time. In April the Emperor declared war on Austria in support of the movement for Italian independence, and after two costly French victories peace was signed in July. Though Britain also supported the movement for independence, the war appeared an adventure reminiscent of the first Napoleon. Palmerston became Prime Minister again in June. In July, in response to widespread popular concern, the Government passed the Volunteer Act and Tennyson called to the volunteers

Form! Form! Riflemen form!
Ready, be ready to meet the storm.

Suddenly, 'the nation ceased to look back to the last war with France and began to prepare for the next'[2] In August Palmerston set up the Royal Commission to consider the defences of the United Kingdom.

In the circumstances Palmerston cannot simply be accused of folly. He was the most experienced statesman of his time - twice Secretary for War and four times Foreign Secretary - and for fifteen years he had been actively concerned about the parlous state of our defences. The building of the Suez Canal which he thought would open Egypt to the French and threaten India, and Napoleon's war with Austria, had added to his distrust of the Emperor whose mind was in his view 'as full of schemes as a warren is full of rabbits'. In the face of such a potential threat, and in view of the shortage of troops at home and the increasing dispersal of the navy, it was time to put our defences in order.

That Palmerston exploited the popular alarm and the swing in public opinion which occurred in 1858-59 to promote his aim of strengthening the country's defences is not in doubt. But this is no more than politicians have done over the centuries. The previous government had already authorised work on the Antony Line in 1858. But to maintain that Napoleon III would in no circumstances have invaded is to be wise after the event. He had the harbours, the men, the railways and the temptation due to our weakness on land, in addition to his and his generals' inclination.

Yet, shortly before he died in 1865 Palmerston wrote to our ambassador in Paris 'all old sentiments of rivalship and antagonism as between Englishmen and Frenchmen are on our part extinguished'! What had happened to change his views? The many uncertainties of 1859 had mostly been resolved. The unquantifiable results of the development of reliable steam power, the building of the first ironclads and the revolution in gunnery, which all combined to shake British confidence in the effectiveness of the Royal Navy, had been if not resolved at least accepted. The two Powers had approached the outbreak of the American Civil War in 1862 in a spirit of rivalry, and yet had ended it with a common policy.

By then France had a new rival on land in the growing power of Prussia. By 1864 a balance of naval power was becoming accepted, helped by the results of the Declaration of Paris on maritime law following the end of the Crimean War. HMS *Warrior* had proved a much more formidable man-of-war than *La Gloire*. Britain's confidence was further strengthened now that the Army's numerical weakness was reinforced by the new fortification system. Palmerston had reason to feel secure once more.

Was the scheme of defences recommended by the Royal Commission strategically sound? There were those, especially in the Navy, who maintained that the defence of the landward approaches to the dockyards, which accepted that a large army with its heavy equipment could be put ashore in England, was strategically unsound. Anyway, the enemy could land at a number of undefended ports on the east coast. The naval opposition to the Royal Commission's proposals maintained to the end that the only adequate defence against invasion was 'a large well-manned and well-disciplined fleet'.[3] The Royal Commission did not accept that the Navy could guarantee to prevent an invasion force landing in all circumstances and though there remains the suspicion that like many military planners they tended to over-estimate the capability of the enemy and under-estimate the strength of the defences, this was the basis of their proposals.

The French naval bases were at Dunkirk, Cherbourg and Brest. The best coastline from which to launch the main invasion force with its many shallow draught vessels was still the coastline from Dunkirk to the Seine. There the crossing to England was the shortest and the best landing beaches were opposite. But the enlarged base at Cherbourg was also capable of launching 20–30 000 men across the Channel overnight.

The principal British bases were at Chatham, Portsmouth and Plymouth, with smaller defended harbours at Harwich and Pembroke Docks and harbours of refuge at Dover and Portland. There could be no doubt that these harbours must be defended from attack by sea. The Royal Commission quickly abandoned the idea of attempting to defend the whole of the coast, although there were still the Martello towers put up as beach defences 50 years before in Essex, Kent and Sussex. It considered that the defence of the two largest dockyards at Portsmouth and Plymouth both from the land as well as from the sea was vital to the maintenance of the fleet in action, a fleet which due to increasing technology became more and more dependent on dockyard facilities.

The Royal Commission rejected the expansion of the regular army for historical and political reasons, and on grounds of finance. The weakness of its strategy lay thereafter in the fact that London lies only 80 miles from the Sussex coast and that as the centre of government and Empire its capture would have ended any war. Provided they could comprehensively defeat our fleet in the Channel and given good weather, the French could have landed a sufficient force on the Sussex coast - 30 000 men initially rising to 100 000 in three or four days - to mask Portsmouth rather than to capture it and reach London in the face of the small force of 10–20 000 regular and militia troops which could have been opposed to them in the time. This was not a possibility which the Royal Commission satisfactorily addressed, and it was not until Cardwell brought 25 000 regular troops home from the colonies in the early 1870s that this danger was removed.

Such an invasion would have required military skill, good organisation and favourable weather. It would have been hazardous but it was an operation which Napoleon and the young generals which he was promoting in the

French army would have relished and of which their army was capable.

What of Cherbourg in this operation? Its squadron, with that at Brest, would have formed the main fleet whose task was to defeat our Channel fleet and drive it into Spithead. But it is likely that it would also have been used as the base for a strong raiding force whose object was to destroy Devonport Dockyard from where naval reinforcements could come and where damaged ships could be refitted. Such a raid would be likely either immediately before, or simultaneous with, the main invasion. This is another reason why Plymouth and Devonport were fortified on the land side.

Taking Plymouth as an example, were the layout and type of defences recommended by the Royal Commission likely to be effective? Helped by the topography of the Sound the proposed outer and inner coast defences were very strong. There were weaknesses at Polhawn, where the abandonment of Knatterbury left it seriously exposed to fire from ships standing off to the south, and as a result of the delays in the completion of Breakwater Fort, though the longer range of the guns eventually mounted at Picklecombe and Bovisand reduced its importance.

In the event the implementation of the Commission's plans was seriously delayed by the rapid development of rifled guns with their greater range and much greater power of penetration. The original object of the casemates for the coast batteries was to protect guns on wooden traversing siege carriages, such as had been mounted *en barbette* on the earlier batteries, from the front and overhead. The development of heavy rifled guns meant that greater protection was required in front so they were given iron shields and the top tier of Breakwater Fort was encased in iron. As heavier RML guns became available they were mounted in the original casemates but on cast iron platforms.

The weakness of these casemated batteries was that they were an obvious target for attack. Also, the effectiveness of an arc of casemates was not tested in firing trials until 1872. It was not until after the humiliating experience of the Navy in its bombardment of the obsolescent Egyptian coast defences at Alexandria in 1882 that it was realised that well spaced guns in sunken pits protected in front by earth and concrete were more effective. They are extremely difficult to knock out, and being open and separate can be manned more efficiently by their detachments when firing.

The land defences originally recommended at Plymouth by the Royal Commission appear to have been an overreaction to the actual threat - of a strong raid rather than of an invasion on this part of the coast - and it is not surprising that they were reduced by the Cabinet. But as a result of the severity of these reductions any depth in the defences was eliminated and the Saltash defences were never authorised. The omission of the latter was explained as not so serious because of the difficult country to the north of the Lynher estuary and the fact that the British army of the time with its Crimean and colonial experience was accustomed to throwing up effective earthwork defences quickly.

Nevertheless the omission of permanent defences covering Saltash remained a calculated risk since as Jervois pointed out in a letter in April 1861 to Lord Herbert (Secretary for War 1859-60) 'the use of the other defences to the Westward is to some extent neutralised and the line of the North East defences is subject to be turned'.[4] He recommended that the complete circuit of the works at Plymouth should be completed by building the inner portion of the Saltash position first to link up with the works on either side. But Herbert said it was not advisable to bring the matter up at that stage - and so it went on.

To the west, Tregantle and Scraesdon were both powerful forts. But without the ditch linking them and the intermediate work originally proposed, an enemy could pass between them in small numbers by day and without difficulty at night, so that the vulnerable east face of Tregantle, which included the keep, would soon find itself under bombardment from the rear. The reserve of men for which Tregantle's huge barracks were built would be needed to counter this threat, but where would the troops come from?

The North Eastern Defences as eventually built bore little relation to those recommended by the Commission and lacked any depth. However, each of the three groups of forts and batteries was well sited and capable of defending itself to the front, and to the rear against infantry only. Crownhill Fort alone was strong enough to hold out indefinitely if surrounded. There were large enough gaps on either side of it which, though covered by fire by day, would enable the enemy to pass through in strength at night. Everything depended on Crownhill's ability to hold out and the existence of reserve units in the garrison capable of determined and effective counter-attack.

The Staddon position was a strong one especially after the building of the additional Fort Stamford and of the scarp wall to Bovisand, covered by two small batteries. But although Fort Staddon had a fine field of fire to the north there was no permanent fortification covering the Kingsbridge road and the approach to Laira Bridge, in spite of the fact that in July 1861 the combined Defence and Fortification committees approved a proposal to build a work at Pomphlett as a *tête de pont* to Laira Bridge - when funds were available. There was no fort at Cattedown as originally proposed and to the north Laira Battery was 2500m from Laira Bridge. As at Saltash, earthwork defences would have been improvised here in the event of an attack from the east.

A much wider question is whether these fortifications, planned just as rifled guns with their greater penetration and plunging fire were being introduced, were effectively designed to meet the threat which these guns represented. Experience from 1862 onwards in the American Civil War showed that the massive brick walls at Fort Pulaski, and later at Fort Sumter, were vulnerable to fire from rifled guns but only after prolonged bombardment. The exposed stone face of the keep at Tregantle was criticised by General Todleben and the stone revetted embrasures of the Haxo casemates in the earlier forts would have been little less vulnerable to accurate bombardment.

On the other hand they were not expected to have to face a prolonged siege. The bomb-proofing of the vulnerable parts of the later forts would have been effective but it was not until Crownhill was designed that the value of earthworks as a protection against modern artillery was properly appreciated or the importance of concealing from enemy view both the outline of the fort itself and its principal features.

However, the Fortification Committee in general terms, and Lt. Col. Jervois and his Royal Engineer officers in detail, appear to have used the money allotted to Plymouth, after the sharp reduction in the Commission's original estimates, to good effect. The casemated coast batteries were to a standard general pattern. Bovisand was quickly reduced to a single tier of guns because of the relatively narrow entrance which it covered. Two tiers of guns were definitely necessary at Picklecombe to cover the wide expanse of Cawsand Bay and the principal channel into the Sound.

Of the land defences, Tregantle and Scraesdon had been designed and their construction begun before the Royal Commission reported. If they had been started three years later as part of the overall plan, the relatively large sum of money spent on them could have been better used both in terms of the general design of Tregantle, the provision of a military road from there to Scraesdon and of an intermediate work to fill the gap.

On Staddon Heights a naturally strong position was further improved and Staddon Fort represents an advance in fortification terms on Tregantle. The elimination of the original keep was a sensible economy and does not appear to reduce the strength of the fort proportionately. Stamford Fort strengthens the northern flank but was probably responsible for the over-expenditure on this position, together with the military road and the three earthwork batteries, even after its original design had been much simplified.

The North Eastern Defences are in many ways the most controversial. They were the last to be designed and finished and suffered from the need to save money in the end to cover the overrun on the Staddon Defences. They consist of eleven works, forming three defensive positions together with the most important single work, Crownhill Fort. They cover four miles of undulating country yet they cost only 22 per cent more than the two forts at Tregantle and Scraesdon. They make remarkable use of the ground available to produce strong positions at Forder and Efford. On the other hand there is little depth to the positions and considerable gaps either side of Crownhill, which rely on the guns of Crownhill to cover them with fire.

Their success is a tribute to the pragmatic approach of Burgoyne and Jervois: each fort or battery is to a different plan, adapted to the ground whilst providing the basis of defence in the form of a ditch and rampart and a gorge wall

covered by a guardhouse. Only at Bowden and Forder does economy appear to have been carried too far, in terms of the lack of proper caponiers at Bowden and of a ditch round Forder. Even this criticism might have been modified if we could see the positions now as they were actually built.

In general the failings of the fortifications which the Royal Commission recommended stem partly from the huge task which it was set and the target which in consequence it set itself. Even after reductions made by the Cabinet in the original recommendations, there were over 80 works to be built in the south of England. Yet the Commission recommended - hoped - they would present some form of earthwork defence within three-four months and would be completed in four years. Although at this time men like Brunel were tackling huge new engineering and construction projects with success, this was an impracticable objective. Only at Portsmouth and Dover had land defences been built of relatively up-to-date design. There was no general staff to coordinate the plans,and only a handful of trained staff officers in the Army. The achievements of the Inspector General of Fortifications' department and of a selected group of Royal Engineer officers was remarkable in the circumstances.

Even with Jervois' untiring efforts the survey work, the preparation and approval of plans and the organisation of a large number of contractors, mostly inexperienced in the building of fortifications, was bound to take far longer than anticipated. There were certain special problems created by the whole conception of sea forts and the decision almost immediately to fit the casemated batteries with iron shields, which caused exceptional delays. The continuous development of new types of guns in the 1860s - RBLs and then RMLs - caused repeated delays in arming even the coast batteries. It was 12 years before all the coast batteries at Plymouth had their shields and 20 years before Breakwater Fort began to receive its guns.

As it was, the need for speed resulted in lack of financial control. This can be seen from the relative cost of the North Eastern Defences as compared with Tregantle and Scraesdon started five years earlier. The latter cost altogether £245 000. This is understandable in the case of Tregantle with its keep and large barracks, but at Scraesdon much money was spent on the building of the remarkable tunnels and galleries in the north or lower section of the fort, which Colonel Westmacott, CRE Western District, later considered unnecessary. The figures for these two forts compare with £168 000 for Staddon and Stamford together. Crownhill Fort, which was built largely by direct labour cost only £77 000, but it has no keep and lacks some refinements. The total cost of the eleven works of the North Eastern Defences - the last to be finished - was only £318 000. With no previous experience of financial control of such a large operation perhaps the waste of money in the early stages was inevitable, but it certainly resulted in some unacceptable economies in the later works.

The attention of the Royal Commission was drawn to the limited number of Royal Artillery men likely to be available to man the defences. This in particular made the assumptions of the Commission on the manpower needed for the defences unrealistic. To take an extreme example, there were fewer men of the Royal Artillery in Plymouth at the time than the total number of guns originally recommended for Plymouth by the Royal Commission.

It has been shown in Chapter 7 that even counting the militia and volunteer artillery, the gunners would have been very thinly spread. Their efficiency in action would depend on their experience on the guns they were to man

and their level of training especially since the rate of fire of the guns of the time was very slow anyway. The manning of the land forts and batteries - even half of them at any one time as suggested by Jervois - required not only relatively large numbers of gunners, but also substantial garrisons of infantry, of which much the more effective would be the militia. Though the best of the militia regiments were considered capable in emergency of taking the field alongside the regiments of foot, their state of training varied and they were often under strength. The volunteers in theory provided the additional numbers required, yet in the early 1850's when the idea had first been mooted the military establishment from Wellington downwards dismissed such a force as of negligible value. Although Burgoyne modified an earlier scathing comment, doubts remained as to their effectiveness even when manning fixed defences.

The most obvious failure in the Royal Commission's plan was the subsequent delay in arming the fortifications once they were completed. When the Commission recommended the emplacement of so many guns it presumably had reason to believe that they could be produced. But it was not to know that the Armstrong gun would prove to be sufficiently unreliable in naval service for the design to be superceded within about seven years by a later generation of RML guns of ever increasing size and cost. Even the coast batteries had not received their full complement of RMLs until the early 1870s. Meanwhile they were armed with the largest smooth bore guns available which were nevertheless ineffective against the armoured warships being built by the French.

The systematic arming of the land forts was even further delayed, and only carried out piecemeal with whatever smooth-bore and (converted) RML guns were available until 1885. In that year a comprehensive survey showed that although Tregantle and Crownhill had the major part of their approved armament; in the other forts and batteries there were only a few guns at best. Thereafter a real effort appears to have been made to bring the armament up to the level approved at that time, though this must be partly due to the fact that the Armstrong guns rejected by the Navy were available in large numbers at last.

This failure to arm the land forts adequately, and earlier, appears at first sight to be inexcusable. But there was one overriding excuse for the delays. The threat of invasion from France, against which the fortifications had been built, had been removed in the year 1870 by the utter defeat of the French army in the Franco-Prussian War, after which the Emperor Napoleon sought asylum in England.

One particular question remains as to the effectiveness of many of the Plymouth land forts and batteries. Although they were built with sites for one or more mortar batteries, there appears to be no reference to mortars once they were completed. The first of the proposals for armament in 1875 refers only to 8-inch rifled howitzers which though introduced in 1872 were not in full production until 1880. The absence of a high trajectory weapon to search the steep valleys in front of Staddon Heights and the North Eastern Defences would have been a serious weakness in the defence before this.

Some critics have dismissed the Palmerston Forts as ineffective on the grounds of their design. This applies to the land forts rather than to the coast batteries. The latter, once fitted with their iron shields, were considered effective until the early 1880s. By then the size of the guns mounted in ships and experience at the bombardment at Alexandria resulted in the abandonment of casemates for coast guns. With much improved range-finding and fire

control methods, the trend began towards fewer guns widely spaced and protected only in front with earth and concrete, which offered both a very small target and one which could be camouflaged.

The most weighty critic of the land defences of this time was Sir George Sydenham Clarke who was Superintendent of the Royal Carriage Department at Woolwich from 1894. Writing in 1890 he characterised the works of the 1860s as of 'large size, high command, broad and deep ditches, tall caponiers. The trace (outline) is fairly simple though the interior arrangements are sometimes complicated. There are keeps in some cases, and two storied casemated barracks are to be found. Unlike the Paris forts of 1840 the gorges are specially treated.'[5] He went on to say 'the guiding principles of these works seem to have been to provide large enclosures secure against assault - so long as they were not subjected to the fire of siege guns'.[6] They achieved a high standard of security but 'this ideal was only obtained by an expenditure so heavy as to cause a reaction which prevented the defences themselves being properly completed'.[7]

He went on to criticise the lack of a scientific approach to the subject of fortification and remarked that 'some of these works might have been designed by clever cadets, quick to recognise the niceties of technical artifice, but unable, from sheer immaturity of thought and want of study, to grasp the broader aspects of the science and its relation to war'.[8]

To what extent the latter judgment is justified by the works at Plymouth is a matter of opinion. At least the designs improved as the works progressed. Tregantle, one of the first forts to be completed and impressive in appearance, attracted criticism both from Todleben and Clarke. There was too much stonework exposed to fire, especially the huge barracks and the exterior of the keep. Clarke described the keep as being 'designed so as to ensure priority of destruction from the artillery of the attack'.[9] Tregantle also has a ditch which is unnecessarily wide, with only the lower half vertical and revetted in places, and the arrangement of the caponiers is elementary. Some lessons had been learned before Staddon and Stamford were completed. The ditch had been deepened, the counterscarp steeply graded throughout and the layout of the caponiers greatly improved by the time it came to Crownhill. The ditch and ramparts at Crownhill are so well concealed that even local residents are not aware of the fort's existence!

In some ways the three defensive positions centred on Agaton Fort, Eggbuckland Keep and Efford Fort are the most interesting. These were each designed for mutual defence making the best use of the ground in the area. The Efford/Laira position is a strong one due to the very steep slope to the east. There is a suspicion that the need for economy reached its peak by the time the Eggbuckland position was finished. When the 1869 Committee visited Bowden Fort it said that 'little had been done to this work since the failure of the contractor' (in 1866) and the final cost of this battery was under £16 000. The defence of the ditch - the place where an attack was to be halted - was left to its single storey 'caponiers' with rifle slits only, no guns. The ditch round the battery was not covered by gun-fire except from the guardhouse at the gorge. The rifle galleries were mutually supporting but this was not considered sufficient elsewhere, and being built on the level of the bottom of the ditch they were vulnerable to attack by infantry.

As always, finance played a major part in the eventual design of the works. The figures are given at Appendix E. There is some reason for the high cost of Tregantle because of its isolated position and because it was a base for a large garrison. The same cannot be said for the equally costly Scraesdon. The fact that they were the first to be completed and were built by contractors may explain much of the difference in the cost between them and Crownhill. The latter was built largely by direct labour and was a much more compact, and in the end effective, design. With no previous experience of financial control of such a large construction project perhaps the waste of money in the early stages was inevitable, but it certainly counted against the completion of the later works - the North Eastern Defences - to a standard equal to the rest.

The aim of this book has been to set the fortifications recommended by the Royal Commission of 1860 in perspective and to counter tendencies to be wise after the event. The key to the reaction of the government at that time was the appreciation that the Royal Navy could no longer guarantee our shores against attack. The weakness of the army at home had long been known. In the face of a real threat of invasion its powers of resistance had to be strengthened - by fortification.

The view of well-informed contemporaries as to the degree of threat in June 1860 is best expressed by Earl de Grey, the Under Secretary at the War Office, who wrote 'War stands close to us and must, I think, come before long if the present reign in France continues'[10]. Palmerston's view must have been similar, hence his appointment of the Royal Commission. He was supported by a remarkable reversal in the attitude of the public at this time.

The Commission carried out its task with commendable speed and made recommendations designed to enable the forces available to meet the threat. But the Commission and later the Cabinet appear to us today to have failed to appreciate many of the problems arising from its recommendations, especially the likely delays caused by the huge and unprecedented construction programme and the need for very large numbers of guns, though they had little alternative but to accept them. The lack of existing fortification systems to build upon in most places meant that a huge programme was inevitable.

But at this stage one must not forget the spirit of the time when the Royal Commission reported. This was the 'can do' Britain when huge engineering and construction projects - ships, railways, tunnels, bridges - were attempted for the first time and successfully completed. It possibly never occurred to those in authority that the programme of construction that they were setting in motion was impracticable, particularly on the planned time scale.

It was unfortunate that in addition the arming of the fortifications was delayed by the need to produce so many guns of new design. As a result the forts would have been only partly effective against an invasion had it come at the time when it was most expected.

Also, although fortification was in principle a way of overcoming the shortage of regular troops, the substitution of relatively small numbers of militia and large numbers of volunteers whose main asset was their enthusiasm was a considerable risk.

For these reasons it is not possible to reject outright the charge that the land forts were 'follies'. But the only alternatives were an even more costly programme of fortification on the scale originally recommended by the Royal Commission or a large increase in the strength of the regular army which on grounds of continuing cost and popular prejudice was politically impossible. The fact is that they proved a successful deterrent to a raid on Devonport.

Plymouth's huge casemated coast batteries are a remarkable monument to the government's determination to secure the second most important dockyard in the country from attack by sea. Given the topography of the Sound they would undoubtedly have been effective in their role,

when armed with RML guns, in spite of the delays in completing Breakwater Fort.

Once the land defences had been armed they should have been effective against the strong raid which they were designed to defeat. But in the event much would have depended on the leadership and skill of the commander of the garrison in organising the widely varied units under his command and inspiring them with confidence and determination. In the Civil War two hundred years earlier Plymouth's Parliamentarians had confounded the enemy by their spirit and resolution in defence. The same qualities would have been needed in the 1860s.

*   *   *   *

The ring of Palmerston Forts at Plymouth is still complete though many are grossly neglected. Some have suffered modification at the hands of their present owners, the destruction of gateway arches being the most obvious. Inside, several have been built on and everywhere most of the interior fittings have been vandalised.

Though the coast batteries are familiar to every sailor who comes into the port, many of the land forts and batteries are now concealed by surrounding buildings or by trees which have grown on the ramparts and in the ditches. Apart from Crownhill Fort which has recently been faithfully restored to its original condition by the Landmark Trust, those works occupied by the Ministry of Defence - Tregantle, Staddon and to a much less extent Scraesdon - have been best preserved.

The defences planned by the Royal Commission were substantial structures designed to last and their ramparts are scheduled as ancient monuments. But this has only partly protected them from piecemeal modification in the past. Fortunately their present condition has been recorded in the Plymouth Defences Survey over the last five years so supervision will be simpler in future. But the ease with which earth-moving equipment has destroyed more modern batteries round Plymouth shows that vigilance is required not only from all the authorities concerned but also from the public.

References

[1] FORT 14. Peter Kent. p. 39

[2] *Island Fortress*. Longmate. p. 324

[3] Admiral Sir Charles Napier, June 1860

[4] FORT 8. p. 83

[5] *Fortification*. Clarke. p. 77

[6] Ibid p. 77

[7] Ibid p. 78

[8] Ibid p. 78

[9] Ibid p. 136

[10] *JSAHR* Vol. 37 1959. Barrie Rose p. 97

Stamford, still life

APPENDIX A

Appendix 5 to the Report of the Royal Commission. PRO.WO 33/5
(See Map II and Plate 23)

Memorandum on Defences proposed for Protection of the Naval Arsenal at Devonport and Plymouth by Major W. F. D. Jervois, Assistant Inspector-General of Fortifications.
26 February 1858

1. In addition to the protection of our ships and extensive Government establishments at Devonport from bombardment, or from actual capture, the existence of a fortified position at this point, within which might be collected all the available resources of the western part of England, would, in the event of our losing our superiority at sea, be of great value in preventing an enemy establishing himself in those districts; the resources of which, if left at his command, would enable him to maintain himself there for a time and thereby force the country to accept disadvantageous terms of peace.

In case of general descent upon England, it would also threaten the rear of any force marching towards London from the westward.

LINES OF ATTACK TO WESTWARD

2. A land attack may be made upon Devonport either from the west or from the east. If attacking from the west, the enemy would have no base of operations nearer than Fowey Harbour, about twenty miles distant, although he might make use of the tidal harbour of Looe, eight miles nearer Devonport, as an auxiliary for landing troops and heavy guns. Fowey Harbour is not, however, sufficiently large as a base for an extensive operation, and the most probable object in making an attack from this side would be to destroy the Naval Arsenal and ships, and, having done so, to retire. He might, however, land a force to the westward, with a view of co-operating with an attack from the east, crossing the Tamar either by the Saltash Bridge, or at a point higher up the stream.

3. From the west, the enemy would most probably advance through East Looe to St Martin's and Hessenford (in preference to the coast road, which is very indifferent), and when near St Germains he must either direct his march along the peninsula between the St Germains River and the sea, or, crossing the St Germains under Shevioc, he would proceed along its left bank, and effect his object from the heights about Trematon Castle or Saltash; or he might, before reaching St Germains, turn off through Landrake towards Trematon and Saltash, but by this route the country is much more difficult.

4. The advance along the peninsula between the St Germain's River and the sea would be best prevented by establishing a line of works across the narrow neck immediately in front of the village of Antony, where a strong position can be taken up, only a mile and a-quarter in length; and the burning of the Arsenal etc., from about Saltash, would be rendered impossible by the occupation of the high ground in front of that village, where is a good position only about a mile long, which if fortified, would also form a tête du pont on the western side to the great railway bridge, now in course of construction across the Tamar.

5. It would, however, still be open to an enemy to land in Cawsand Bay, and to burn the Dockyard, etc., from Mount Edgcumbe. With reference to this, during the French revolutionary war, six small redoubts (which it is desirable to repair) were thrown up on Maker Heights, between Cawsand Bay and Millbrook Creek, and these, together with the battery at Picklecombe Point, bearing on the western entrance to the Sound, are all the existing defences on this side of Devonport.

EXISTING DEFENCES TO WESTWARD

6. There are differences of opinion with respect to the practibility of landing troops and guns in Whitesand Bay, but at all events this contingency may be met by very small means.

The points then to be considered, with reference to the western defences of Plymouth, taking them in order, commencing at the western entrance to the Sound, are:

1st. The prevention of a landing in Cawsand Bay.

2nd. The prevention of a landing in Whitesand Bay.

3rd. The prevention of an advance along the peninsula between St Germain's River and the sea.

4th. To provide against the destruction of the Arsenal and ships from the ground about Saltash.

PROPOSED DEFENCES TO WESTWARD

7. A landing in Cawsand Bay might be prevented:

1st. By erecting a battery on the knoll just above the village of Cawsand, from whence the shore on either side would be effectually enfiladed. This battery, which might be made to act as a keep to guns placed at intervals in its front, may be for about ten pieces, with accommodation under its terre-plein for about 100 men.

2nd. By placing about eight guns, which would afford a cross fire on the bay, at Hooe Lake Point, about 2,000 yards distant from the knoll just mentioned, with a defensible guard-house on the height in its rear. This battery would also bring additional fire to bear on the western entrance to the Sound.

The left redoubt (No. 4) on Maker Heights would, to some extent, aid in the protection of Cawsand Bay, but, as it is about 300 feet above the sea, its fire would be too plunging to be of much use for that object.

8. As regards a landing in Whitesand Bay, although boats may be beached on its sandy shore during fine weather, it is bounded by cliffs of considerable height, up which there is access only at a few points where there are gullies and cart tracks, or where the cliff, as at its eastern part, being of earth has to some extent fallen away. It would certainly be a hazardous operation to attempt to force a landing at these places; but it is submitted it would, nevertheless, be injudicious to leave them entirely undefended, considering that, in case, through any unforeseen circumstance, the attempt were successful, the line in front of Antony would be turned.

It would be only necessary, however, to provide cover for a few men, and to place some guns securely in position at the most accessible points; these objects would, perhaps, be best attained by the erection of towers, four of which would probably suffice, one at the Coast Guard Station, another about 1,000 yards from it, a third about 1,800 yards further westward, a fourth about 1,500 yards from the latter and about the same distance from the main work on the left of the Antony line. Each of these towers might be for five guns and about fifty men.

POSITION IN FRONT OF ANTONY

9. With reference to the third line of attack, it should be observed that the main ridge of the peninsula, to the west of the Hamoaze, which runs parallel to the shore of Whitesand Bay, has its main spur branching off through Antony to Torpoint, opposite the Dockyard. At the junction of this spur with the main ridge, and at a distance of about 6,000 yards from the Dockyard, is the proposed position in front of Antony. There is no position nearer Devonport affording similar advantages.

10. There is however, another strong position of the same length (viz. 1 1/4 mile) across the peninsula, at Craft's Hole, but it is not considered so desirable as a permanent line of defence, it being about 1 mile farther from Devonport, and subject to be outflanked from ground on the left bank of the St Germain's River, whilst it is not nearly in such close connection with the left of the proposed position at Saltash.

11. The right flank of the Antony line will be in a secure position at Screezen Hill, behind a creek running in front of Wacker Mill, from whence is commanded the approach by the new turnpike road from Cornwall to Devonport, and the St Germains River both up and down the stream.

The left flank of the position will be just above Lower Tregantle and Higher Blerack Farms, on a hill on the main ridge; on its right, dividing the watercourses in the direction of the St Germain's River, from those running to St John's Lake, and its left resting on the sea, with which it would be connected by a line of parapet and ditch; - it effectually commands the road along the ridge, as well as the connecting branch between it and the new turnpike road, also the ground both in front and rear of the line; and its capabilities generally mark it out as the site for the main work of the position, of which it may be considered as the key.

It will be necessary either to take it or to detach a considerable body of troops to mask it, before an advance by an enemy towards Devonport along the western peninsula could be effected.

12. The ground midway between the two flanks would be well commanded by the works on either side, especially by that at

Tregantle; but as the distance between those works will be nearly a mile, it is desirable to have an intermediate post.

13. The forts on either flank will be provided with towers at their gorge, so that they might be held by a small body of men against a coup de main. For the intervening work, however, it is proposed to adapt a different arrangement, and to place a keep, well covered by a glacis, on a knoll half way between the works on the flanks, on the site best adapted for keeping up the connection between them; whilst the work would be about 300 yards from it, and rather in advance of the line between it and Tregantle Fort, in such a position that it would enfilade the enemy's approaches along the ridge in front of the main work.

The forts thus described will mutually support each other, and will be about 700 yards apart;- that on the left will be for about sixty guns, and the other two for about thirty-five guns each. There will be a bomb-proof barracks in them for about 1,000 men.

14. An advanced work, which would delay the attack on the main line, may be thrown up with advantage on Delabole Hill, and batteries on the ridge about 700 yards in front of the main work, and on the narrow tongue of land in front of Screezen Hill, would also give additional strength to the position, by flanking parts of the ravine, otherwise unseen, under that hill. Some guns should also be placed at the head of the valley, between Screezen Hill and the intermediate tower to command a part of that valley not seen from the other works. But none of these need be of permanent construction.

BARRACK ON MAKER HEIGHTS

15. As a reserve to afford support, in case of necessity, to the Antony position, as well as to aid in the defence of Cawsand and Whitesand Bays, it is proposed to place a defensible barrack for 1,000 men,, and a battery of Field Artillery, in rear of the redoubts on Maker Heights, where this force would be in a position also to defend those redoubts, and from whence it could be thrown across the Hamoaze to the eastward if required.

CONNEXION BETWEEN ANTONY AND SALTASH POSITIONS

16. Between the right of the Antony and left of the Saltash positions, the StGermains River affords a good defence, being 700 yards broad, until at a distance of about two miles from Screezen Hill, and close to the left of the Saltash line, it narrows to about

half that breadth. Gunboats may be placed in the St Germains River to play on the right flank of the Antony line; also to prevent the possibility of the passage of the river by an enemy, as well as to bear on the ground in front of the left of the Saltash position.

SALTASH POSITION

17. With respect to the latter, which will provide against the fourth line of attack to the westward, there will be two works, about 700 yards apart, on the high ground above Saltash, mutually supporting one another; one will be on the hill over which the old turnpike road runs, and the distance between it and a creek running up from the Tamar, under South Pill, being only about 500 yards, it will in conjunction with gunboats in the Tamar, and a battery on a knoll commanding the bridge which crosses the mouth of the creek, close the right of the line;- the other, on a knoll close to the village of St Stephens, between that village and the first-mentioned work, will, together with an advanced flèche in its front, keep up the connection with a breastwork thrown up along edge of the high ground above a deep ravine and creek on the left of the position; the flanking parts of the breastwork will be for light guns or howitzers, and at about 450 yards in rear of it will be a tower, forming a keep to the whole of the left of the line, commanding the reverse side of the breastwork, as well as the interior of the work on the right of St Stephens, from which it will be about 300 yards distant, this tower will also command the mouth of the creek which closes the left of the line, and which will be further flanked by gunboats, as before stated.

18. Old Trematon Castle, on the other side of the creek, and about 600 yards in advance of the main line, should be occupied as an advance post to which there would be a good communication by means of the railway bridge about to be constructed opposite Antony passage.

The distance of this position is 4,300 yards from Keyham-yard; its distance from the magazine establishment at Bull Point being, however, only 2,000 yards, it might be possible to bombard that establishment, notwithstanding the works at Saltash, but it would not be sufficient inducement to undertake an operation merely with a view to its destruction, especially as the magazines are of bomb-proof construction.

19. As regards the two works on the heights, the right would be for about forty guns, including those in a tower at its gorge. The

work near St Stephens will mount about thirty guns, and the tower in its rear about ten.

With respect to the barrack accommodation in these works, it would be for about 600 in all, including the accommodation in the towers; but there would be bomb-proofs under the ramparts in addition, to be used in case of actual attack.

20. It is not considered necessary to provide barrack accommodation on this position on the same scale as for that in front of Antony, as troops can be more readily thrown up to it by the railway from Devonport and Plymouth; and the large work on St Budeaux, hereafter to be mentioned, would be less than a mile in its rear, and could also afford effectual support.

EXISTING DEFENCES TO EASTWARD

21. The existing defences on the eastern side of the Hamoaze are:

1. The unfinished lines of Devonport, which cover only the Dockyard and Gun Wharf.
2. Plymouth Citadel, commenced by Charles II, about 200 years ago, and intended, it is believed, as a Royalist stronghold, as well as to command the Catwater and approaches to the harbour, but, of course, having no reference to the Naval Arsenal, which did not then exist. It, however, acts, to some extent, as an outwork to the lines, from which it is 2,200 yards distant, and will also co-operate very advantageously with part of the defences now proposed.
3. There are also two small, insignificant square redoubts, of field profile, about 1,000 yards in advance of the lines, and 2,000 yards apart, one on a commanding position to the north-east of the lines, called Mount Pleasant, the other, surrounded by houses, on Stonehouse Hill, nearly midway between the Citadel and lines, which is also capable of bringing a distant enfilading fire to bear on a part of the course by which ships must approach the harbour.
4. The batteries of Nicholas Island, Eastern King and Western King, as well as those on the right of the lines, also command the passage to the Hamoaze.
5. The battery at Staddon Point commands the eastern entrance to the Sound, and there is also another battery on Staddon Heights, bearing on the Sound, but it is at too great an elevation to be of much use.

LINES OF ATTACK TO EASTWARD

22. In the case of attack from the eastward, the movements of an enemy would of course depend on whether his object were the actual destruction of the Government establishments (for which purpose he must obtain possession of them) or whether he desired merely to do as much damage as possible by distant bombardment.

If he meditated a prolonged operation he would, of course, require a harbour of sufficient capacity to keep up the requisite supplies of troops, stores, guns and ammunition, for which purpose the Dart, which is only twenty five miles distant from Plymouth, would give every facility.

23. Landing in Torbay, he would make a flank march, and seize the harbour of Dartmouth, either to the right or left of which he might take up positions, out of which it would be impossible to drive him with any force we could collect for the purpose; thence, proceeding westward by the road towards Modbury and Plymouth, he might receive a fresh accession to his force by the inlet running up to Kingsbridge; continuing his advance he would seize the Yealm, which, although not sufficient as the sole base for operations on a large scale, would be valuable as a subsidiary harbour, close to Plymouth, to which Artillery, troops, stores, etc., might be brought round from the main depot at the Dart, only thirty miles distant by sea.

24. If he intended a hasty attack, with a view of doing as much damage as possible and retiring, the Yealm would probably become his base in the first instance; and if he could not seize it by a sea attack, he could land to the eastward of it, and turn any defences that might close its mouth.

Advancing from Brixton on the Yealm, either through Elburton or Plympton, there is nothing to prevent his entering the town of Plymouth. Probably he would bombard the Citadel from Staddon Heights and the ground above Turnchapel, taking in reverse its northern front, and then approaching, under cover of the houses of the town, close up to the work, he might carry it by escalade.

25. The Citadel taken, the battery on Nicholas Island would be turned, and the enemy might, in this case, move his base of operations to the Catwater itself, the battery at Staddon Point for the protection of the eastern entrance of the Sound being already in his hands.

From Plymouth, the enemy would probably proceed to possess himself of the small redoubt on Stonehouse Hill, 1,200 yards from the Citadel, and, being of an insignificant field profile, and approachable under cover of streets and houses, might be carried by a coup de main; - he may then destroy the Victualling Establishment, and the sea batteries at Eastern King and Western King would be turned.

26. The Dockyard and Gun Wharf, covered by the Devonport lines, which are at present incomplete, are not secure against a coup de main.

Keyham Steam Yard, which is outside the lines, and is only protected by the insignificant outwork on Mount Pleasant, would be at his mercy.

27. It should be remarked, that although the preliminary operation of taking the Citadel would most probably be undertaken in case the enemy desired to obtain a firm hold of the place, he might, nevertheless, run into and destroy the Dockyard and Steam Yard without incurring this delay, keeping the fire of the Citadel under by batteries established on Staddon Heights.

DEFENSIVE POSITIONS TO EASTWARD

28. To obtain a line of defences to cover the Victualling-yard, Dockyard, Gun Wharf, and Steam Yard, which shall be tolerably free from obstruction by houses, the shortest position that can be taken up rests on Weston Mill Lake on the left flank, and on the Catwater on the right, being about three miles in length in a straight line.

The works which it would be necessary to establish on this line would be-

29. Two on the feature to the north of Keyham Yard; a new work on Mount Pleasant; one in front of the Stoke Reservoir; another on the hill above the Cemetery; two small intervening works between the Cemetery and Borough Jail; one in front of the Borough Jail, near Lipsom [sic] Terrace; and another on Catdown.

By consulting the plan, it will be seen that this position is defective; that it is weak by reason of its saliency at Lipsom; it would not include within it the magazines at Bull Point; would leave the Saltash Bridge in possession of the enemy, and enable him to take the Saltash position in the rear; moreover, it would not protect the Arsenal and ships from bombardment from the heights about St Budeaux and Tor.

30. By throwing up the left of the line, however, from the point near Lipsom Terrace, and passing through Tor to a knoll above Burrington House at the head of Weston Mill Lake, and occupying, in addition, the heights behind St Budeaux by a defensive work, these objectioins can be avoided without increasing the length of the position, except in so far as the occupation of the ground about St Budeaux is concerned.

31. This line would be a slight curve, the chord of which will be four miles, with a rise of a little more than half-a-mile, having no prominent salient presenting a favourable point of attack, and would be on an average 4,000 yards from the outside of the Government establishments, which it will, therefore, protect effectually from bombardment; it will include within it the magazines at Bull Point, and will cover the Saltash Bridge; whilst the work on St Budeaux will, as before remarked, be in a position from which effective support could be afforded to the Saltash position, should it be requisite. It is, in short, the only position which can be taken up on this side of Devonport which will meet all requirements. The two main works on its right will, as in the other position, be at Catdown and near Lipsom Terrace.

POSITION ON STADDON HEIGHTS

32. To secure this line from being taken in reverse from the ground on the left bank of the mouth of the Catwater, as well as to prevent the enemy seizing the batteries protecting the eastern entrance to the Sound, also to prevent his occupying ground which it would be most important to him to seize, it will be necessary to take up a position on Staddon Heights, under cover of which troops might also be thrown across the Catwater, to act on the flank or rear of an enemy approaching Plymouth.

The ground on that point of the heights nearest the Citadel, and between Hooe Lake and the Sound, is well adapted for defence, and can be effectually occupied by three redoubts, mutually supporting one another, and in a straight line half-a-mile long, with the flanks resting on precipitous ground on either side, and secured by lines of field-work, connecting them with the Sound on one side, and with the head of Hooe Lake on the other.

The centre redoubt will probably be for about thirty-five guns, including some in a tower at its gorge, and those on either flank for about fifteen guns each.

They will be provided with bomb-proof cover under the ramparts, and there will be space in the tower for about 200 men. As this position can be supplied with troops from the Citadel, it is considered unnecessary to have in it any further barrack accommodation.

POSITION BETWEEN STADDON HEIGHTS AND THE TAMAR

33. The work at Catdown, for about thirty-five guns, will flank the right and left of the positions on either side of the Catwater respectively, will bear on the iron bridge in its front and roads leading thereto, and together with that on Lipsom Terrace (for about forty-five guns), and the Citadel, each about 1,500 yards from the other, will put the intervening space under three fires; so it will only be necessary to have a small intermediate work for ten or twelve guns between it and the Terrace. This intermediate work will be open in rear to the fire of the Citadel, from which it will be about 1,000 yards distant.

34. Lipsom Fort will command the valleys in which the railway and main roads to Plymouth from the eastward run. It should be defiladed from the work on its left (the site of which is 100 feet higher), and would thus be seen into from the Citadel. In front of it, a field-work should be placed, to see up the valley towards Compton.

35. The next work to the left will be for about thirty guns, and 800 yards distant from the Terrace, on the hill between Compton and the railway tunnel. Field batteries to see down valleys on either side of it would be desirable. It will be 600 yards from a large fort behind Compton Hall, the approach to which along the ridge in its front will be flanked by it.

The latter will be the main central work of the line; its site will be on a hill which divides the waters running towards the Hamoaze from those running towards the Plym River. It will command the approaches from Dartmoor and from Plympton by the Efford Bridge to Plymouth and Devonport, and will be capable of bringing a reverse fire to bear on a great part of the ground between the rear of the line and the Government establishments. Being in a situation of such importance it is recommended that this work should be capable of mounting sixty guns.

36. About 600 yards in front of it, on the ridge towards Efford, it will be desirable to have an outwork to command ground otherwise unseen, as well as to delay the attack on the main work. This, however, need not be a permanent construction.

37. At Tor House, about 450 yards from the central fort, will be a small work for about twenty guns, which will command the valley running down to the Plym, flank the approach along the ridge, and the main work on its right, give a close fire on the roads which unite in front of it, and will also command the head of the valley and ground in front of Weston Peveril, where will be a work on a knoll about 650 yards distant.

This latter will also command the main road to Devonport, as well as the road to Keyham, along the ridge between Keyham Creek and Weston Mill Lake. It will be for about forty guns.

38. The connecting work between Weston Peveril and that at St Budeaux will be about the same size as that to its right, and will be about 1,000 yards distant from the former, and 1,200 yards from the latter; but there are good sites on either side of it, as shown in plan, for field-works to keep up a close connection with the works on its flanks.

39. The work on the left flank being in a very influential position will be for about sixty guns. The left of this fort will be so arranged as to flank a steep feature which connects it with the Tamar, and along the edge of which an entrenchment should be thrown up, with a field redoubt, on a conspicuous knoll, in its rear.

40. The left of the line will be further secured by gunboats in the Tamar, and may be additionally strengthened by field works thrown up on the hill in front of the village of St Budeaux, on Honiknowle, and on the knoll in advance of Burrington Farm.

41. As regards the accommodation for troops in this line, there will be casemated Barracks for about 500 men in each of the large works at St Budeaux and Compton Hall, for about 400 in the Lipsom work, 300 in each of the two works at Burrington House and Weston Peveril, and for about 100 and 200 respectively in the towers at the gorges of those at Catdown and to the left of Lipsom Terrace, about 2,300 in all.

The Barracks already provided in the Citadel render unnecessary any further accommodation than that proposed on the right of the line.

42. As regards the nature of the works generally, they will have straight faces, flanked by well-covered caponieres, and will be provided with towers at their gorges, to enable a small number of men to secure them from a coup de main. They will be traced, so

as to bring a fire to bear on the reverse side of the position, and thus co-operate with field-works, which may be thrown up successively in rear to supply the place of any intervening work which may have fallen into the enemy's hands. The work at St Budeaux will be of a different description from the others, in consequence of the nature of the ground; it will probably consist of two bastions, with towers at their gorges, and connected by a curtain with a casemated barrack in the rear, well screened on the reverse side of the hill.

43. But it is not proposed to enter now into a description of the precise plan of the works, which may form the subject of a future paper, should the general project be approved.

INTERIOR LINE OF DEFENCE

44. With respect to an interior line of defence to the eastward, to act as a keep to the outer position, it would be desirable to finish the lines of Devonport, already advanced so far towards completion, and to have a new work for about thirty guns and 300 men on Mount Pleasant, which, although somewhat obstructed by houses, and not sufficiently distant to prevent a bombardment, is a very influential position for preventing the actual capture of the Arsenal, and the occupation of it by an enemy would lead to the instant fall of the place. The redoubt at Stonehouse Hill might also be improved, and would act as an outwork to the right flank of the lines.

Some heavy guns might also be advantageously mounted there, to rake the passage to the eastward of Nicholas Island.

SEA DEFENCES

45. This leads to the general consideration of the sea defences of Plymouth generally.

They are already of considerable power, except as regards the two entrances to the Sound, which are only at present imperfectly defended by two batteries of nine guns each. It is recommended therefore, that under each of these - the one at Picklecombe, the other at Staddon Point - there should be established heavy batteries for about sixty guns, in three tiers, two of which will be in casemates, and that works of a similar description should be erected at each extremity of the breakwater. It is considered that, with these batteries it would be a hazardous operation for a squadron to attempt to force the passage to the Sound. If not constructed at a time of expected attack, their want might be supplied, although in a far inferior degree by floating defences.

An additional tier of twenty-five or thirty guns in Haxo casemates, under the present battery on Nicholas Island, and some guns placed on either side of the work at Eastern King, would afford a great accession of strength at a comparatively small cost.

46. On the site of Western King Battery, at which, although it is peculiarly well situated for the defence of the entrance to the Hamoaze, by reason of the enfilading fire which it can bring to bear on the channel, there are, at present, only seven guns, it would be desirable to establish a heavy battery of twenty or perhaps thirty guns, which might be distributed in two tiers, the lower one in Haxo casemates.

With these additions it is considered that nothing further would be necessary to the sea defences.

47. It may be objected that the works proposed in this Memorandum are very extensive, but, irrespective of other considerations adverted to at the commencement of this paper, it may be urged, so are the the establishments they are designed to protect, both as regards money value and national importance; and although their cost will, no doubt, be great, yet it will be comparatively trifling when compared with continental works having a similar object.

It may also be urged that we shall not have sufficient troops for their defence, but this objection will have less weight when it is considered that the works are divided into four positions, separated from each other by rivers, and that it would be next to impossible to attack any two positions simultaneously; moreover, in the longest line, viz., that between the Tamar and Catwater, the works are divided from each other in most instances by ravines, which would divide the attacking force into several detachments, between which there could be no direct communication.

48. To the same objection it may also be answered that, possibly, the very existence of the works would put the idea of attack out of the question, and that, with the inferior number of our regular forces, we should be much better prepared for resistance with the works than without them. When it is considered moreover, that the population of Plymouth, amounting to more than 100,000 persons, would, together with the surrounding rural districts, probably afford at least 10,000 fighting men, who would be capable of doing good service in the defence of works; it is conceived that, in conjunction with about 6,000 or 8,000 regular troops, militia, and sailors etc., a sufficient garrison would be obtained.

Undoubtedly, the local forces would require some organization, but, as the duties would be so entirely local, and would moreover have a close connection with the defence of their own homes, it would only require a slight encouragement during peace, to render them available for any emergency which might arise in time of war.

49. At this stage of the proceeding, it is of course impossible to give an accurate estimate of the expense of the proposed works; but, as stated at the end of this Memorandum, the probable ultimate cost will be about £1,740,000.
Of this sum, more than £300,000. is for the purchase of land, and there is also included in it the cost of accommodation for upwards of 7,000 men, which may be put down at about £600,000.

50. It is to be observed, that although the whole of the proposed works may not be executed at the time of attack, the defence capabilities of the place will be greatly improved, according as each work and position is completed.
The War Committee of the Cabinet, on the 17th November last, directed that the position in front of Antony should be proceeded with, and negotiations are now in progress for the purchase of the necessary land for that object. Sums have also been taken in the estimates for 1858-59, as part payment for the land, as well as for the commencement of Tregantle Fort.

Wm F.D. Jervois
Assistant I.G.F. War Office.
26th February 1858

In the original paper there follows a detailed 'LIST OF WORKS' proposed for the defence of Naval Arsenal at Devonport and Plymouth, distinguishing those proposed for permanent construction, from field works, which would give additional strength to the positions. The totals are given below:

	No. of Positions	No. of Guns	Guns in Field Works	No. of Men Men in Casemated positions
LAND DEFENCES	21	685	162	5,820[†]
ADDITIONAL SEA DEFENCES[‡]	6	295	12	1,530

There is also a list showing the 'Order of Relative Importance of the Several Positions' as follows:

1. Tregantle and Antony 2. Cawsand Bay. 3. Staddon Heights. 4. Mount Pleasant. 5. Saltash. 6. St Budeaux. 7. Between St Budeaux and Staddon Heights. 8. Devonport 9. Whitesand Bay Towers. 10 Barrack on Maker Heights.

The sea defences are to be proceeded with in the following order:

1. Picklecombe Point. 2. Staddon Point. 3. Western King. 4. Nicholas Island.

with the order of relative importance of works within each position.

The paper concludes with the following table:

PROBABLE COST.

Antony Position	£270,000	including cost of land
Cawsand Bay	17,000	including cost of land
Staddon Heights	120,000	including cost of land
Mount Pleasant	50,000	including cost of land
Saltash Position	140,000	including cost of land
St. Budeaux	140,000	including cost of land
Between St Budeaux & Staddon Heights	540,000	including cost of land
Completing Devonport Lines	70,000	including cost of land
Whitesand Bay	23,000	including cost of land
Barrack on Maker Heights	120,000	including cost of land
Additional Sea Defences	50,000	including cost of land
	£1,740,000	

Or, £80,000 a-year for about 22 years
A further note points out that the reason why this sum (whose addition is wrong as shown in the report) is much more than the cost of the completion of the works proposed at Portsmouth is that so many of the works required there have already been completed.

[†]All casemated except for 1120 at Maker Heights.
[‡]Includes 120 guns and 600 men for batteries at either end of Breakwater

APPENDIX B

PROGRESS IN THE BUILDING OF THE PLYMOUTH DEFENCES 1860-1885.

Extracted from 'Precis of Correspondence relating to the Defences of Plymouth, prior to April 1893' (PRO WO 33/2772. *(Crown copyright material in the Public Record Office is reproduced with permission of the Controller of Her Majesty's Stationery Office).*

7.2.60

Royal Commission Report published

28.8.60

Defence Act passed

12.10.60

1. Plans approved by Defence Committee for:-
    Picklecombe Battery
    Staddon Point Battery (Bovisand)
    Breakwater Battery
    Drake's Point Battery (Drake's Island)

2. Land to be purchased for Staddon Heights position, to include a fort at Staddon Heights and another near Turnchapel.

27.10.60

Design approved for fort behind Breakwater - two tiers of casemates of granite with iron shields - 33 guns in casemates, 7 on roof.

10.11.60

General design of North Eastern Defences and extensions to Western and Eastern King approved.

2.2.61

Design for Polhawn Battery approved.

7.5.61

Design for casemated battery at Mount Edgcumbe Garden approved.

17.7.61

Lt.Col. Jervois reported that the cost of land for the North Eastern defences would be £350,000 against £200,000 provided in the Defence Loan. Fortification Committee after a visit to the area reported that a very good line of similar length and about 1 mile in advance of it was obtainable based on high ground north of St Budeaux through Knackers Knowle (Crownhill) in the centre to Efford Warren. This would cost £130,000 less and would be the best way of using £600,000 allotted for the North Eastern Defences. This was approved but CRE's proposal of a continuous rampart and ditch with three forts was rejected.

The suggested ground was to be occupied by batteries eventually called:

Ernesettle	Forder
Agaton	Austin
Knowles	Efford
Woodland	Laira
Bowden	

supported by strong self-defensible keeps serving as bomb-proof barracks and depots at:

St. Budeaux	Eggbuckland
Widey	Efford Warren.

Only Eggbuckland Keep was built. Accommodation was provided instead at Ernesettle, Agaton, Woodland, and Efford.
The hill in front of Knackers Knowle was to be occupied by a detached advanced work (Crownhill Fort). Covered communications to be made between keeps and batteries and between the keeps themselves. The lane from Ernesettle to Crownhill and on to Bowden was improved and protected from the north by a bank, and a sunken military road was built from Bowden to Laira and on to Crabtree.

20.1.62

1. Plans approved for Ernesettle, Agaton and Knowles Batteries.

2. Ordinary permanent barracks to be built in rear of Staddon Fort in place of casemated barracks in keep.

3. A work to be built near Pomphlett Farm (as originally proposed) to act as a *tête du pont* to Laira Bridge.

Neither 2 nor 3 were built. The keep at Staddon was not completed and casemated bomb-proof barracks facing the gate were built instead.

27.5.62

Royal Commission reassembled to consider the building of sea forts at Spithead and the Breakwater recommended one inside the Breakwater, not on it or at either end as originally suggested.

29.10.62

1.Barracks included in the design for Scraesdon to be omitted - bomb-proof casemates under the ramparts will be sufficient.

2.Barrack accommodation not needed in peacetime may (casemates excepted) be omitted from all new works.

20.4.63

Plans approved for:

Woodland Battery	Crownhill Fort
Bowden Battery	Efford Fort
Forder Battery	Laira Battery
Austin Battery.	

28.4.66

Breakwater Fort. In view of the advance in artillery since the original design and the probability of a hostile squadron bringing concentrated fire to bear, one tier of iron-faced casemates to be substituted for two. The top to be prepared for two turrets each of two of the most powerful guns

(i.e. 17 in casemates, 4 in turrets = 21).

16.2.67

'Five powerful guns behind earthworks' to be mounted *en barbette* on the upper battery of Drake's Island.

16.11.68

The Moncrieff system was considered in connection with Drake's Island and the Fortification Committee recommended that the parapet on Drake's Island, where 5 23-ton guns are to be mounted, be prepared for guns of Moncrieff pattern in case the system is hereafter adopted.

9.2.70

The Defence Committee considered a letter from Sir L. Simmons who said 'The present system is an artillery defence, supplemented by submarine mines; whereas according to the proposition I now venture to submit submarine mines would constitute the main defence, with guns to support and protect them' and he gave corresponding proposals for the reduction in the armaments.

His detailed suggestions for Plymouth included:

1. 4 turret guns on the Breakwater to be omitted. - the Committee pointed out that no funds had been approved for these.

2. A large proportion, if not all, the shields on Drake's Island could be omitted.

3. Garden Battery is a useless work - The Committee pointed out that there was 26 feet of water over the Bridge at high water. Garden Battery would be useless only on the principle of planning absolute reliance on the outer line of torpedoes (mines).

31.10.70

The Defence Committee considered whether it was possible to save money by reducing the number of RML guns on the fortifications. No reduction was recommended apart from the two left emplacements on Drake's Island which became an artillery store.

19.12.70

Plymouth to be allotted 10 of the 10-inch RML's available in March 1871. It was decided to allot them to Bovisand (4) and Picklecombe (6).

17.6.72

Inspector General of Artillery proposed heavy RML guns at Mount Wise and No. 4 Redoubt on Maker Heights. The Defence Committee recommended 3 10-inch 18-ton RML's at No. 4 Redoubt.

25.10.72

The Defence Committee submitted a memorandum on the use of rifled guns, exclusive of heavy RML's. The 64-pounder RML converted gun is to be substituted in almost all cases for the present obsolete smooth-bore ordnance. 'The armament of the new land defences, which have not yet received any guns, was left for future consideration'.

2.4.73   The Defence Committee considered the armament of Breakwater Fort. At present it has only 8-10-inch 18-ton guns which are incapable of dealing with ships of the 'Devastation' class. Breakwater should be the most heavily armed fort in view of its central position. The Committee suggested 11 36-ton guns on the front and sides and 7 18-ton in the rear.

25.11.74

The Secretary for War decided the turrets on Breakwater Fort were to be omitted and some 38-ton guns to be mounted. The Defence Committee recommended:

14 - 12.5-inch 38-ton RML guns
4 - 10-inch 18-ton RML guns.

5.1.75

The Defence Committee recommended a scale of armament for the land works not yet armed. All guns under cover in casemates to be mounted in position and the bulk of the armament of Ernesettle, Agaton and Knowles to be housed in the Gun Wharf (in the present Morice Yard).

The total guns in the armament table amounted to:-

7-inch RBL	209
64-pounder RML	49
8-inch rifled howitzer	45
SB flank guns	132

10.5.77

The Defence Committee recommended the SW face of Fort Stamford should have 2 10-inch RML covering Jennycliff Bay. No. 4 Redoubt, Maker Heights, should have 2 12.5-inch 38-ton in place of 3 10-inch 18-ton RML.

31.7.80

Inspector General of Fortifications' report on the works built under the Defence Loan:- Due to the progress in artillery since 1860 and in spite of the margin of safety allowed in the original designs, magazines in many cases require further protection and additional traverses are required.
Plymouth sea defences are satisfactory once the armament is completed but Polhawn requires improvement and heavier guns.
The land defences have been pushed so far to the front that they satisfy modern conditions. The Saltash defences have been omitted - a serious gap - and this partly neutralises the remainder. On the west flank of Staddon an advanced work is desirable.

2.80

A detailed report by Col. Nugent was attached:

SEA DEFENCES.

Breakwater Fort is receiving guns now.

Picklecombe and Bovisand are now fully armed and equipped.

Some shields on Drake's Island are not yet fixed.

Garden Battery now armed with heavy guns.

Eastern and Western King and the sea front of the Citadel have been re-modelled for medium guns.

An equipment of submarine mines has been provided for the entrance to the Sound.

LAND DEFENCES.

Staddon position is complete including 2 heavy guns at Stamford.

The north east defences are in good order i.e. 3 forts, one central and one on each flank and 7 intermediate batteries.

The development of siege artillery makes the occupation of high ground at Saltash 'more necessary than ever' but any work should be in advance of the line originally recommended. A central work should be at once constructed.

The Western Defences are in good order and the military road complete to Polhawn where heavier guns are needed.

The gap between the Laira and Staddon positions needs attention.

22.3.82

Officers commanding Royal Artillery and Royal Engineers proposed to the Defence Committee to demolish the land fronts of the Citadel. The armament was:

1 9-inch RML
28 medium rifled guns
69 SB guns.

The rifled guns are mounted mainly on the Harbour fronts. The Citadel covers part of the gap between the Staddon and the North Eastern positions and acts as a depot for stores and for the garrison. The ravelins are of no use.

The Committee recommended that the armament of the of the land fronts be removed and the outworks and counterscarp demolished. Removal of part of the ramparts was considered in connection with the construction of new buildings. The Committee considered a proposal for the demolition of Devonport Lines. Between 1860 and 1865 £12,000 had been spent on the Lines and on Mount Wise batteries as an inner line of defence, but

such a line should be further out to cover the Steam Yard at Keyham. It was recommended that the part of the Lines from Devonport Road to Passage Hill be removed, leaving Mount Wise battery and the part overlooking Stonehouse Pool untouched.

22.6.83

The Defence Committee considered the outstanding items needed to complete their approved armament. Bovisand, Picklecombe and Drake's Island particularly required additions.

6.1.85

The War Office addressed the Treasury (without succes) on the incomplete state of the defences of the military forts and urged the need for £2.25m additional expenditure over the next five years. Two 50-ton and two 38-ton guns should be mounted above Bovisand and Picklecombe.

27.5.85

The Defence Committee submitted a memo to GOC Western District on the temporary defences to be planned for the Saltash position. The probable time available for preparation was fourteen days. Ten 20-pounder guns to be allotted to Devonport for this purpose and kept ready at Woolwich.

12.6.85

Deputy Adjutant-General RA addressed the Adjutant-General on the incomplete state of the defences of the military forts. At Plymouth 'there are no works for the defence of the Sound or its approaches capable of resisting a modern attack, and the land forts are practically without any guns'.

3.12.85

The RA and RE Works Committee submitted reports on the revision of the armaments at Plymouth to meet modern conditions. Heavy long range guns were to be mounted in advanced positions (Penlee, Whitsand Bay, etc.) and the minefield protected. The revised armament tables were produced for the land defences, including 5-inch BL guns, and 'great importance should be attached to the position of moveable armament'.

12.12.85

In forwarding the above report the Adjutant-General pointed out that the Defence Loan was devoted to fortification works, and the armaments were to come from the Ordnance estimates. This it had been impossible to do. At Plymouth the land defences 'are unarmed and consequently inefficient though the works were finished 12-14 years ago'.

12.12.85

The Secretary of State for War proposed to submit a scheme for funds to cover the armament report if assured that the estimates are final.

Note: The variation in the description of RML guns is due to the fact that they were being developed and increased in size rapidly during this period and the weight of the gun is the most accurate description. For example 12-inch guns varied in weight from 23 tons to 25 tons.

APPENDIX C

FEATURES OF THE FORTIFICATIONS

THE LAND FORTS AND BATTERIES

To appreciate the importance of the various features of the fortifications it is important to know how they were designed to play their part in defeating an attack. There are variations, particularly between the earlier forts and the later ones, but the general principles are as follows:

Each fort or battery was surrounded not only by the sloping ground of the glacis but by a further area beyond over which the War Department had clearance rights to remove obstructions, which could be exercised in an emergency. The glacis extended for 200–300 yards from the ditch and was cleared and graded so that its slope was as far as practicable in extension of the line of fire of the guns on the ramparts. In the major forts it ended at the parapet of the covered way which was about 30 feet from the edge of the ditch. In the early stages of an attack the defending riflemen could move along the covered way under cover of its parapet into position to fire from the raised banquette or fire step. They could later withdraw through the main gates, or into the ditch and up ladders into the sally ports alongside some of the caponiers.

Before an attack the enemy would have moved into position such guns, especially any heavy siege guns and mortars, as he had been able to bring up and would bombard the fort with the object of disabling the guns on the ramparts and knocking down the scarp wall in selected places so as to make an assault practicable. In the case of the Plymouth forts, all the scarp walls were revetted with stone and in many cases were cut out of solid rock, in which case any fall of debris from the scarp wall would be limited. The enemy would hope that shells which landed in, or burst over, the fort whose interior they could not see would cause casualties to the garrison, destroy accommodation and might even fire a magazine. In the Plymouth forts all casemates were bomb-proofed with a covering of 6 feet or more of earth and even in the earlier ones barracks were protected from the enemy side by earth on their exposed side or by a large earth traverse across the fort which would stop horizontal fire from cannon.

The enemy advance would be led by a line of skirmishers followed by the main body of the infantry in close formation - in line or in column - and these formations would be engaged by the guns of the fort firing shot or shell. As they attacked up the glacis the guns would load with grape and later cannister as the range shortened. The enemy would also be engaged by riflemen from the parapet of the covered way or from the ramparts.

When the attacking infantry reached the parapet of the covered way they would, in the case of the principal forts, for the first time see the *chemin des rondes* at the top of the scarp on the other side of the ditch from which they would come under further rifle fire. They were faced by a ditch about 30 feet deep and up to 45 feet wide sloping steeply down at the counter scarp and with a vertical scarp wall on the other side. Once in the ditch they would be fired on with cannister shot (110 balls in each round from the early 32-pdr SB.BL) by the guns in the caponiers and by fire from the rifleman in the galleries alongside the guns. If the scarp wall had been brought down by the fire of their own guns, providing a possible way into the fort and shelter on the far side of the fall from the fire of the caponiers, they would try and rush the defences by charging through the breach on to the rampart. Otherwise they would have to close up to the caponier and try and silence the guns and the riflemen with their own rifle fire and with grenades thrown through the embrasures. Re-forming, they would then launch a deliberate attack on the scarp wall of the fort using scaling ladders and grappling hooks, or after blowing a further breach in the scarp wall.

Glacis

The ground for several hundred yards beyond the ditch of a fort or battery was cleared of vegetation and where possible levelled and graded so that it provided a slope in prolongation of the line of fire of the guns and the rampart. This was important if the gunfire was to achieve the greatest effect. In addition, under the Defence Act of 1860 the War Department had clearance rights over a considerable additional area of land around the fort

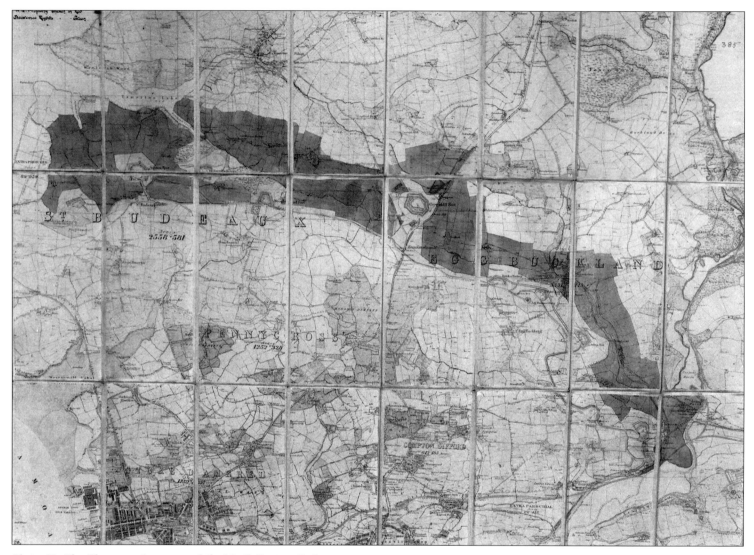

Plate 47: *The Clearance Area around the North Eastern Defences.* (PLYMOUTH PROPRIETORY LIBRARY)

beyond the glacis which could be cleared of buildings, trees etc. in an emergency. The extent of the clearance area of the North Eastern Defences is shown in Plate 47.

COVERED WAY
In the major forts the glacis does not always end at the counter-scarp of the ditch but in a bank about 8 feet high and 30 feet from the edge of the counterscarp. This forms a 'covered' way, i.e. one that is covered from fire, along which the defending riflemen can move and take up positions on the fire step or banquette. The covered way was also the place where the garrison could assemble for a sortie.

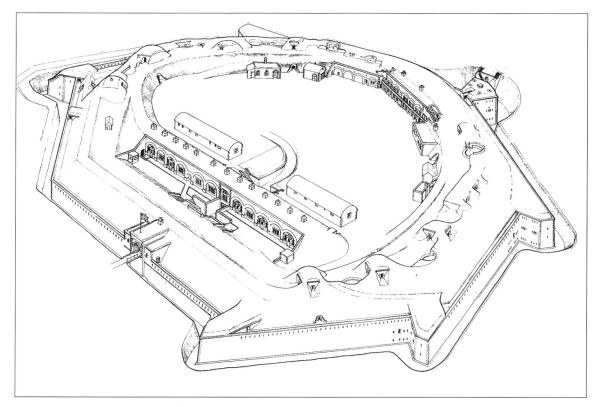

Plate 48: *Panorama of Crownhill Fort.* (LANDMARK TRUST ©)

Plate 49: *Crownhill Fort. Mini-caponier (left) and the countermine gallery (right).* (ANDREW PERRY AND AUTHOR)

To get to the covered way steps, or an iron ladder in some places, led up from the bottom of the ditch to the top of the counterscarp, with a break in the steps crossed by a small metal bridge which could be dropped quickly by pulling out a pin if the attackers threatened to use it themselves. The defenders could get into the ditch from the fort or battery through a 'sallyport' or doorway in the scarp wall, alongside the caponier at first floor level and approached from the rifle gallery there. From the sally port the defenders could drop a ladder into the ditch to make a sally or to clear the ditch of enemy.

In 1863 Du Cane[1] was suggesting putting small iron blockhouses holding five or six men and with 'secure communications to the interior' in the covered way or in the *chemin des rondes* (see p.150), but this idea does not appear to have been put into practice, at least at Plymouth.

COUNTERMINE GALLERY
(Plate 49)
Crownhill Fort has the only known countermine gallery incorporated into fortifications recommended by the Royal Commission. Its entrance is opposite the north double caponier and is covered by a single gun

embrasure in the caponier. The landing in front of the entrance to the tunnel is half way up the counter scarp and is approached by a pair of stairways down from the covered way. There are no steps down to the floor of the ditch but there are the remains of the metal fixings for a removable (?) metal ladder to enable the defenders to climb up to the landing. From the landing a 4 feet wide tunnel runs north into the bank of the counter scarp under the covered way to the remains of the leats which originally supplied water to Plymouth and Devonport, which cross it at right angles.

It was obviously necessary to provide access to the tunnels of the leats which otherwise would invite the mining of this part of the glacis. This tunnel is referred to in the 1869 report as being 'available as countermine if required'.

DITCHES

The faces of the land forts and batteries were protected by ditches, normally 30 feet deep and 45 feet wide. The scarp walls were vertical, or nearly so, and the counterscarps were steeply sloped at 70–80°. The ditch at Tregantle, an early construction, is both wider and in places shallower. Also, the top half of the counterscarp is a bank sloping at about 45° and the lower half a vertical revetment. Efford Fort and Laira Battery which stand on a promontory overlooking the Plym estuary, relied for the defence of their outer faces on a long, steep and reinforced scarp. The principal forts - Tregantle, Crownhill and Staddon - were entirely surrounded by ditches apart from the sea face at Tregantle and in front of the gate at Staddon.

Of the minor forts, although their gorges were well covered by fire neither Scraesdon nor Agaton had a proper ditch along the gorge, although there was one at Stamford, Austin, Efford and Woodland, and a ditch in front of the gate at Ernesettle. Of the batteries, Bowden was entirely surrounded by a ditch but the others had shallow ditches or the military road along the gorge. However the gorge walls were in every case covered by musketry, and in some cases gun fire, either from the guard room or from galleries on the flanks.

General Todleben[2] suggested that instead of the ditch being narrowed at the salients of the caponiers it should be wider as there as they are the places most liable to assault, being deprived of the flanking fire of artillery and exposed to the danger of being crossed by portable bridges. Jervois replied that if the ditch were widened there the caponiers would be exposed to be breached by artillery fire. In our new works, he said, the ditch is always made so wide that it cannot be crossed by a portable bridge.

DROP DITCHES
(see Plate 33)

Often the faces of casemates, caponiers or musketry galleries were protected by a deeper section of ditch in front of them to prevent easy access by an attacker, as at Tregantle, Staddon, Scraesdon, Agaton, Bowden, Stamford and Polhawn. Most of these have subsequently been filled in.

CAPONIERS AND COUNTERSCARP GALLERIES
(Plate 50)

The ditch was the principal defence against assault but needed to be covered by close range fire throughout its length to be effective. This fire came from a series of caponiers, or rifle galleries in the counterscarp, each covering the ditch on one face of the fort. The ditch in the rear, or the gorge wall in the case of most batteries, was covered by the fire of the fortified guardhouse.

The caponiers jutted into the ditch and were approached by tunnels under the rampart of the fort. Built of masonry and bombproofed on top with earth, they were entirely below the level of the top of the counterscarp and therefore not exposed to direct aimed artillery fire. But because the enemy could place his guns in prolongation of the line of the ditch and put the armament of the caponiers out of action by firing along the ditch without even seeing them, the caponiers on the flanks of the fort had to be carefully sited with the face which was armed towards the rear. The other face was banked and revetted so as to be able to withstand artillery fire.

There were normally at least

Plate 50: *Caponiers and scarp rifle galleries.* Left: *Crownhill Fort, Haxo embrasure, chemin des rondes and scarp rifle gallery.* (ANDREW PERRY); top left: *Crownhill Fort caponier.* (AUTHOR); above left: *Tregantle Fort - double caponier.* (EXETER ARCHAEOLOGY ©); top right: *Tregantle Fort - single caponier.* (EXETER ARCHAEOLOGY ©); right: *Agaton Fort - interior of the rifle gallery.* (EXETER ARCHAEOLOGY ©).

two guns in any caponier side by side firing along any section of a ditch. The weakness of this arrangement was that any substantial breach in the scarp wall would produce a fall of debris which would hide the part of the ditch beyond the fall from fire. In the principal forts another pair of guns were on an upper level and in some cases there was a third level above with only musketry loops.

Single caponiers are by definition those covering one section of the ditch; double caponiers were built in the salient angle of the fort, ie, facing the likely direction of attack, and covered the sections of the ditch on either side. The double caponiers at Agaton, Crownhill, Stamford and Staddon are covered against attack on their outer faces by 'mini' caponiers (Plate 49) though this design had not apparently been developed when Tregantle had been completed. There the 'double' caponiers consisted of two single caponiers at an angle like donkey's ears. Of the 16 gun embrasures - four on each face of each caponier - the four on the inside of each caponier faced obliquely at the opposite one and beyond to the counterscarp wall only 30–40 yards away.

Since attackers once in the ditch could close with the face of the caponiers and attack the embrasures, the faces themselves were covered by fire from rifle galleries built into the scarp of the fort alongside, with angled loops firing across the face of the caponiers, and also in some cases by drop ditches in front of the embrasures.

In some cases - Crownhill and Staddon - inside the double caponiers there were musketry racks and most caponiers had fireplaces showing that they could be used as temporary accommodation, especially where the embrasures and loopholes had removable glazing. Most of the fittings have long been removed.

Where a section of ditch is not covered by a caponier it is covered instead from a counterscarp gallery built in the outer face of the ditch and approached by a tunnel from within the fort that goes under rampart and the ditch. The disadvantage of these galleries is that, apart from the fact that there are often only rifles firing from them, the men were relatively isolated from the rest of the garrison. At Austin for example the defenders of the western counterscarp gallery were at the far end of a subsidiary tunnel running along the counterscarp from a caponier.

At Bowden Battery although there are two 'caponiers' in the ditch they are only in the form of low single-tier rifle galleries with no gun embrasures. The NE one is 'L' shaped and so covers the north and east faces. Admittedly the guns in the double caponier at Forder could fire along the ditch on either side in support of Bowden and Austin. But the ditch to the west was only

straight as far as Forder Hill Bridge and fire across the re-entrant beyond would strike the caponier at the NE salient of Bowden.

CHEMIN DES RONDES
(Plate 51)
Crownhill Fort is entirely surrounded by a wall about 7 feet high standing at the bottom of the lower slope of the rampart and on top of the scarp wall. It is pierced with musketry loops throughout its length and is placed at such a level at the foot of the rampart that it cannot be seen or fired upon directly by attackers until they reach the top of the glacis. There is a walkway on the berm behind it, which is covered with earth to form a gallery along the NNE and NNW faces of the fort from which directions artillery fire would initially come in the event of an attack. Consequently defenders could move to any part of the ditch under attack without being seen or directly fired upon and could themselves fire on the covered way, or down into the ditch. A *chemin des rondes* also covered part of the ditch around Tregantle, Scraesdon, Staddon and Stamford Forts. At Tregantle it is in the simpler form of a substantial parapet at the top of the scarp with a fire step inside it and at Scraesdon it is entirely covered.

A *chemin des rondes* effectively raises the height of the scarp and prevents any part of the rampart brought down by gunfire from falling directly into the ditch.

Plate 51a and b: *Chemin des rondes* (above) *at Tregantle, and* (opposite page, inset) *at Crownhill Fort.* (AUTHOR)

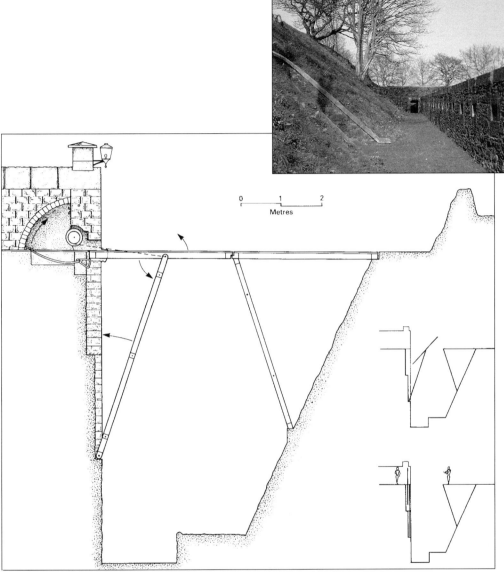

Plate 52a-c - top: *The gate at Stamford Fort* (Exeter Archaeology ©); above: *Drawbridge mechanism at Bowden Battery.* (Author); left: *the operation of the drawbridge at Polhawn Fort.* (Andrew Perry)

DRAWBRIDGES
(Plate 52a-c)
The main approach to any work was by a wooden trestle bridge with a drawbridge at the inner end, the gateway being closed by substantial doors. The original doors appear to have had rifle loops in them. At Staddon the gateway is protected by a machicolation above, from which suitable objects could be dropped on an attacker in case the drawbridge was not raised in time. Polhawn has an unusual drawbridge with a quick release mechanism in case of a surprise attack (see Plate 34 and above left).

GUARDHOUSES
(Plate 53)

Entrance to the forts is through a guardhouse, normally containing guardrooms and detention cells on either side of the passageway, with rifle loops for the guard to cover the bridge and the passage into the fort. The original main doors remain at Stamford, with rifle loops in them and a sallyport door also with loops. At Staddon and Scraesdon the entrance is also covered by rifle loops and gun embrasures in the projecting angles of the fort on either side (bastionettes). In these and some other forts the guardroom is incorporated in the main accommodation block. In the batteries the guardhouse is usually a building on its own and normally forms the only accommodation in the battery, often with the main magazine underneath it. From there rifle loops, and in some cases gun embrasures, cover the gorge wall!

Plate 53a–f: *Guardhouses and gateways;* top left: *Austin Fort*; middle left: *Knowles Battery*; lower left: *Woodland Fort*; top above: *Staddon Fort - note drawbridge mechanism in position.* (COURTESY R.C.F. SERPELL); middle above: *Efford Fort c. 1810*; above: *Crownhill Fort.* (ALL AUTHOR).

KEEPS
(Plate 54)

Tregantle is the only fort in the Plymouth defences with a self-defensible keep within the fort. The object was to hold out - possibly for no more than a few hours but perhaps for up to two days - if the fort itself was occupied by the enemy until relief arrived. It had guns in casemates firing into the interior of the fort and an upper tier of guns on the roof firing over the ramparts, as well as those firing outwards as part of the main armament. The interior face of the keep was surrounded by a ditch with a drawbridge leading to its entrance. Round the counterscarp of the ditch was a continuous counterscarp gallery linked to the rifle galleries in the east section of the ditch and so to the main guardroom. It was intended that Staddon should have a keep but this was modified on grounds of expense, although there was still in effect an inner line of defence formed by a substantial parados, with a fire step on top, to the rear of the gate. A keep was also proposed for Scraesdon originally.

General Todleben was concerned that the masonry of the keep facing the interior of the fort was exposed and was liable to be battered by artillery fire from in front of the fort. He suggested covering it with a short glacis. Jervois gave a number of reasons why he had turned down this idea. In particular, if the glacis was to protect the scarp of the keep effectively it would prevent the guns from sweeping the interior of the fort and it would itself take up much of the interior..

Plate 54a-d: above: *Tregantle Fort from the air* (CORNWALL ARCHAEOLOGICAL UNIT © ACS. 3134); top right: *The keep, north-east face*; middle right: *the interior*; lower right: *the ditch with counterscarp gallery* (ALL AUTHOR).

Plate 55: *Murder hole at Staddon Fort.* (AUTHOR)

MURDER HOLES
(Plate 55)
At Staddon Fort, in addition to the machicolations over the gate there are two slits at the foot of the parapet wall on either side of the gateway enabling rifle fire to be brought to bear on the approaches to the gateway and the bridge. A similar slit exists at Polhawn to cover the rifle loops which fire along a short ditch to the north of the battery. When George's Bastion in Devonport Lines was re-modelled in the early 1860s murder holes were incorporated in the face.

RAMPARTS
(Plate 56)
The main defence of a fort or battery above the level of the scarp wall was a deep earth bank or rampart 20–25 feet high in most cases and with a forward slope which General Todleben thought generally was too steep. He always made his 2-of-base to 1-of-height whereas we used 1-to-1 or 45°. Jervois stated that 1.5-to-1 (34°) was used in many of our works and pointed out that an increase in the width of the slope added to the size of a work and the expense of excavation.

'The trace of the rampart does not follow the line of the ditch, but is arranged so as to afford a fire of artillery and musketry nearly equally upon the front and flanks, whilst the ditch is arranged so as to complete the enclosure with as few sides as possible, in order to simplify the arrangements for flanking it '.[1] In other words, the outline of the ramparts which were to hold the guns in positions to cover the required ground to the front and flanks of the fort/battery dictated the general design of the fortification and its ditch.

On top of the ramparts were the gun emplacements on the terreplein, firing either over high parapets (up to 6 feet) or from within Haxo emplacements. Within the ramparts were bomb-proof expense magazines to service the guns on either side, which in effect acted as traverses.

In the batteries and some of the forts the forward slope of the rampart ends at the top of the scarp. At Crownhill and elsewhere where there is a *chemin des rondes* it ends ten feet or more inside the top of the scarp. Jervois said that the rampart should be 'so retired from the escarp, that the continuation of its exterior slope strikes about two-thirds down the escarp wall ; thus even if the scarp were breached, the rampart would not be brought down'. But this is not always the case, not even at Crownhill where the *chemin des rondes* is covered over on the two north faces to form a gallery.

At Tregantle in the north-west face the rampart is indented in two places, producing at one point a substantial triangular space within the scarp wall covered by musketry fire from galleries within the ramparts. This 'sawtoothed' rampart (*crémaillère*) effectively increased the length of the rampart on this face and the number of guns which could be mounted to cover the important gap between Tregantle and Scraesdon.

Also at Tregantle there remains a 'V' shaped embrasure in the parapet which has been partly filled in for the gun which was last mounted there (Plate 57) and represents an earlier type of embrasure. In 1864 General Todleben objected strongly to some masonry in the throats and sills of the embrasures on the terreplein and this was thought objectionable by some of our own officers. Jervois in his comments said that it was to keep the embrasures in proper order in peacetime and was only where guns would always be mounted. Iron shields would be provided in case of attack. It is likely that this type of embrasure, characteristic of forts of an earlier period, was originally built in other positions at Tregantle and elsewhere.

Plate 56a-d: *Ramparts and gun emplacements*: top above: *Tregantle Fort*; above: *Staddon Fort*; above right: *Ernesettle Battery*; middle right: *Crownhill Fort*. (ALL AUTHOR)

Plate 57 - lower right: *Emplacement at Tregantle* (EXETER ARCHAEOLOGY ©)

As there were three different scales of armament proposed between 1875 and 1893 the gun emplacements which we see now represent at least modifications, and more often a complete re-design, of those originally built. Already in 1869 the report says 'the character of the works has been materially altered, and a much smaller number of heavy rifled guns substituted for the numerous 68-pdrs and 8-inch guns then contemplated' (in the 1860 report).

The open gun emplacements which we see now were designed to fire over deep earth parapets up to 6 feet high, the height depending upon the platform and carriage of the guns mounted there. The earlier parapets are revetted with stone but by the time the later modifications were incorporated this had become concrete. Where the parapet is high the guns were on special blocked up carriages, and although these appear unwieldly (see Plate 42) they enabled the gunners to remain protected from enemy fire except when in the act of loading the gun.

Those forts and batteries whose layout was brought up to date have each gun position, or at least each pair of guns, separated by an earth traverse from the next one. For every two guns the traverse was larger and contained within it an expense magazine (Plate 58). Sometimes these had a further magazine chamber below from which shells were raised using a davit, and cartridges brought up on a hand-operated lift.

Set in the inner face of the ramparts there were sometimes casemates to provide accommodation close to the guns and to the double caponier or mortar battery, if there was one, in the salient.

Also within the salient of the fort where the rampart was thickest the main magazine was normally sited, with its entrance into the fort to the rear (Plate 59).

Plate 58a-c: *Traverses and expense magazines* - left: *Tregantle Fort - main traverse*; top above: *Agaton Fort, expense magazine*; above: *Crownhill Fort - interior of expense magazine.* (ALL AUTHOR)

Plate 60: *Barbette gun emplacement, Crownhill Fort.* (AUTHOR)

Plate 59a and b: Main Magazines - top: *Crownhill Fort, exterior;* (AUTHOR) above: *Scraesdon Fort, interior.* (EXETER ARCHAEOLOGY ©)

BARBETTE GUN EMPLACEMENTS
(Plate 60)
Many of the open emplacements for 64-pdr RMLs have a single circular racer with a centre pivot provided by a 32-pdr gun barrel.

Some of the earlier emplacements for 7-in RBLs for example, and also all those firing through an embrasure of any kind, have a pair of racers, inner and outer. In some cases there are also the remains of the granite sets on which a racer, usually the outer one, was mounted for an earlier type of platform. The racers now in position in most cases correspond with the armament shown in the armament table of 1893.

MONCRIEFF EMPLACEMENTS
(Plate 61)
Some time after 1870 most of the principal forts had their ramparts modified to take one or two of the concrete emplacements nearly ten feet deep for a gun on a Moncrieff disappearing carriage. The guns were usually 7-in RBLs but there were later 5-in BL guns on these mountings. The emplacements were usually at the salients of the fort and they have characteristic 'diamond-toothed' racers.
The disadvantage of the Moncrieff system was its expense and the fact that though it offered excellent protection from horizontal fire there was no protection from vertical fire. It proved unsatisfactory with larger calibre guns than the 9-inch RML.

Plate 61: *Moncrieff emplacement - Crownhill Fort.* (AUTHOR)

HAXO CASEMATES
(see Plate 41)
Bomb-proofed casemates on the ramparts of forts and batteries of this period are so called after General Haxo who first proposed them. Those guns which fire in the general direction from which an attack is likely to come only require protection from a parapet in front, but on the flanks guns and their detachments are liable to enemy fire from the side. Haxos in this position were bomb-proofed on the top and the sides, but open to the rear so that the gun smoke could escape. Where guns were sited towards the rear of the fort or battery and were therefore liable to fire from behind, the Haxos were entirely earthed over, suffering the disadvantage that gun smoke might blow back into the casemate and make the work of the detachment difficult. The disadvantage of Haxo emplacements is that they often stand out in silhouette on the ramparts in the earler forts and their stonefaced embrasures were vulnerable to accurate fire from rifled guns. Guns in Haxo casemates had limited traverse so that they were interspersed with *barbette* emplacements with 360˚ traverse.

ACCOMMODATION
(Plate 62)
In the main forts where there is accommodation for up to several hundred men this is either in casemates built into the ramparts, or in barracks often on either side of the gate. Sometimes there is a long earth traverse across the middle of the fort which often has additional accommodation in casemates, and also magazines, within it. At Stamford the two-storied barracks on either side of the gate is bomb-proofed with a bank of earth on the vulnerable east side.

TRAVERSES
Large traverses were built or later added across the parade (the interior) of Tregantle, Scraesdon, Efford, Stamford and Staddon to cover magazines or accommodation from horizontal gunfire. At Tregantle the huge barracks for two thousand men is only partly covered from fire by a traverse across the middle of the fort. The arrangement reflects the early design of the fort and its completion before long range guns and plunging fire were factors to be seriously considered. If it had been designed later the barrack accommodation would have been largely in casemates in the traverse. Both at Tregantle and at Scraesdon the traverses do not cover the barracks round the gates.

Plate 62a-e: *Accommodation - barracks and casemates.* Above: *Tregantle Fort, barracks.* Opposite - above left: *Scraesdon Fort, casemates;* above right: *Stamford Fort- barracks;* below left: *Efford Fort, casemates;* below right: *Crownhill Fort - officers' casemates.* (ALL AUTHOR).

MAGAZINES

Ammunition - cartridges, shot and shell - were stored in three ways. Each fort had its main magazine in brick-vaulted chambers covered with many feet of earth. These were either in the main rampart with the entrance facing away from the likely direction of fire, or similarly placed in the main traverse across the fort if there was one. In the batteries the main magazine was usually

under the guardhouse. In the case of Bowden, Forder and Austin ammunition was stored centrally in Eggbuckland Keep with a smaller magazine under each guardhouse, except at Forder where there was no guardhouse but communication with Eggbuckland by tunnel. At Ernesettle Battery the 1869 report recommended the building of a new magazine as the early arrangements were not satisfactory. This is the only free standing magazine now to be seen in the defences and is of course bomb-proofed. At the entrance to the main magazine was a space which later became called a 'shifting lobby' where the men working in the magazine left their boots, matches and any metal object which could cause a spark in the powder magazine where the cartridges were filled with gunpowder.

Nearer to the guns, ammunition was held in expense magazines either let into the ramparts and bombproofed or, in the case of mortar batteries, in magazines off the passage leading to them under the ramparts. The guns in caponiers were normally supplied from expense magazines at the rear of the caponier, close to the tunnel from the fort. Expense magazines in the principal forts often had magazine chambers below. These lower magazine chambers were sometimes connected to a tunnel through which they could be supplied from the main magazine or from within the fort. In other cases there was no entrance other than from the hatch to the casemate above, so that in peace time ammunition was first lowered down in the same way as it would be lifted up in action. This was presumably an economy measure to avoid building additional tunnels to these small magazines.

The standard method of raising ammunition from magazine level to the level of the gun platforms was by rope and tackle from a davit in the case of the land fortificatons. Few of these remain but there is one on the east rampart of Fort Stamford. In the casemated coast batteries the tackle was attached to a ring bolt in the roof above the shaft. Various forms of lift were later developed, especially for cartridge.

Ready-use ammunition was stored in ammunition recesses or cupboards alongside the emplacement or in the casemate.

All cartridge magazines, even the expense magazines on the ramparts, were ventilated from small passageways or from channels running round the outside of the inner wall. These carried air from the outside to the interior, even when the doors of the magazine were shut, through a series of slits in the brickwork wall.

The lighting of main magazines was normally from a separate lighting passage running right round the magazine. Lanterns carrying two or more tallow candles were placed in rectangular openings in the brick wall of the magazine, separated from the interior by a fixed glass plate. In this way there was no possibility of a naked light being in contact with the air of the magazine.

There was lack of uniformity in the design of magazines at first, due to the inexperience of the designers and the contractors, but this was corrected by later modifications following the 1869 report. The systems of ventilation and lighting were standardised

and there were modifications to the design of the magazines on Drake's Island to protect the expense magazines further and to improve the rate at which ammunition could be passed to the guns. Standing orders for expense magazines issued in 1863 are given at Plate 63 below.

W. O. Form 929.

STANDING ORDERS

FOR

ARTILLERY EXPENSE MAGAZINES.

1. No light to be used in any Magazine unless an Officer or the Authority in Charge be present.

2. Any person entering a Magazine with Cigar, Pipe or Lucifer Match in his possession, is to be made Prisoner and reported immediately.

3. Magazine Slippers are to be put on at the Door by all persons before entry.

4. Magazines are to be aired and swept daily (Sundays and rainy days excepted).

5. Magazines are not to be left open without a Guard.

6. Magazine Doors and Windows to be closed upon any sign of Thunder, Lightning or Rain.

7. Passage Ways are to be covered with Hide, or overlaid with folded Hair Cloth.

8. Cases and barrels must not be lodged in contact with the masonry of Walls.

9. No stowage or shifting of Cartridge, or issue of Powder from Cases or Barrels, is permitted within Magazines or outside thereof within reach of the Doors.

10. No friction or detonating Tubes are to be kept in or about the same Magazine with Powder, nor are filled shell to be admitted.

11. Common Tubes, Fuzes, Quick and Slow Match and Portfires, are to be kept in Lobbies, if possible, rather in Magazines.

12. Oiled rags, cotton waste, oakum, or cloths for cleaning are not to be kept in Magazines or Lobbies.

13. The contents of Magazines are always to be shown upon the Inventories.

14. All Boxes, Cases and Barrels are to be labelled.

15. No open or empty Packages of any kind are to be left in Magazines.

By Order,
C. BINGHAM.
Deputy Adjutant General Royal Artillery

Horse Guards,
16th March, 1863.

NB. To be affixed to the inside of the outer Doors and the inside and outside of the inner Doors.

Plate 64: *Mortar batteries* - top left: *Crownhill Fort, open battery.* (AUTHOR); lower left: *Staddon Fort, inside casemated battery.* (AUTHOR); below top: *Fort Nelson, Portsmouth, casemated 13-inch mortar battery.* (AUTHOR); below: *Gun drill on 13-inch mortar.* (ROYAL ARTILLERY HISTORICAL TRUST).

MORTAR BATTERIES
(Plate 64)

In a number of forts and batteries which overlooked steep valleys or gullies, especially in the North Eastern Defences, there were one or more sunken mortar batteries. These were normally in a salient of the fort outside the main rampart but covered from the enemy by a subsidiary rampart between them and the top of the scarp. They were approached by tunnels through the ramparts in which there was a magazine for their ammunition.

In two places, at Staddon and Ernesettle, there were casemated mortar batteries (see Plate 64). Here the mortars were emplaced within a series of arched bays facing on to a steep and high ram-

part along the scarp. Since mortars fire at a fixed angle of 45° they can be placed under the arches while able to clear the rampart. Such batteries which were much more expensive than the open batteries were necessary where the valleys which the mortars were required to cover were in front of the fort and the mortars therefore required additional protection from incoming gunfire.

Although mortars are included in the armament described in the reports up to 1869, they are not referred to in the armament tables from 1875 onwards, presumably because the Royal Artillery were by 1868 (Jervois) considering the development of rifled howitzers which would produce vertical fire with much greater accuracy.

MILITARY ROADS

In the Western Defences, Scraesdon and Tregantle were never linked by a ditch and rampart or by an intermediate work as originally proposed, nor was the battery recommended in 1860 built on Knatterbury Hill. However Tregantle Fort was linked to Polhawn by a military road along the coast. This would have enabled the considerable reserve of troops from the fort to take up positions to oppose a landing in Whitsand Bay, protected by the height of the road above sea level or where it is lower at Polhawn by a bank and parapet on the sea side of the road.

The forts and batteries in the North Eastern Defences were linked by a substantial military road running from the gate of Ernesettle Battery through Knackers Knowle village round to below Laira Battery at Crabtree. Movement along this was covered from enemy fire by a high bank on the north or east side. Spurs led off from this road to those forts and batteries which are sited in advance of it. These spurs were banked on both sides. A military road also ran behind the Staddon Defences from Stamford Fort, past Staddon Fort to Watch House Brake.

Plate 65: *Eggbuckland Keep and Forder battery* (top left). (F.M. GRIFFITH, DEVON COUNTY COUNCIL ©, 10.1.92).

EGGBUCKLAND KEEP
(Plate 65)

This was the only one of the four defensible barracks proposed in August 1861 which was actually built. Its importance lay in the fact that it was sited on the high point which commanded the rear of Bowden, Forder and Austin batteries whose positions had had to be pushed forward in order to cover the steep slope down into Forder valley. It provided accommodation for the garrisons of these batteries apart from the limited accommodation in their own guardhouses. It was connected to Forder by an underground tunnel which led into the battery and continued beyond into the important double caponier at the salient of the battery, whose guns covered the ditch running towards both Bowden and Austin batteries on either flank. But there was a slight curve in the ditch at Forder Hill Bridge so the guns could not cover all the way to Bowden. Towards Austin the ditch bent slightly at Goosewell Hill Bridge and ended behind the fort at the gorge ditch.

Eggbuckland Keep was described in 1869 as having 'revetments 30 feet high flanked by musketry, and completely protected by a glacis. The two-storied casemated barrack contains accommodation for 230 men and ample stores for powder and shell'. It was the main magazine for Austin, Forder and Bowden batteries.

MAJOR SCARPS AND DITCHES

Bowden, Forder and Austin, with Eggbuckland Keep, form a single defensive position. Whereas on either flank Bowden and Austin have their own ditches, Forder in the centre is only covered on its two principal faces by a long arrow-shaped ditch which runs from the face of Bowden, in front of Forder and ends at the rear of Austin (Plate 66). This ditch was covered by a substantial double caponier at the salient of Forder and to some extent by that battery's main armament. General Todleben did not like this idea because he thought that in the event of an attack the central battery, i.e, Forder, would be far too concerned with defending itself from the front to fire in support of the batteries on either flank, but Lt-Col. Jervois pointed out that this was being treated in some respects as a single position on the hill.

Efford Fort is protected mainly by a ditch but on its north face has only a steep revetted scarp, and Laira likewise has a scarp to the east and south east.

On Staddon Heights a revetted scarp 20 feet high was cut into the slope of the hill to the east of Staddon Fort and ran from there to the south in front of Brownhill Battery, before turning west towards Watch House. Due to a re-entrant the scarp ends west of the turn and is replaced by a free-standing scarp wall between the

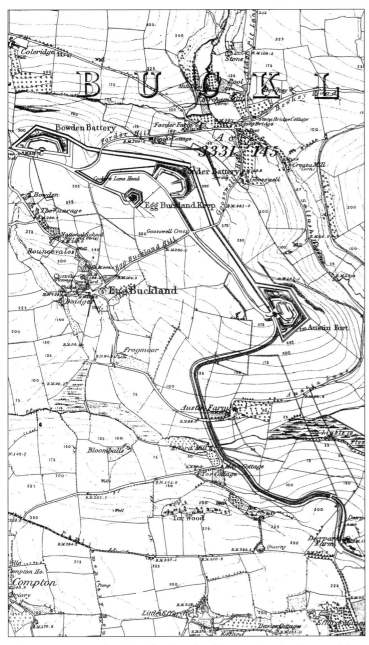

Plate: 66 *Map showing the Bowden Battery–Austin Fort position, 1882.* (PRO WO 78/2314/9).

small batteries at Twelve Acre Brake and Watch House Brake which were designed to cover it with fire. A separate ditch runs down the hill below Watch House to Bovisand Battery and is covered by two rifle galleries (Plate 67).

Plate: 67 *The ditch down to Bovisand Battery.* (AUTHOR).

WELLS AND SPRINGS
When questioned by the 1869 Committee, Lt. Col. Jervois confirmed that there were sufficient wells and springs within the North Eastern Defences to supply any number of men likely to be encamped there, and the same applied to the other forts.

Plate 68: *Devonport Lines - panorama of 1872.* (ILLUSTRATED LONDON NEWS).

DEVONPORT LINES
(Plate 68)

The work on the Lines which had been begun in 1853 was completed in 1863, by which time the ditch had been deepened and the scarp raised to conform with the standard of the time. In addition the Lines had been extensively realigned on the east and NNE and an existing quarry face converted into a vertical scarp facing east above Stonehouse Creek.

THE COAST DEFENCES.

Of the coast batteries at Plymouth the four principal ones were built in the form of an arc of granite casemates. The longest battery was at Bovisand with 23 casemates and there were 21 at

Picklecombe and Drake's Island. At Picklecombe two tiers were built making a total of 42 casemates in all and this is the only battery of its size in the country apart from Garrison Point at Sheerness. Garden Battery was much smaller, with only seven casemates.

The existing redoubts at Eastern and Western King were extended on either flank (Plate 69). Seven and nine earthwork emplacements respectively were built with underground magazines

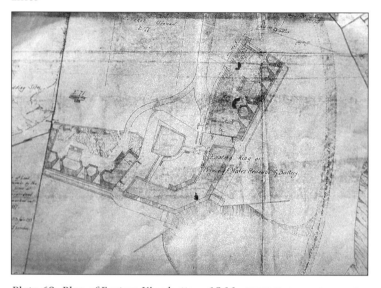

Plate 69: *Plan of Eastern King battery, 1866.* (RCHME. CROWN © PLM 536)

After many changes in the design Breakwater Fort was eventually armed with 18 guns; the four smaller ones faced into the Sound. At Cawsand there was a barbette coast battery with nine guns, five facing north east, two east and two south east. Polhawn also had seven guns in casemates of a simpler and less substantial design than the larger batteries, presumably because the casemates were not considered liable to heavy gunfire from the front as they faced west along Whitsand Bay.

The standard granite casemates originally proposed for the principal batteries had a recessed granite embrasure but these were not apparently completed in this form except possibly at Garden Battery. The front of the other casemates was left open after the decision was taken in 1863 to fit iron shields. However at Polhawn the original design, entirely of granite, was completed, and remained so as frontal attack was unlikely.

Plate 70a-c - top left: *Bovisand Battery, inside casemate.* (AUTHOR); left: *Bovisand Battery notice of gun mounted.* (AUTHOR); above: *Staddon Fort, inside caponier.* (EXETER ARCHAEOLOGY ©).

CASEMATES
(Plate 70)
Faced with heavy granite blocks and with substantial overhead cover of rubble, the casemates of the principal batteries were vaulted with brick and the arches connecting them to each other had substantial brick pillars. Large ring bolts in the ceiling and on either side were for lifting or moving the guns whose plat-

forms traversed on two iron racers. These platforms and the carriages which slid on them when the gun recoiled were originally of oak. But with the introduction of the much heavier RML guns both the platforms and the carriages were made of wrought iron (see Plate 71, over).

The introduction of iron shields was not without its problems. The weakest point was where the iron and granite joined, since on the outside the corners of the granite were liable to be knocked off and inside the granite was cut away to allow the working of the gun when traversed. The total traverse of the gun was usually 60° and elevation and depression were each 10°. On this basis, by designing the carriages so that the gun when traversed pivotted about a point one foot from the muzzle it was found that for the original 7-in Armstrong gun the embrasure in the shield could be as small as 2 feet wide and 3 feet 3 inches high.[4]

The casemates were linked to each other by arches on either side which were in peacetime closed by wooden partitions. The archways to the rear of the guns were sometimes closed partly by a low brick wall but the remainder of the opening was of wood and was glazed. Where the casemates were over the magazines, as at Bovisand (Plate 72) and Picklecombe, there was a circular

Plate 71: *A reproduction 9-inch RML gun in an open emplacement at New Tavern Fort, Gravesend.* (AUTHOR)

hole lined with wood in the floor to the right front, which with the davit above it formed a cartridge hoist from the front passage of the magazine below. In this shaft was a voice pipe for communication between the magazine and the gun detachment.

Between each pair of guns was a smaller arch in the dividing wall to the rear of which was a hole with a davit or ring bolt over it forming a shell lift from a recess in the rear passage of the magazine.

SHIELDS
(see Plate 29)
There were four different patterns of shields in the Plymouth batteries.[5] The earliest type was fitted to Garden Battery, the first to be completed, and the latest pattern was used on Breakwater Fort. There were variations in the other two designs within the battery on Drake's Island.[3]

The most common type of shield found on Bovisand, Picklecombe and Drake's Island is composed of blocks, plates or wide bars of wrought iron (depending on the manufacturer) usually 5–6 inches thick with 3–4 inches of iron cement as a buffer between and usually five plates wide. The shields fitted later were designed to stop an 11-inch shell fired from a range of 1000 metres or more.

On and round the shield are a variety of fittings for rope mantlets.

MANTLETS
An essential part of the equipment of a casemate was the curtains or mantlets of heavy rope suspended from, and covering the rear of the shields. These could be moved when the gun traversed so that the two curtains fell closely either side of the barrel when the gun was run out preparatory to firing.

The principal function of a mantlet was to protect the gun detachments from the shower of metal splinters resulting from a direct hit on the shield and its instant distortion. It also served to prevent much of the heavy acrid smoke from the gunpowder charge from being blown back into the casemate and it deadened the concussion both of firing and of a direct hit on the shield. It offered some protection from small arms fire and case shot at long ranges. To prevent the rope catching fire from the gun flash the mantlet had to be washed with a saturated solution of calcium chloride and regularly wetted with it during action.

There were variations in the system of hanging and sliding the mantlet in different batteries but the object was the same: to hold them close around the gun in any position and to cover as far as possible the area of the shield.

MAGAZINES
These varied in position according to the size and situation of each battery but the principles were the same.

Complete protection from fire from the sea was given by many feet of earth/rubble/stone in front as laid down in the regulations (later a minimum of 17 feet).

At Bovisand and Picklecombe, and also in different circumstances at Breakwater, the magazines were under the gun casemates and connected to them by shell and cartridge hoists. Cartridge and shell were in separate magazines, one for each pair of guns, and were moved by separate routes until they reached the gun. In the cross passage from the rear (shell) passage and before the door to the cartridge store, was what later became known as the 'shifting lobby' where the ammunition numbers left their boots, matches and anything metallic before putting on their felt shoes and aprons and going through into the cartridge store.

Shell were moved by hand trolley and put into a lifting rack at the hoist (Plate 73). Once on the casemate floor they were moved by trolley to the gun and hoisted to muzzle level by tackle attached to the tubular bar running along the top of the shield. Improved methods were developed later. Cartridge were moved by hand through a hatch, to prevent the possibility of a flashback reaching the magazine, to the hoist and then to the gun. There

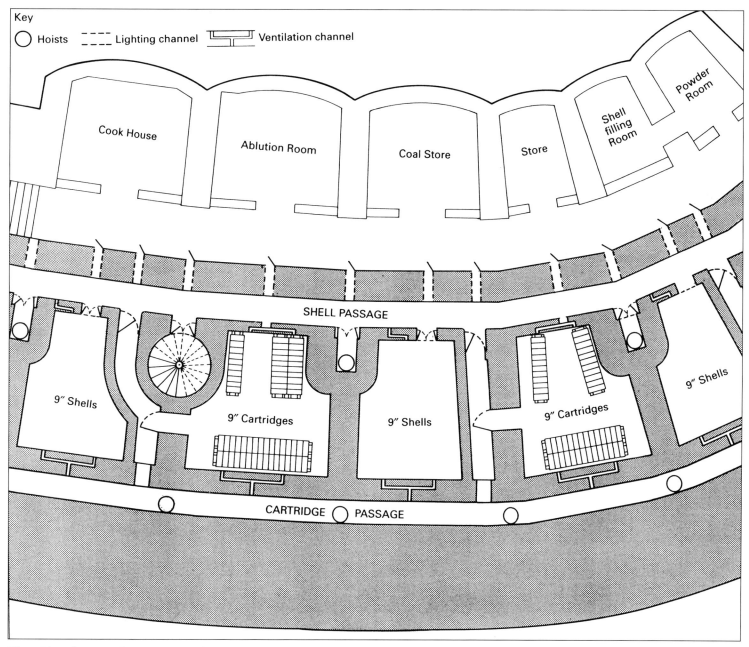

Key

◯ Hoists   - - - - Lighting channel   ⊔⊓ Ventilation channel

Cook House

Ablution Room

Coal Store

Store

Shell filling Room

Powder Room

SHELL PASSAGE

9" Shells

9" Cartridges

9" Shells

9" Cartridges

9" Shells

CARTRIDGE ◯ PASSAGE

Plate 72: *The magazines at Bovisand.* (FROM PRO 600 78/3857)

was a cartridge hoist to each gun and a shell hoist to each pair of guns.

On Drake's Island the magazines were in the rock behind the broad open passageway running behind the casemates. There expense magazines, connected by passages to the main magazines deep in the rock, had doors and hatches onto the passageway, through which shell and cartridge were passed and ferried on munitions trolleys to the various casemates (see Plate 37).

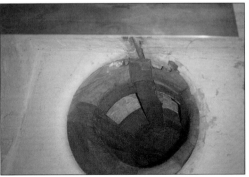

Plate 73a-e: *Details of the magazines at Bovisand Battery* - top left: *cartridge passage;* lower left: *cartridge hoist;* above left: *typical shell trolley* (AUSTIN C. CARPENTER); above right: *exterior lighting passage;* right: *cross passage to cartridge magazine (at left) lit by a lighting recess.* (ALL AUTHOR).

Plate 74: *Garden Battery - above: the casemates* (Author); right: *the water gate* (Ian F. Angus).

At Garden Battery (Plate 74), because it is just above sea level, the magazines are in rear of the casemates and on the same level. Shell and cartridge were moved by trolleys to the casemates. At Cawsand and Polhawn the magazines are in the rock under the batteries.

LIGHTING PASSAGES
(Plate 73)
No naked lights were permitted in the magazines so lighting had to be external and separated from the interior by a fixed plate of glass. The main source of light was from a lighting passage running round or alongside the magazine with places for lamps so designed as to throw light on to the interior of the magazines or onto the passageway and hatches.

The lamps themselves were large lanterns containing two or more thick tallow candles each of a different sizes so that when the smallest burnt out it was replaced by a whole candle and the light was never out.

Although not shown on the original plan of the magazines at Bovisand, in the rear or shell passage there were a series of shafts in the vault of the passageway from which lanterns appear to have been lowered from the walkway behind the casemates to light the shell passage, presumably because the initial lighting system was inadequate. These are now covered over at the top.

References

[1] *Duties of the Corps of Royal Engineers*. New Series. Vol XII 1863. Du Cane p.14
[2] (PRO WO55/1548/23)
[3] *RUSI Journal* Vol.XII 1868, Jervois p.558
[4] Du Cane, Ibid p.19
[5] *Drake's Island* 'Report of a Joint Working Party from the FSG and UK Forts Club' 1978. Foss et al.

APPENDIX D

NOTES ON THE INDIVIDUAL FORTS AND BATTERIES

NOTES

1. Details of the armament of each land fort and battery at certain dates are given after the historical notes. This is mainly to indicate the relative importance of the particular site at the time in the eyes of the committee who allotted the guns available.

The dates refer to different sources of information. The 1869 Report gave the guns the site was designed to mount. The 1875 details are from the first armament table recommended by the Defence Committee on 5.1.1875 (see Appendix B) but there is no indication whether they were ever mounted. The coast defences were not referred to in this table.

The figures for 1885 and 1893 are taken from the detailed armament tables prepared by the Royal Artillery and Royal Engineers Works Committee in those years.[1] The 1885 figures given here are those shown under the column headed 'Mounted'. (In this table alone the position of each group of guns on the site is given). The figures for 1893 are taken from the column 'Mounted or on charge at the station'. Any guns which in 1885 or 1893 were shown as unmounted are marked *.

Details of the armament of the coast batteries are as they were individually known after the 1869 report.

2. Descriptions of the guns are abbreviated as follows:

7-in Armstrong Rifled Breech-Loading (mounted in casemates or in Haxos)	= 7-in RBL
32-pdr or 8-in Smooth-Bore converted to 64-pdr RML, or 64-pdr RML, 64-cwt, built as such	= 64-pdr RML
32-pdr Smooth-Bore converted to breech loading for use in caponiers, (in 1875 referred to simply as SB flank guns)	= 32pdr SB.BL

8-in Rifled Muzzle-Loading Howitzer	= 8-in How
5-in Breech-Loading Gun	= 5-in BL

3. The expression 'musketry' and 'musketry galleries' was used frequently in the report of the 1869 Committee, although rifles were by then in general use, so it is used here.

4. The area now known as Marsh Mills was then the site of the first bridge over the marshes and its contemporary name is used - Longbridge.

AGATON FORT

A minor land fort in the North Eastern Defences with four faces, forming the centre of the western position and covering the valley down to Tamerton Creek to the west. It is flanked by Ernesettle and Knowles batteries. This position was linked to Crownhill Fort to the east by Woodland Fort.

There was one Haxo casemate on the right flank and two mortar batteries, each of 3 mortars, in the NW and East salients. The ditch extends round four faces and was covered by the fire of a large double caponier, with a mini-caponier, in the north salient, a single caponier covering the East face and a counter-scarp gallery covering the west face. There is no ditch along the gorge, which is covered by a musketry gallery.

There were seven expense magazines on the ramparts. The main magazine is under the SE corner of the rampart and there was another magazine opposite the officers' quarters under the curved traverse. Casemates along the gorge provide accommodation for about 60 soldiers. The officers' quarters were in a free-standing building at the gorge.

Designed by Capt Du Cane, the fort was begun in 1863 and completed in 1870-1 at a cost of £41 133.00. Work was begun by George Baker & Co and completed under the Royal Engineers.

Armament:
1869	20 guns (1 in a Haxo), 6 mortars.
1875	15 7-in RBL, 5 8-in hows, 10 SB guns
1885	3 7-in RBL + 7 7-in RBL*
1893	5 64-pdr RML

AUSTIN FORT

A minor land fort in the North Eastern Defences on a spur over-looking Leigham and Marsh Mills and forming the right flank of an arrow-shaped position with Forder Battery in the centre and Bowden Battery on the left.

The three faces are surrounded by a ditch which is covered by counterscarp galleries, (with gun casemates and musketry galleries according to the 1869 report), in the east and NE salients linked to the fort by a single tunnel. Beyond the ditch is a further scarp cut in the hillside and facing NE. Unusually, the gorge is protected by a ditch, the North part of which is the end of the main ditch which also covers the front of Bowden and Forder. A large central guardhouse in the gorge covers the ditch on either side with two tiers of guns and musketry. There are three mortar battery positions in the south, east and NW salients.

In the guardhouse is accommodation for about 60 men with a reserve magazine below.

Designed by Capt Du Cane, the fort was begun in 1863 and finished in 1869-70 at a cost of £20 607.00. Construction was started by George Baker & Co and completed under the Royal Engineers.

Armament:	1869	15 guns, 5 mortars
	1875	10 7-in RBL, 10 8-in Hows, 4 SB flank guns
	1885	None in position, 5 7-in RBL*, 3 8-in Hows*
	1893	4 64-pdr RML

BOVISAND BATTERY

A large granite casemated coast battery covering the eastern entrance to the Sound, designed for 50 guns in two tiers in 1861, with a large detached magazine in rear. Re-designed in 1864 for RML guns in a single tier of 23 guns, which were to have iron shields and magazines below. There was much discussion in the 1869 committee about the layout and lighting of the magazines whose hatches and cartridge lifts were modified as a result.

Designed by Major Porter. Built by Geo. Baker & Co at a final cost of £58 264.00, excluding the iron shields, and completed by the Royal Engineers in 1869.

Armament:	1872	1 10-in RML, 22 9-in
	1880	13 10-in RML, 9 9-in RML
	1885	13 10-in RML, 9 9-in RML
	1893	14 10-in RML, 8 9-in RML, 6 6-pdr QF*

BOWDEN BATTERY

A land battery in the North Eastern Defences forming the West flank of the Bowden–Forder–Austin position and covering the upper part of Forder Valley. It is 1200 metres from Crownhill Fort to the west, and is surrounded by a ditch on three faces and at the gorge. The ditch on the north face continues across to Forder Battery and is partly covered by its double caponier - as far west as Forder Hill Bridge. The ditches on the three faces are covered by a double 'flanking gallery' at the NE salient and a single one at the NW salient. Neither gallery has gun embrasures. The gorge on the other hand is covered by a small guardhouse with a magazine under and with single gun embrasures on two levels on each flank. The two mortar battery positions are in the NE and west salients.

This was probably the last of the batteries to be completed and was the cheapest. Money seems to have been saved by not building proper caponiers with gun embrasures. On the other hand the battery has natural advantages. The slope of the glacis to the north is about 1 in 3 and the scarp on the north face, due to this, rises as much as 45 feet from the bottom of the ditch.

Designed by Capt Du Cane, it was begun in about 1864 and not finished until about 1872, at a cost of £15 891.00. Construction was started by George Baker & Co and completed under the Royal Engineers.

Armament:	1869	12 guns, 3 mortars
	1875	8 7-in RBL, 4 8-in Hows, 2 SB flank guns
	1885	1 7-in RBL*
	1893	4 64-pdr RML, 2 7-in RBL

BREAKWATER FORT

A sea fort behind the centre of the Breakwater to cover the gap between Bovisand and Picklecombe. The first design in 1860 was for a granite fort with 4 floors and two tiers of gun casemates. The foundations laid in June 1862 were swept away within two months by an August gale. Work began again in March 1863. Later tests showed that only an iron structure could withstand the fire of the heavier guns being developed and work did not go beyond the foundations until 1866 when it was redesigned with two floors: one tier of guns surrounded by an iron shield nearly 3 feet thick and magazines below.

The 1866 design included two turrets on top of the ironwork, mounting 'four of the largest guns', and 17 guns in casemates. Eventually the turrets were omitted and the approved armament in 1874 was:

14 12.5-in RML
4 10-in RML

The first 12.5-in RML was mounted in 1879 and the fort was fully armed by 1880. The 10-in guns faced the inner waters of the Sound.

The shield round the upper tier had been built with small 'ports' (embrasures) in anticipation of the development of muzzle-pivoting or 'small port' carriages which pivoted about the muzzle when elevated or depressed. This was one cause of delay in arming the fort.

In 1885 it was decided to remove alternate 12.5-in guns as they were too crowded and replace them with 6-pdr QF guns.

Designed by Capt Siborne. The main contractor was Henry Lea & Sons of London and the ironwork was by the Millwall Iron Co. The final cost was estimated in 1869 as £167 062, or £12 000 over the original estimate.

BROWNHILL BATTERY

A subsidiary land battery on Staddon Heights, the second of the two works recommended by the Royal Commission to hold the Heights. It stands above the valley down to Bovisand Bay, with its glacis running down to the scarp from Staddon to Bovisand, and covers the ridge beyond to Down Thomas. There are five faces protected by only a narrow ditch. The gorge has a loop-holed wall at its more exposed south end with musketry loops angled to the south and covering the gap between it and Watch House Brake Battery. There was originally no accommodation and only four bomb-proof traverses containing expense magazines in the ramparts.

From the 1880s onwards the expense magazines were used to store guncotton for the Bovisand submarine mining system. Designed by Capt. Du Cane. Built by George Baker & Co? Cost included in figure for Brownhill - Watch House Brake position of £25 768.

Armament: 1869   13 guns
            1875   8 64-pdr RML
            1885   Nil
            1893   6 8-in Hows

CAWSAND FORT

Begun before 1860 as a minor coast battery to cover Cawsand Bay, it was extended in the rear to provide a defence against a surprise landing on Whitsand Bay designed to turn the defences of Cawsand and so open up the best landing beach in the Sound. In evidence to the 1869 report it was said to have 13 guns, 9 facing the sea and four towards the land. In the report itself these were described as 68-pdrs, 8-in guns and 7-in RBLs.

On three faces its scarp walls are reinforced by the steep sides of the spur between the villages of Kingsand and Cawsand on which it stands. The NW face, overlooked by Wringford Down, is covered by a narrow ditch in which there is a small bastion with rifle loops towards the north and caponiers/demi-bastions at either end. There were quarters for officers and about 80 soldiers.

Its designer is not known; it could have been Major Porter who designed the main coast batteries, or Capt Du Cane who was responsible for finishing Tregantle and designing Polhawn. Begun before 1860, it was finished by 1863 at cost of £16 171.00. The name of the contractor is not known.

Armament: 1869   13 guns
            1885   9 64/32 pdr RML, 4 8-in SB guns
            1893   9 64-pdr RML

CROWNHILL FORT

This is the principal land fort in the North Eastern Defences, standing in the centre and 400 metres in advance of the general line. It is built on a knoll, formerly known as Knackers Knowle, which not only commands in front the saddle across which runs the main approach road to Plymouth from the North but also the two valleys running east and west down to Longbridge and Tamerton Creek respectively. General Todleben in 1864 described its position as 'magnificent' and the 1869 Committee called it 'the key of the North Eastern Defences'.

Because of its exposed position it was designed for all-round defence to an extent unlike that of any other fort in the defences, being roughly circular with seven faces, all with ramparts. The ditch around it is excavated from solid rock and is covered by one double and five single caponiers with two guns covering each section of the ditch supported by rifle galleries above and below as well as on the scarp.

There is a covered way round the top of the counterscarp. Round the scarp is a *chemin des rondes* which on the north and NE faces is covered over to form a gallery. Opposite the double caponier which is protected on its front faces by a small double musketry gallery, or 'mini' caponier, is a tunnel half way up the counterscarp leading to the Plymouth and Devonport leats which pass under the northern glacis. On the east rampart is a double Haxo casemate open at the rear and there are four more single

Haxos facing SE and SW. Some time after 1870 two emplacements were built on the east and NW salients for Moncrieff pattern disappearing mountings for 7-in RBL guns. There are two mortar batteries in the NW and SW salients approached by tunnels under the ramparts, in which are magazines. In 1880 the SE caponier was used for gun drill trials in connection with the introduction of the 32-pdr SB.BL.

There was bomb-proof accommodation in two ranges of casemates for officers and 300 men. There is a gun shed for the moveable armament on field carriages, allotted to the sector from Crownhill to Ernesettle, and a stable. Some of these could be used to reinforce the guns of the fort, particularly on the rampart facing south overlooking the gate where there are no permanent gun emplacements but the rampart has a low parapet.

The large main magazine is in the north rampart and there are six bomb-proof expense magazines on the ramparts. The four individual Haxos have magazines under them from which shells were raised by davits and cartridges by lifts.

The fort has been in continuous use by the Army since it was built. From 1899 until after WWI it was the depot of the Royal Garrison Artillery for the Western District and its successors, and also a barracks for an infantry battalion from time to time. In WWII it became a local defence strongpoint, and an AA Gun Operations Room and Garrison HQ afterwards.

Designed by Capt Du Cane, it was begun by George Baker & Co in about 1864 and completed in 1872 under the Royal Engineers at a cost of £76 409.00.

Armament:	1869	32 guns, 6 mortars
	1875	23 7-in RBL, 6 8-in Hows, 15 SB flank guns
	1885	13 7-in RBL, 14 32-pdr SB.BL, 2 6.6-in Hows*, 2 8-in Hows*, 8 7-in RBL*
	1893	5 64-pdr RML, 11 7-in RBL, 14 32-pdr SB.BL, 6 25-pdr RML

DEER PARK EMPLACEMENT

This was an earthwork gun position for emergency use covering the re-entrant leading from Longbridge and running behind Efford Fort to the high ground that dominates the Efford/Laira position.

1869	5 guns
1875	4 64-pdr RML
1885	Nil

No guns appear to have been permanently mounted here. They would have been supplied from the moveable armament in Efford Fort.

DRAKE'S ISLAND

The large casemated battery on the Island was the pivot of the Inner Line of sea defences of the Sound, covering from South through East to NNW. Begun in 1860, the casemates were probably completed by about 1864 apart from the iron shields, and were temporarily armed with 68-pdr SB guns. In 1868 it was proposed to mount 5 23-ton guns on the existing Upper Battery and it was recommended that the two left casemates (20 and 21) should be converted into an artillery store.

The main magazine (see Plate 37) on the north side of the Island is cut into the rock and is linked to the line of expense magazines by tunnels to either end of them and to the tunnel which runs immediately behind them. These expense magazines have hatches opening on to the wide open passageway running behind the line of casemates. From the hatches shells and cartridges were carried on trolleys to the casemates.

The 1869 report referred to the need to complete a fourth expense magazine and to give them all more protection against plunging fire. The expense magazines for the Upper Battery are connected to the main magazine system below by lifts and hoists in two places.

There was already adequate accommodation on the island for gunners in the barrack block, and for officers and the master-gunner in the Commanding Officers House.

Designed by Major Porter, the main battery was begun in 1860 and completed about 1864 at a cost, apart from the iron shields, of £34,808. The contractor is not known.

Armament	1869	21 9-in RML
	1885	Upper Battery - 2 12-in RML, 3 11-in RML Casemated Battery - 13 9-in RML
	1893	as above

EASTERN KING

The limestone redoubt built in 1849 was improved as a minor coast battery by the addition of earthwork gun positions - 4 on the east flank and 3 on the west - and underground magazines. The work was begun at the end of 1860 and completed by 1863. The guns mounted were originally 68-pdrs but by 1885 a total of 17 64-pdr RMLs were mounted on the old redoubt and the new battery. This was reduced to 7 64-pdrs, on the new battery only, in 1893.

EFFORD EMPLACEMENT
The gap of 400 metres between Efford Fort and Laira Battery where there is a re-entrant and the approach is less steep, was covered by a ditch flanked by two guns in a flanking gallery approached by the tunnel running down from Efford past the five Haxo casemates (see Plate 28 and below). This ditch joined the ditch covering the gorge at Efford Fort. Overlooking the ditch were earthwork emplacements for 4, later 6, guns.

Armament	1869	4 guns
	1875	4 64-pdr RML
	1885	Nil
	1893	2 64-pdr RML, 6 8-in Hows*

EFFORD FORT
This land fort, 1200 metres south of Austin Fort, was built on the spur which overlooks Longbridge and the approaches from there into Plymouth ie, to the west and NW up Forder Valley and Hartley Vale, and to the SW by the road via Crabtree and the Embankment. Owing to its position on a steep-sided spur it is an irregular shape with five faces, and it relies partly on the steepness of the natural scarps for protection, with a ditch where this is practicable. The gorge is protected by a 20 feet high loopholed wall and covered by a ditch and a substantial defensible guard-room with gun embrasures in two tiers. The SE casemates are in a traverse which includes the main magazine.

The three Haxo casemates on the ramparts are connected by lifts to magazines below and in the natural scarp below the rampart to the SSE are five more Haxo casemates approached by a sloping tunnel which leads towards Efford Emplacement below (see Plate 28). The tunnel goes further down to a series of caponiers and rifle galleries covering the vulnerable re-entrant to the south of the fort (for details see *The Historic Defences of Plymouth.* pp. 186-7). The 1869 committee commented that the left flank of the fort was liable to enemy fire from the high ground to its rear and recommended that a further traverse be built.

There is accommodation for a total of 108 officers and men, the latter in a double row of bomb-proof casemates facing each other and probably built later than the ramparts. There is also a shed for moveable armament for the Crownhill-Laira sector.

Designed by Capt Du Cane, the fort was begun after the rest of the North Eastern Defences in about 1864-5 and completed about 1870 at a cost of £50 403. The contractor was George Baker & Co and it was finished under the Royal Engineers.

Armament:	1869	21 guns in fort, 5 in Haxos below
	1875	19 7-in RBL, 5 64-pdr RML, 3 SB flank guns
	1885	6 7-in RBL, 5 7-in RBL*
	1893	2 5-in BL, 3 64-pdr RML, 9 7-in RBL

EGGBUCKLAND KEEP
This unusual two-storied fortified barracks is said to be the last 'keep' built in Britain. It stands on the higher ground behind the Bowden–Forder–Austin position and denies it to an enemy. It housed the garrison for Forder Battery with which it was connected by a tunnel. It also housed the major part of the garrison for Bowden and Austin, together with the reserve of ammunition for the entire position. It is surrounded by a ditch and the five sections of this, including the gorge, are covered by musketry galleries in small caponiers - one double one in the north salient and three single ones.

The casemated barracks inside has accommodation for 230 men. It was probably begun after most of the North Eastern Defences, owing to the various changes of plan, and finished in 1872. In 1875, five 7-in RBLS were recommended but by 1885 it remained unarmed.

Designed by Capt Du Cane, it was started by George Baker & Co and completed under the Royal Engineers at a cost of £14 642.

ERNESETTLE BATTERY
This land battery forms the left flank of the North Eastern Defences and overlooks the Hamoaze. Standing on a spur it has four faces protected by a ditch which is covered by flanking rifle galleries. The gorge is angled and in two sections. The entrance section facing SW is protected by a ditch and covered by a rifle gallery, the other facing south has a flanking gallery but no ditch. Both are overlooked by a 30ft high loopholed wall. Unusually, it has a casemated mortar battery in the NW salient covering both the ground sloping down in front and the estuary itself.

There is a casemated barracks for 60 men. Three large traverses on the ramparts enclose expense magazines. The detached bomb-proof main magazine near the centre of the gorge was an improvement following the 1869 report.

Designed by Capt Du Cane, the battery was begun about 1863 by George Baker & Co and completed under the Royal Engineers in 1868 at a cost of £17 630.

Armament: 1869 15 guns, 6 mortars
1875 8 7-in RBL, 2 8-in Hows
1885 2 7-in RBL
1893 3 64-pdr RML, 2 5-in BL

FORDER BATTERY

A land battery forming the salient of the Bowden–Forder–Austin position, it covers the Forder valley and across to Estover. Of the five faces, only the principal ones facing north and NE are covered by a ditch which extends on either side as far as Bowden and Austin respectively. There was no wall at the gorge separating the battery from the military road. Entrance to the battery was from the military road or through a tunnel from Eggbuckland Keep. This continued on to the large counterscarp gallery (or 'reverse caponier') with casemates for four guns in two tiers in the salient of the ditch, which covered both arms of the ditch. In emergency the whole of the terreplein of the battery could be swept by fire from Eggbuckland Keep.

Designed by Capt Du Cane, the battery was begun in about 1863 by George Baker & Co and not finished until about 1871 under the Royal Engineers, at a cost of £16 443.

Armament: 1869 16 guns
1875 12 7-in RBL, 6 SB flank guns
1885 Nil, 6 7-in RBL*
1893 4 64-pdr RML, 1 7-in RBL,
2 32-pdr SB.BL

GARDEN BATTERY (Plate 73)

The smallest of the casemated coast batteries, its 7 guns covered the channel between Drake's Island and Western King. Because of its low site near the water's edge the magazines are on the same level as, and in rear of, the battery. The 1869 committee did not consider them secure against frontal fire and they were modified. Designed by Major Porter the battery was begun in 1862 and finished in 1863. The total cost, apart from the shields but including the later modification to the magazines, was £9 702.

Armament: 1869 7 68-pdr SB
1885 7 9-in RML
1893 4 64-pdr RML*, 3 6-pdr QF*

KNOWLES BATTERY

A small land battery in the North Eastern Defences on a spur between Agaton and Woodland, it covers a re-entrant out of sight of either. Of its three faces the NNE and NNW were protected by a scarp and wide ditch extending beyond the battery to the west. There is no flank defence for the ditch which is designed to be enfiladed by the guns of the forts on either side. The fire of the east face covers the re-entrant. The angled gorge is protected by a 30ft high loopholed wall and the entrance was flanked by gun and musketry fire from the large two-storied guardhouse which contains the main magazine.

There were three expense magazines in traverses on the ramparts and one Haxo casemate.

Designed by Capt Du Cane, the battery was begun about 1863 by George Baker & Co an.d completed under the Royal Engineers about 1870 at a cost of £19,562.

Armament: 1869 13 guns
1875 9 7-in RBL, 3 SB flank guns
1885 1 7-in RBL, 3-7-in RBL*
1893 3 64-pdr RML, 2 7-in RBL

LAIRA BATTERY

A small land battery on a spur on the extreme right of the North Eastern Defences, it covers the approach to Plymouth from Longbridge via Crabtree. There was a ditch on the north and NE faces and from east round to south it was protected by a scarp. The gorge is closed by a wall and is enfiladed by the fire of Efford. The south face which has an unusual triple Haxo emplacement is enfiladed by Laira Emplacement which stands above and behind the battery. There was accommodation for 2 officers and 30 men in casemated barracks.

Designed by Capt Du Cane, the battery was begun after the rest of the North Eastern Defences in about 1865, by George Baker & Co, and completed about 1871 under the Royal Engineers at a cost of £16 805.

Armament: 1869 13 guns
1875 11 7-in RBL, 2 SB flank guns
1885 3 7-in RBL, 5 7-in RBL*
1893 3 7-in RBL, 2 64-pdr RML

LAIRA EMPLACEMENT

A small L-shaped earthwork battery facing east and south on the high ground west of Laira Battery and overlooking it. There were two expense magazines for the gun emplacements. Two of these face east covering the right of Laira Battery and four south over the Laira estuary and beyond.

Armament: 1869   6 guns
             1875   6 64-pdr RML
             1885   Nil
             1895   4 8-in Hows

PICKLECOMBE BATTERY
The 1869 report describes it as 'designed in 1860 as a granite case-mated battery for 42 68- and 110-pdrs in two tiers, and 16 guns on the platform, all protected by iron shields, with a large detached magazine in rear. It was re-modelled in 1864: the magazines were removed to the basement under the gun case-mates, the two tiers of guns were retained, but the guns on the platform were given up. It is now intended to mount 42 12- and 18-ton guns, (9- and 10-in RML), protected by iron shields, which also cover the vertical space between each casemate.' Concern was expressed by the Committee about the effect of the concussion of guns firing above or below the men while loading in view of the arrangement of the shields.

The magazine arrangements were similar to those at Bovisand and the same comments were made on them by the Committee. The limestone barracks behind the battery, completed in 1848, was used as accommodation.

The battery was designed by Major Porter and the cost, excluding shields, was £80 876. It was built by Hubbard & Co and appears to have been finished about 1866. The first 6 10-in, 18-ton, RML guns were mounted in 1871 and the shields were installed in 1872-3. The first firing trials of a casemated battery with iron shields were carried out here on 27-28 November 1872.

Armament: 1869   42 9-in and 10-in RMLs
             1885   4 7-in RML, 14 9-in RML, 18 10-in RML
             1893   as above, plus 6 6-pdr QF*

POLHAWN BATTERY
A small self-contained casemated coast battery built of stone in an isolated position below Rame Head. It covers Whitsand Bay to the west. Because of the possibility of landings, even if only raids, in Whitsand Bay and the fact that it is built into the steep, scrub-covered slope of Rame Head, it was designed as a small self-contained fort with a narrow ditch. This is covered by fire from rifle galleries, including two small 'caponiers', a double one covering the south face and a single one covering the west.

Its features include a murder hole covering the rifle gallery on the east flank and an unusual drawbridge which gives access to

the battery at roof level and has a quick-release mechanism. This drawbridge has recently been restored (see Plate 34).

The 1869 Committee commented that Polhawn needed re-modelling if it was to mount the heavier guns by then considered necessary to oppose ironclad warships; this was never done. Without the battery originally proposed on Knatterbury Hill whose fire would have covered its SW flank, Polhawn was vulnerable to bombardment from the open sea.

The magazines are under the gun casemates and there is accommodation for the garrison.

Designed by Captain Du Cane, it was begun in 1861 and completed about 1864 at a cost of £8850. The contractor may have been F. Roach & Co of Plymouth who built Scraesdon.

Armament: 1869   7 68-pdr BL
             1885   7 64-pdr RML
             1893   7 64-pdr RML

SCRAESDON FORT
A large fort of irregular shape built on Berry Hill near the village of Antony, it forms the north end of the Western Defences which were earlier known as the Antony Position. The main, or upper fort, has four short faces with casemates under and covers the likely enemy approach from the west round to the ESE. The lower part of the fort overlooks the Lynher estuary to the north and the high ground beyond. On the north side of the main fort is a long line of casemates bombproofed on the north side and forming a traverse from which the ground falls away sharply to the north so that the lower fort is some 80ft below.

The original design involved the construction of 'an interior enclosed keep within the work on the upper level, to be formed by a range of casemated buildings with parapet on top running completely around and parallel to the exterior sides...' (as quoted in 1869). This idea was abandoned and so was the 1869 Committee's recommendation of a massive traverse across the interior of the upper parade to cover the line of casemates to the North of it and the entrance to the main magazine.

The fort is entirely surrounded by a ditch covered by a double caponier, with a mini-caponier, and five single caponiers. These have two guns in each of two tiers except on the relatively inaccessible faces of the lower fort. The ditch round the latter slopes steeply down to the north and is covered by a high loopholed scarp gallery of massive construction due to the steep and rocky nature of the position. There are two Moncrieff emplacements in the west and SW salients of the upper fort and a triple Haxo casemate in the lower fort facing north whose guns cover the high ground north of the Lynher.

There is ample accommodation for a large garrison in the casemates, and there is accommodation for officers in the massive gatehouse which has gun embrasures on the roof and whose entrance is covered from either flank by musketry fire.

Designed by Capt. Crossman, construction was begun early in 1859 by F. Roach & Co of Plymouth and was largely completed by 1868. The total cost was £137 411, above the original estimate due to the cost of the scarp galleries which Col. Westmacott, Commanding Royal Engineers Western District, thought unnecessary (1869 Report).

For a detailed description of this unusual fort, see *The Historic Defences of Plymouth* pp 84-87.

Armament:	1869	57 guns
	1875	25 7-in RBL, 6 8-in Hows, 10 SB flank guns
	1885	5 7-in RBL, 19 7-in RBL* 2 8-in Hows*
	1893	8 7-in RBL, 1 64-pdr RML, 2 5-in BL, 2 32-pdr SB.BL

STADDON FORT

This was the major land fort facing east at the centre of the Staddon Position, which covered with its guns both Staddon Heights to the south and round to the north as far as the Kingsbridge–Laira road. It is linked to Stamford and Watch House by a military road and from the fort to the south runs the 20ft high scarp to Brownhill, Watch House and Bovisand.

It was originally designed with a self-contained hexagonal keep which was omitted due to its cost (£52 000). The west half of the design of the hexagonal keep exists around the gate, the other half being closed off by a large parados. The fort is surrounded by a ditch and a *chemin des rondes* except around the projecting and heavily defended gateway which was covered by gun and musketry fire as well as by machicolations and two murder holes above.

The two long principal faces to the east have rifle galleries over the scarp and there are rifle galleries round the recessed gateway. There is a double caponier, with a mini-caponier, in the east salient and a single one on either flank covering short faces, all with two tiers each of two guns. The west faces are covered by guns and musketry in the angles of the scarp. In the ditch on either flank are stone steps up the counterscarp which can be broken halfway up by the removal of a pin in a platform.

The original armament was 16 guns on the terreplein, 12 on the keep where there are embrasures on the top, 6 in haxo casemates and 6 mortars. The latter were in arched casemates behind the double caponier facing East. Two Moncrieff emplacements were added later.

There is ample accommodation for officers around the gateway and for 250 soldiers in three lots of casemated barracks.

Designed by Capt. Du Cane, building began by George Roach & Co of Plymouth in about 1861 and it was completed 1869 at a cost of £112 844.

Armament:	1869	34 guns, 6 mortars
	1875	25 7-in RBL, 2 64-pdr RML, 4 8-in Hows, 30 SB BL flank guns
	1885	2 7-in RBL, 2 8-in hows*, 10 7-in RBL*
	1893	6 7-in RBL (2*), 5 64-pdr RML, 2 5-in BL, 8 32-pdr SB.BL, 2 machine guns

STAMFORD FORT

A five-sided land fort forming the left or northern flank of the Staddon Position, it covered the dead ground below and north of Staddon as well as being able to cover in a coast defence role Jennycliff Bay to the SW. It is entirely surrounded by a ditch covered by a *chemin des rondes* and the fire of a double and two single caponiers, all with two tiers each of two guns. The remaining side which includes the gate is covered by a counterscarp gallery.

The armament was originally to include 7 9-in RMLs facing west in a coast defence role. This was revised in 1877 when 2 10-in RMLs were recommended by the Defence Committee for the SW face to cover Jennicliff Bay. There were two mortar batteries in the east and SW salients. Later a Moncrieff emplacement was added facing east.

The substantial barracks on two floors facing north had ample accommodation for officers and 200 men as well as soldiers' families. It was bomb-proofed on the interior, or SE side. There was also a large central traverse to protect the interior, and the guns firing west and south, from fire from the high ground to the east.

Designed by Capt Du Cane, it was begun in 1861-2 and completed about 1870 at a cost of £70 359. It may have also been built by F. Roach & Co of Plymouth who built Staddon Fort.

| Armament: | 1869 | 20 guns, 6 mortars |
| | 1875 | 5 7-in RBL, 4 64-pdr RML, 3 8-in Hows, 16 SB flank guns |

1885	1 7-in RBL, 2 10-in RML,
	4 7-in RBL*, 1 8-in How*,
	3 64/32-pdr RML*
1893	1 7-in RBL, 2 10-in RML, 5 64-pdr RML

TREGANTLE FORT

This is the largest land fort in the Plymouth defences. It stands on the left flank of the Western Defences on high ground overlooking Whitsand Bay and covers most of the ground towards Scraesdon to the north. It has the only self-contained keep in a fort in the Plymouth Defences, surrounded by a ditch with a counterscarp gallery and with the main magazine under it.

Begun in 1859 it was the first of the major forts to be designed and displays elementary features which had been improved upon by the time Crownhill was built. For example, the ramparts with their Haxos stand out in clear silhouette from the west and NW and there is much stonework exposed to direct enemy fire (especially the embrasures in the keep remarked upon by General Todleben). The double caponier in the north-west salient consists of two single caponiers set at an angle like donkeys' ears so that of the 16 gun embrasures half point at the opposite caponier or at the counterscarp wall no more than 100 feet away. There was a proposal at one stage to build a redan to the north west, covering the double caponier, but this was never carried out.

The five landward faces are protected by a ditch and covered by a double and three single caponiers. The face in which the gate stands is covered by a musketry gallery in the ditch and the two outer faces of the keep are covered by rifle galleries in the ditch and in the counterscarp, linked to the keep and the guardhouse by a system of tunnels. The south face, towards the sea, is recessed so that flanking galleries in the barrack block which constitutes this face cover it with fire.

The ramparts incorporate two Haxos open to the rear and two Moncrieff emplacements added later. The barbette gun emplacements are of varied design and some have been modified from the original simple V-shaped embrasures with granite blocks in their inner angles which were condemned by the 1869 Committee. The important NW face of the ramparts covering the gap in the position across to Scraesdon has been angled in two places to make it saw-toothed (crémaillère) to provide more fire on the gap. The triangular 'garden' (so called) created by this is covered by fire from musketry galleries in the ramparts. There are substantial traverses in the ramparts on the NW and west faces, containing expense magazines.

The 1869 committee reported that a number of changes had been incorporated in the design and others were recommended. In evidence it was pointed out that the keep was set so far back from the rampart to the West - the direction of attack - that it was vulnerable to shot and shell coming over the rampart.

The large two-tiered casemated barracks for 2000 men along the SSE face, is partly covered from horizontal fire from the NW by a traverse across the interior of the fort. There is accommodation for officers south of the gate.

The barracks presents its 45ft high face to the sea 360 ft below and could in theory be fired on from there, though not with the guns and carriages of the early 1860s. The 1869 Committee recommended that a heavy coast battery be built to counter this possibility. The SW face was later re-built incorporating a line of 5 casemates open to the rear covering the bay, and one to the left and below firing down a ditch running to the sea.

The fort was completed by 1865. The 1869 Committee refers to variations made in the original design, including the omission of a small advanced work in front of the salient (to the west). The total cost of the work was £189 999 including minor alterations recommended in 1869 (magazines were damp) but excluding the coast battery added later. This is the most costly work built under the 1860 programme.

The original design was by Capt Crossman, later modified by Capt Du Cane, and the fort was built by Messrs Kirk & Parry. In 1886 trials were carried out in the fort with the 32-pdr SB.BL gun.

Armament:	1869	35 guns, excluding those for the defence of the ditch.
	1875	22 7-in RBL, 13 64-pdr RML, 5 8-in Hows, 24 SB flank guns
	1885	7 7-in RBL, 6 64-pdr RML (coast), 10 8-in SB guns
		15 7-in RBL*, 7 64-pdr*, 4 8-in SB guns*
	1893	5 7-in RBL, 10 64-pdr RML, 6 64-pdr RML (coast)

TWELVE ACRE BRAKE BATTERY

This small earthwork land battery in the Staddon Position covered the ditch running east-west to the south of it. It was begun about 1864 and completed presumably within a short time. There were emplacements for 3 guns and an expense magazine.

Armament:	1869	3 guns
	1875	1 SB flank gun
	1885	1 32-pdr SB*

1892 Re-named Frobisher Battery and
rebuilt.

WATCH HOUSE BRAKE BATTERY

A small pentagonal earthwork redoubt built on the high point which overlooks Bovisand Battery and enfilades the scarp and ditch running east-west and the ditch running South down to Bovisand.

It was begun about 1864 and completed presumably within about a year.

There were emplacements for five guns and an expense magazine.

Armament: 1869 3 guns
1875 3 64-pdr RML
1885 Nil
1893 2 64-pdr RML

WESTERN KING BATTERY

An earthwork open coast battery was added to the existing redoubt here in 1861-2 in the form of five emplacements facing SE and four facing South, together with expense magazines.

Armament: 1869 9 guns
1885 12 64-pdr RML (including 3 in the old redoubt)
1893 9 64-pdr RML

WOODLAND FORT

A minor land fort in the North Eastern Defences between Crownhill and Knowles, it covers the gap between the western group, based on Agaton, and Crownhill 1700 metres to the East.

Its four faces were entirely surrounded by a ditch which was covered by a caponier in the west face and a substantial L-shaped counterscarp gallery covered the North and East faces with gun and musketry fire. A small fortified guard house in the middle of the gorge covered the South section of the ditch with musketry fire.

On the ramparts are two Haxo casemates, one on either flank. Three traverses house expense magazines and there is a main magazine under the north rampart. A casemated barracks under the north rampart provides accommodation for 100 men.

Designed by Capt Du Cane, the fort was begun about 1863 by George Baker & Co and completed under the Royal Engineers in about 1870 at a cost of £27 973.

Armament: 1869 18 guns
1875 12 7-in RBL, 6 SB flank guns
1885 1 7-in RBL, 7 7-in RBL*
1893 3 64-pdr RML, 2 7-in RBL (in Haxos), 2 7-in RBL*

References

[1] (PRO WO33/2772)

APPENDIX E

FINANCE

After the layout of the land defences had been settled and plans for the North Eastern Defences approved in the spring of 1863, work was going ahead on all the works by 1864. The main problem from then onwards was control of the expenditure. In the Fortification Act of 7 August 1862 a schedule gave the estimated expenditure on land and works for each fort and battery at Plymouth and elsewhere, the money expended so far and the authorised expenditure for the next twelve months. The exception was the North Eastern Defences whose plans had not by then been approved. An overall figure - £350 000 - was given for works in this sector.

Successive Acts in the years 1963, 1864 and 1865 brought the expenditure figures up-to-date, authorised the raising of more funds and detailed their expenditure. These schedules showed in the final column the amount required to complete the work.

As a result of Jervois' progress report in February 1867, the Act of 31 May 1867 revised the original estimates of the cost of each work. The individual figures for Breakwater and Picklecombe were increased by £10 000 and £7000 respectively. Each other sector of the defences was bracketed to show an overall figure equivalent to the previous individual totals, except at Maker where the new total was reduced from £35 000 to £15 000 as a result of the decision to omit the works at Maker Barracks. Significantly, the original figure for the North Eastern Defences was now bracketed with that for the Staddon Position.

The report of 1869 on 'the construction, condition and cost' of the fortifications built under the Defence Loan gave the latest expenditure figures and the committee's estimates of the cost of completing the individual works. These figures were the basis of the final Act of 9 August 1869.

The following table gives the original 1862 estimate (Column 1), the estimate of total cost from the 1869 report (2) and how much of each work was covered by the Defence Loan (3). Considerable work had already been done on the Western Defences by 1862 and the cost of this is shown to the right. By 1865 the decision had been taken to modify the casemates of the coast batteries to take iron shields and by 1867 the final pattern had been approved. The cost of the iron shields and their installation was also additional to expenditure under the Defence Loan (Column 4). However the building of the three military roads was covered within the Loan estimates and this is also shown to the right of Column 3.

The varying rates of progress in the different sectors become apparent from the reports of expenditure in the various Acts. The Western Defences went steadily ahead until 1865 but the Staddon Position did not progress rapidly until 1863-65. More than half the work at Picklecombe and Bovisand was not done until after 1865. As for the North Eastern Defences, only £2035 had been paid for by March 1964, though the work went ahead rapidly in the next twelve months and thereafter.

The eventual cost of the various works as given in the table show some interesting comparisons. Tregantle was the first of the principal forts to be completed. It exceeded its original estimate and altogether cost nearly £190 000. Even allowing for the cost of the keep which can be estimated at £40 000–50 000 (it was smaller than the one designed for Staddon) and of the large barracks for 2000 men, it cost about 1.5 times that of Crownhill Fort with much the same area.

Tregantle also shows similarities to the design of the 1847-9 works - too much stonework shows - but it was begun before the effect of rifled guns had been fully appreciated. By the time Crownhill came to be completed, ditches had become narrower and all accommodation was in bomb-proof casemates. Above all, Crownhill is almost invisible from the north and no stonework offers a target apart from the revetments of the embrasures of the Haxos. Built in the light of experience and by direct labour it represents value for money.

In spite of the increase in the number of works in the North Eastern Defences, following the re-alignment of the original position and the building of the military road, the total cost was £322 581 as compared with the original estimate of £350 000. In 1867 this latter figure was combined with the figure for the Staddon Position which was overrunning its estimate, due partly to an overspend of nearly £20 000 on Staddon Fort and also to the cost of the minor works: the military road and the scarp linking Staddon to Bovisand. The final excess here of over £40 000 was partly balanced by the saving on the North Eastern Defences, leaving an eventual excess of £13 000. This and the overspend on the Outer Sea Defences of £9000 was balanced by the saving of over £20 000 on Maker Heights (Maker Barracks and Knatterbury were not built).

DETAILED NOTES ON THE FIGURES BELOW

1. Column (1) below gives the estimates of the cost of individual works shown in the schedule attached to the Fortification Act, 7 August 1862. Although the figures in the schedule are headed 'Estimated cost of works and Land' an overall figure for the cost of Lands is added in at the end of the total cost of all the works under the Defence Loan. This figure is roughly 18 per cent of the cost of the works. There is no way of knowing the estimated cost of the land required at Plymouth other than the figure of £200 000 quoted for the North Eastern Defences. The eventual cost is shown below.

2. Column (2) shows the total cost of each work - work done plus an estimate of the cost of completion - given in the Report of 1869. This figure includes any expenditure on the work before the Defence Loan was passed, covered by earlier Annual Votes. It also includes the cost of shields in the case of the four casemated coast batteries. Where column (3) plus column (4) does not equal column (2) the difference is due to additional expenditure on modifications authorised after the completion of the work and covered by the Annual Fortification Votes.

3. The cost of the military roads was treated in various ways in the figures. For the Western Defences the cost is included in the totals. On Staddon Heights the cost is included in the item for the cost of Brownhill Battery, Watch House Brake, Twelve Acre Brake and the connecting Lines,i.e, all the work outside the two forts. The cost of the military road round the North Eastern Defences was shared between totals for the Ernesettle-Austin sector and for the Efford-Laira position. None of the works on Maker Heights were carried out apart from the battery at Polhawn and the cost of the road was shown as a separate item. The totals shown in column (4) include the cost of the roads.

4. Towards the end of the 1869 Report the position of the Plymouth defences was summarised as follows: 'The cost of the works under the Loan is now estimated at £1 181 341, and of the shields at £134 550, amounting together to £1 315 891. The excess on the estimate of 1867 is chiefly due to the great increase on the iron shields'. The account will then stand thus:

	£
Expenditure on land	282 840
" under Loan	1 315 891}
" Annual Votes	80 186} = 1,396,707
Total	1 679 547

Estimate of Defence Commissioners	2 670 000
Saving	990 543

Note. The report pointed out that the works did not provide the complete protection the Defence Commissioners had proposed in 1860, as there were gaps between the St Germans estuary and the Tamar, and between Laira and Staddon.

FORT/BATTERY	EST 1862	TOTAL INCL SHIELDS		SHIELDS
		EST 1869	AGAINST LOAN	
Sea Defences - Outer	(1)	(2)	(3)	(4)
Picklecombe	85 000	149 126	80 876	68 250
Staddon (Bovisand)	80 000	88 164	58 264	29 900
Breakwater	145 000	167 062	167 062	
Cawsand	10 000	16 171	12 914	(& 3257 earlier)
	---------	---------	---------	
	320 000	420 523	319 116	
Sea Defences - Inner				
Drake's Island	35 000	62 108	34 242 x	27 300
Eastern King	2000	2019	2019	
Western King	3000	3176	2887	(& 289 earlier)
Mt Edgcumbe	8000	18 802	7804 x	9100
	--------	--------	--------	---------
	48 500	86 105	46 952	134 550
Western Defences				
Tregantle	130 000	189 999	135 625	x (& 53 494 earlier)
Scraesdon	130 000	137 411	120 608	(& 16 803 earlier)
	---------	---------	---------	
	260 000	331 777*	260 000*	(*incl road = 3767)
Staddon Position				
Staddon	93 000	112 844	112 120 x	
Stamford	75 000	70 359	70 359	
Brownhill, W. Hse & Lines	25,768	25,768		(includes road)
	---------	---------	---------	
	168 000	208 971	208 247	

Forts or Follies?

North Eastern Defences

Ernesettle		17 630}	17 630	
Agaton		41 133}	41 133	
Knowle		19 562}	19 562	
Woodland		27 973}	27 973	
Crownhill	350 000	76 409}	76 409	
Bowden		15 891}	15 891	
Eggbuckland Keep		14 642}	14 642	
Forder		16 443}	16 443	
Austin		20 607}	20 607	(incl road = 252 955)
Efford		50 403}	50 403	
Laira		16 805}	16 805	(incl road = 69 626)
	----------	----------	----------	
	350 000	(317 498)	(317 498)	Total = 322 581

Maker Heights

Knatterbury	5000			
Whitesand (Polhawn)	10 000	8850	8850	(incl road = 14 626)
Maker Barracks	20 000			
	--------	-------	-------	
	35 000	(8850)	(8850)	Total = 14 626
Devonport Lines	10,000	12,724	9,819	
	========	========	======	
Total	1 181 000	(1 385 848)		1 181 341
		+ roads = 1 396 707		+ shields 134 550
				=======

x = Balance, to make (3)+(4)=(2),
was charged to Annual Vote.

Total £1 315 891

APPENDIX F

NOTES ON THE ROYAL ENGINEER OFFICERS WHO DESIGNED THE FORTIFICATIONS

These notes are based on information supplied by The Library of the Royal Engineers, Brompton Barracks, Chatham, particularly from memoirs in *The Royal Engineers Journal*, supplemented by entries in the *Dictionary of National Biography*. In the case of Captain du Cane the author is grateful to Mr Fred Larimore of Drexel Hill, Pennsylvania, U.S.A. for permission to use his notes on the Du Cane family.

Promotions in the Royal Engineers, or to Army ranks, up to Colonel are not shown below. But promotions to Brevet ranks in recognition of outstanding service are included.

MAJOR W.F.D. (LIEUT-GENERAL SIR WILLIAM, KCMG.) JERVOIS, (1821-1897)

1821	Born 9 Sept.
1837	To Royal Military Academy (RMA), Woolwich.
1839	Commissioned 2nd. Lieut, Royal Engineers.
1839	To School of Survey. His work commended and framed as pattern for students.
1841	To Cape of Good Hope.
1842	Brigade Major to force sent to Colesberg. Built bridge over Fish River.
1847	Made survey of British Kaffraria used 30 years later by Lord Chelmsford.
1848	Recommended by Sir Harry Smith, Governor & C-in-C at the Cape, to Lord Raglan as 'one of the most able, energetic and zealous officers'.
'49-52	Commanded a company of Sappers & Miners at Woolwich and Chatham.
'52-55	Went with his company to Alderney to build fortifications designed to protect the island as 'harbour of refuge'. Worked on details and superintended construction.
1854	Promoted Brevet Major.
'55-56	Commanding Royal Engineers (CRE) London District.
1856	Assistant Inspector-General of Fortifications (AIGF). Worked on proposals for the defence of the dockyards.
1857	Secretary of Defence Committee (DC). It was decided that the design of fortification works should in future be done at an enlarged IGF office under Jervois.
1858	Made maps for siting defences of London.
1859	Met Lord Palmerston and showed him plans for projected defence of Plymouth. Appointed secretary of Royal Commission (RC) on Defences of United Kingdom.
1860	Initial reaction of Defence Committee to RC report was negative. Jervois in a memo showed its inconsistencies. At his suggestion the committees sat together. Opposition to the RC report was based on the assumption that naval superiority would protect us from invasion. Later it was accepted that lack of fortifications would fetter the fleet in its operations and that a naval reverse might result in the destruction of the dockyards. In the end the original RC report was agreed. A Fortification Committee appointed to examine the designs of the works. Jervois made a member and the secretary.
1861	Promoted Brevet Lieut-Colonel.
1862	Appointed Director of Works for Fortifications. A committee to consider the use of submarine mines and torpedos appointed at Jervois' suggestion.
1863	Nominated Commander of the Bath (CB). Sent on mission to Canada to report on defences on eastern coast and at Bermuda.
1864	Sent to Canada again and reported his proposals on defences to Parliament.
1865	Sent to Canada and US.
1867	Promoted Brevet Colonel.
1868	Lectured to United Services Institute on 'Coast defences, and the application of iron to Fortification' with particular reference to Plymouth Breakwater Fort.
1869	Sent to inspect the works at Halifax and Bermuda, and later at Gibraltar and Malta.

1870   Served on the 'Committee on Coast Defence'.
1871-2 Reported on the defences of Aden, Perim, Bombay and the Hooghly.
1874   Created KCMG on recommendation of Canadian Government.
1875   Appointed Governor of Straits Settlements.
1875-6 Suppressed disturbances in Perak & elsewhere and established indirect British rule.
        Suppressed riots by Chinese in Singapore.
1877   Promoted Major-General.
        Sent to review defences of Australia & New Zealand.
1877-83 Governor of South Australia.
1882   Promoted Lieut-General.
1883-89 Governor of New Zealand.
1888   Delivered the keynote speech at the celebrations in Sydney to celebrate the centenary of New South Wales.
1889   On his retirement as Governor he was described by the New Zealand correspondent of the *Sydney Morning Herald* as 'beyond measure, the best and most popular governor that New Zealand has ever had.'
1890   Served on 'The Consultative Committee on Coast Defence Duties'.
1893   Appointed Colonel Commandant, Royal Engineers.
1897   Died 16 August.

CAPTAIN E. F. (MAJOR-GENERAL SIR FREDERICK, CB.) DU CANE, (1830-1903)

Designed at Plymouth: The North Eastern Defences: Ernesettle, Agaton, Knowles, Woodland, Crownhill, Bowden, Forder, Austin, Efford, and Laira. The Staddon Position: Staddon, Stamford, Brownhill, Twelve Acre Brake and Watch House Brake. The Western Defences: Tregantle (partly) and Polhawn.

1830   Born 23 March.
1846   To RMA, Woolwich.
1848   At RMA, Woolwich. Top of class, first in maths and fortification.
1848   Commissioned 2nd. Lieut, Royal Engineers.
1850   At Woolwich with a company of Sappers & Miners.
1851   Assistant superintendent of the foreign department of the International Exhibition.
1851-56 To Western Australia (Swan River Colony) to superintend public works constructed by convicts.

1856   Recalled to England for Crimean War but arrived too late. To IGF office to work on designs and estimates for proposed defences of dockyards and Naval bases.
1858-63 Designed land defences at Plymouth and Dover.
1863   Wrote paper on 'Fortification in Iron' in *The Duties of the Corps of Royal Engineers*.
1863   Appointed Director of Convict Prisons and Inspector of Military Prisons.
        Carried out reorganisation following Prisons Act 1865 and on the abolition of transportation in 1867.
1869   Inspector General Military Prisons and Surveyor General of Prisons.
1872   Described British system to International Prison Congress, London.
1873   Appointed CB.
1877   Chairman, Commissioners of Prisons to carry out Prisons Act.
        Promoted Brevet Colonel.
        Created KCB.
1887   Retired with honorary rank of Major-General.
1888   Published *Punishment and the Prevention of Crime*.
1898   In a lecture to the United Services Institute on 'The Fortification of our Dockyards' he gave a spirited defence of the work of the Royal Commission of 1859-60.
1903   Died 7 June.

He has been described as 'an accomplished man of wide interests, embracing archaeology, architecture and Napoleonic literature. He was an accomplished water-colour artist. Much of what is known of the early appearance of the Swan River Colony, Western Australia, comes from Sir Edmund's water-colours.'

MAJOR W. (MAJOR-GENERAL WHITWORTH) PORTER. (1827-1892)

Designed at Plymouth the Coast Batteries at: Picklecombe, Bovisand, Drake's Island and Mount Edgcumbe Garden.

1827   Born 23 Sept.
1842   To RMA, Woolwich.
1845   Commissioned 2nd. Lieut, Royal Engineers.
1852   In the military jury at the International Exhibition. Feb-Mar 1855 in Crimea. Mentioned in despatches at Sebastopol.
1855   Promoted Brevet Major.

1859-62 Worked on design of coast defences of Milford Haven and Plymouth.
1862-69 Instructor in Fortification at Royal Military College, Sandhurst.
1866 Promoted Brevet Lieut-Colonel.
1872 To Malta and Sicily.
1873 Promoted Brevet Colonel.
1874-76 In Barbados.
1877-81 Commanding Royal Engineers, Devonport.
1881 Retired due to ill-health.

He had a lifelong connection with the Order of St John of Jerusalem and its charitable works. He wrote a number of books including *Life in the Trenches in the Crimea*, *The History of the Knights of Malta* and, of particular interest, *The History of the Corps of Royal Engineers*.

CAPTAIN W. (MAJOR-GENERAL SIR WILLIAM, KCMG.) CROSSMAN. (1830-1901)

Designed at Plymouth: In the Western Defences: Fort Scraesdon & Fort Tregantle (partly)

1830 Born 30 June.
1847 To RMA, Woolwich.
1849 Commissioned 2nd. Lieut, Royal Engineers, and posted to Chatham.
1851 On staff of International Exhibition.
1851-56 To Western Australia (Swan River Colony) to supervise newly arrived convicts.
1856-61 To War Office to work on fortification design under Jervois and with Du Cane.
Designed most of land forts and coast batteries at Portsmouth.
1861 Volunteered for service in Canada.
1862 Secretary of Royal Commission on the Defences of Canada.
1862-66 On return, again worked under IGF.
1866 To China and Japan. Designed consular buildings and new dockyard at Shanghai.
1869 Mentioned in Despatches after Nanking and Yung Chow expedition.

1870 To Aldershot, then War Office. Worked on project for fortification of London.
1874 Assistant Director of Works for Fortifications.
1876 Inspector of Submarine Defences.
1877 Appointed CMG.
1879-80 President of Committee on Siege Operations.
1881-82 Inspected defences of various colonies.
1882 CRE, Southern District.
1884 Appointed KCMG.
1885 Elected Liberal MP for Perth.
1886 Retired as Hon. Major-General.
1901 Died 19 Aug.

CAPTAIN H. T. (MAJOR-GENERAL) SIBORNE. (1830?-1902)

Designed at Plymouth: Breakwater Fort

1830? Born.
1843 To RMA, Woolwich.
1846 Commissioned 2nd. Lieut, Royal Engineers.
1850-53 Active service in South Africa in Kaffir Wars.
1853 In charge of building Boma Pass Road near King William's Town, South Africa.
1855-56 Selected to raise and form a Mounted Troop, Royal Engineers, for 'the care and transport of field stores for the engineer service' in the Crimea. Eventually called A Troop, RE Train. It was hastily formed and had no preliminary training. Inspected by General Burgoyne before embarking. Arrived at Scutari early in 1856 but peace was declared before it got into action.
Jan '60 Appointed to IGF office where he designed the whole of the defences of the Thames and Medway.

Little more of his career is recorded.

1883 Retired as Hon. Major-General.
1902 Died 16 May.

BIBLIOGRAPHY

CHAPTER 1

CHALKLEY, Brian, Editor. *Plymouth; Maritime City in Transition.* David & Charles. 1991
GILL, Crispin. *Plymouth, a New History.* Devon Books. 1993.
OPPENHEIM, M. M. *The Maritime History of Devon.* University of Exeter. 1968
PYE, Andrew & WOODWARD, Freddy. *The Historic Defences of Plymouth.* Cornwall County Council. 1996.
WOODWARD, F.W. *Plymouth's Defences, a short history.* 1990.

CHAPTER 2

BATCHELOR, John & HOGG. Ian.V. *Artillery.* Macdonald. 1972.
CARPENTER, Austin C. *Cannon.* Halsgrove Press. 1993.
HOGG, Ian V. *Fortress, A History of Military Defence.* St Martin's Press, New York. 1975.
HOGG, Ian V. *Coast Defences of England and Wales, 1856-1956.* David & Charles. 1974.
HUGHES, Brig. B. P. *British Smooth Bore Artillery.* Arms & Armour Press. 1969.
HUGHES, Quentin. *Military Architecture.* Beaufort Press. 1991.
HUGHES, Quentin. 'Kronstadt and the Crimean War'. *FORT. 21.* 1993.
MAHAN, D. H. *A Complete Treatise on Field Fortification.* 1836. Re-printed Greenwood Press. 1968
MAURICE-JONES, Col. K. W., DSO. *The History of Coast Artillery in the British Army.* Royal Artillery Institution. 1959.
SAUNDERS, Andrew. *Fortress Britain.* Beaufort Press. 1989.

CHAPTER 3

BARTLETT, C.J. *Great Britain and Sea Power.* Oxford University Press. 1963.
GARBETT, Capt. H. *Naval Gunnery.* Republished 1971 by S. R. Publishers.
GARDNER, Robert. Editor. 'Steam, Steel and Shellfire. The Steam Warship 1815-1905'. Conway's *History of the Ship.* 1992.
HAMILTON, C. I. *Anglo-French Naval Rivalry, 1840-1870.* Clarendon Press. 1993.
HOUGH, Richard. *First Sea Lord.* George Allen & Unwin. 1969.
HUGHES, Quentin. 'The Duke of Wellington's Warning of Invasion'. *FORT. 9.* 1981.
HUGHES, Quentin. 'Wellington and Fortifications'. *FORT. 15.* 1987
HUMBLE, Richard. *Before the Dreadnought. The Royal Navy from Nelson to Fisher.* Macdonald & Jane. 1976.

KENT, Peter. 'The Militant Trinity: the role of Wellington, Burgoyne & Palmerston in fortification policy; 1830-1860'. *FORT. 14.* 1986.
LONGMATE, Norman. *Island Fortress.* Random Century. 1991.
LYON, David. *The Ship: Steam, Steel and Torpedoes.* National Maritime Museum. HMSO 1980.
MORDECAI, Major Alfred. *Military Commission to Europe in 1855-56.* Ordnance Dept, US Army. 1860.
RIDLEY, Jasper. *Lord Palmerston.* Constable 1970.

CHAPTER 4

CRICK, Timothy. 'Fortifications from Vauban to Jervois'. *FORT 24.* 1996.
ENCYLCLOPEDIA BRITANNICA. 1977-78. 'Fortification'.
HOWELL-EVERSON, Douglas. 'Victorian Fortress Strategy in the UK'. *FORT 15.* 1987.
JERVOIS, W. F. D. 'Observations relating to the Works in Progress for the Defence of the Naval Ports, Arsenals and Dockyards'. *Professional papers of the Royal Engineers. New Series IX. XIX.* 1860.
JERVOIS. W.F.D. 'Short description of Works proposed and in progress at Alderney Isle'. *FORT 8.* Supplement. 1980
KENYON, John R. 'James Ferguson: a critic of early Victorian military architecture'. *FORT 8.* 1980.
MITCHELL, Gerry & COBB, Peter. 'Fort Nelson and the Portsdown Forts'. *Solent Papers* No. 3. 1987.
MOORE, David. 'Fort Brockhurst and the Gomer - Elson Forts'. *Solent Papers* No. 6. 1990.
PARTRIDGE, Michael. *Military Planning for the Defence of the United Kingdom, 1814-1870.* Greenwood Press, Connecticut, USA. 1989.
WROTTESLEY, Lt-Col. Hon. George. *Life and Correspondence of Field-Marshal Sir John Burgoyne.* Richard Bentley & Son. 1873.

CHAPTER 5

BAINBRIDGE, Maj-Gen. 'Notes on Changes in the Construction of Fortifications'. *RE Papers.* New Series. Vol. 13. 1864.
CUNLIFFE, Col. OWEN. 'Fortifications versus Forts'. *Duties of the Corps of Royal Engineers.* New Series Vol.XIII 1864.
DU CANE, Maj-Gen. Sir E.F. 'The Fortification of our Dockyards', etc. RUSI Journal. XLII. 1898.
HUGHES, Quentin. 'Russian views on the English Defences in 1864'. *FORT 7.* 1979.
HUGHES, Quentin. 'Letters from the Defence Committee in 1861'. *FORT. 8.* 1980.

JERVOIS, Capt. W. F. D. 'Coast Defences and the application of Iron to Fortification.' RUSI Journal. Vol. XII. 1868.
MCDONALD, Kendall. Ed. Mary Bax. *The Bovisand Book.* 1981
PORTER, Whitworth. *History of the Corps of Royal Engineers. Chatham.* 1889.

CHAPTER 6

BAKER-BROWN, Lt-Col. RE. *The History of Submarine Mining in the British Army.* W. & J. Mackay. 1910.
DU CANE, Capt. E. F. RE. 'Fortification in Iron'. *RE Papers.* New Series. Vol 12. 1863.
FOSS, Christopher, etc. 'Drake's Island. Report of a Joint Working Party from the FSG and UK Forts Club'. 1978. (In Plymouth Local Studies Library).
JEWETT, Llewellyn. *History of Plymouth.* W. H. Luke. 1873.
WOODWARD, F. W. *Drake's Island.* Devon Archaeological Society. 1991.

CHAPTER 7

BURNS, Lt-Cdr KV, DSM *The Devonport Dockyard Story.* Maritime Books. 1984.
CALLWELL, Maj-Gen. Sir Charles & HEADLAM, Maj-Gen. Sir John. *The History of the Royal Artillery Vol.I . 1860-1899.* Royal Artillery Institution. 1931.
FISK, Col. *Annals of the Militia, being the Records of the South Devon Regiment.* Wm. Brendon, Plymouth. 1873.
LITCHFIELD, Norman. *The Militia Artillery, 1852-1908.* Sherwood Press. 1987
LITCHFIELD, Norman & WESTLAKE, Ray. *The Volunteer Artillery, 1849-1908.* Sherwood Press. 1982.
NAVAL & MILITARY RECORD. *Devonport's Old Battalion of Workmen.* 3.6.1925.
ROSE, Barrie. 'The Volunteers of 1859'. *Journal of the Society for Army Historical Research.* Vol. 37. 1959.
ROWE, John. *Devon Soldiers.* North Devon Athenaeum. 1990
WESTLAKE, Ray. *The Rifle Volunteers.* Picton Publishing. 1982.
WHITFELD, Henry Francis. *Plymouth & Devonport: in times of war and peace.* E. Chapple, Plymouth. 1900.
WORTH, R.N.FGS. *History of Plymouth.* William. Brendon, Plymouth. 1890.

CHAPTER 8

BARNETT, Corelli. *Britain and her Army, 1509-1970.* Allen Lane. 1970.
BARTHROP, Michael & TURNER, Pierre. *The British Army on Campaign 2. The Crimea 1854-56.* Osprey. 1988.
CHESNEY, Lt-Col. Sir G. *The Battle of Dorking. Reminiscences of a Volunteer.* William Blackwood. In book form 1875.

GRIFFITH, Paddy. *Forward into Battle. Fighting tactics from Waterloo to Vietnam.* Antony Birch. 1981.
HASKELL, Frank A. *The Battle of Gettysberg.* Eyre & Spottiswood. 1959.
MCLYNN, Frank. *Invasion from the Armada to Hitler, 1599-1945.* Routledge & Kegan Paul. 1987.
ROBERTS, Col. H. C. B. *Weapons of the British Soldier.* Seeley Service Co. Ltd. 1960.

CHAPTER 9

CLARKE, Sir George Sydenham. *Fortification. 1890.* Re-printed Beaufort Press.

PRINCIPAL DOCUMENTS IN THE PUBLIC RECORD OFFICE

ADM1/5543 Report of the Committee of Harbour Defences - Plymouth. 23.10.1844.

ZHC1/2477 Report of the Commissioners appointed to consider the Defences of the United Kingdom. 1860.

ZHK1/1747 Report with reference to the progress made in the construction of the Fortifications for the defence of the Dockyards and Naval Arsenals, &c of the United Kingdom. 20.2.1867.

ZHL1/1884 Report of the Committee appointed to enquire into the construction, condition and cost of the Fortifications. 1869.

Documents prior to the enactment of the
Royal Commission's Report

WO55/1548/19 Duke of Wellington's memorandum on Works for the Defence of the Naval Arsenals and Dockyards. 20.12.1944.

WO55/1548/21 Lord Palmerston's Report on the Defence of the Country. 17.12.1846.

WO33/8 Memorandum on Defences proposed for the Protection of the Naval Arsenal at Devonport and Plymouth. W. F. D. Jervois. 26.2.58. p.495-580. (Also in WO33/5 p.71.)

WO33/8 Memorandum on Defences for Plymouth. J. F. Burgoyne. 4.3.1858. p.65.

WO33/5 Report by a committee under the Presidency of the Commander-in Chief on the best means of repelling the invasion of the United Kingdom. 7.5.1858. p.1.

WO33/65/507 Report of the committee on Home Defences. 26.5.1858, including Memorandum on Defences proposed for Protection of the Naval Arsenal at Devonport and Plymouth (Incorporated in the report of the Royal Commission as Appendix 5 and herein as Appendix A)

WO33/5 Memorandum on Popular Fallacies with regard to our Security against Invasion. J. F. Burgoyne. June 1858. p.78.

WO33/5 Memorandum relative to the Protection of Dockyards and the most important Harbours of England, also on the Defence of the Country against Invasion. W. F. D. Jervois. 29.10.1858. r.95.

WO55/1548/22 General Sir John Burgoyne's Report on the Defences of Plymouth. 10.11.58.

WO33/7 Memorandum on the probable effects of rifled cannon on the Attack and Defence of Fortifications. J. F. Burgoyne. 7.2.1859. p. 018.

WO33/7 Report of the Committee on the influence of the new Rifled Cannon on existing fortifications and plans. 1st Report. 22.2.1859. p. 126-28.

WO33/9 Papers respecting National Defences. 2.2.1860 - 3.8.1860. p 885-897. (Letters and memoranda relating to the Royal Commission's report).

WO33/9 Minute of the Defence Committee on the Report of the Royal Commission 9.4.1860. p.771.

WO33/9 Memorandum on National Defences. J. F. Burgoyne. 1860. p. 888. (His comments on the Royal Commission's Report)

WO33/9 Report on the Armstrong gun. 1.5.1860. p. 813.

WO33/9 Ordnance Select Defence Committee. Report of a committee on Coast Batteries. July 1860. p. 1029.

Documents after the enactment of the
Royal Commission's Report.

WO33/2772 Precis of Correspondence relating to the Defences of Plymouth, prior to April 1893. See Appendix B for extracts up to 12.12.1885.

WO55/1548/23 Report on General Todleben's visit to England 1864. 1.2.1865.

WO33/26 Report on progress in the Construction of Fortifications for the Defence of the Dockyards & Naval Arsenals. W. F. D. Jervois. Feb. 1874. p.555.

PRINCIPAL MAPS AND PLANS IN THE
PUBLIC RECORD OFFICE

WO 78/4481 Prince of Wales Redoubt, Eastern King. MPHH 629. Pt. 3.1847

WO 78/2569 Proposed reform of Devonport Lines. 1854

WO 78/483 Early plan of Scraesdon Fort. 1859

WO 78/4367 Early plans including
  Part 1. Staddon Position
          Polhawn Fort
          Saltash Position
          North Eastern Defences (3)
          Stamford Fort 1860-62

  Part 2. Staddon Fort
          Turnchapel (Stamford) Fort
          North Eastern Defences   1860-61

WO 78/3847 Site plan of Bovisand Battery and plans of Watch House Brake and Twelve Acre Brake Batteries. 1870-76

WO78/623 Plan of Staddon Heights Position. 1872

WO 78/566 Map 1/10 000 showing North Eastern Defences and Clearance Areas. 1878

WO 78/5056 Site plan of Garden Battery with conversion details. 1880

WO 78/5050 Site plan of Picklecombe Fort and plans of QF battery and search lights. 1880 & 1901

WO 78/4200 Site plan of casemated battery and main battery on Drake's Island, 1895 (and amendments, 1899)

WO 78/2314 Survey 1/2500 for War Department showing all Plymouth defences, 1896 - and other 1:10 000 surveys of the defences. 1882-1911.

GLOSSARY OF FORTIFICATION TERMS

(With acknowledgements to Andrew Saunders and also David Moore)

ADVANCED WORKS - Additional works beyond the GLACIS but still commanded from the main defences.

BANQUETTE - An infantry firing step.

BARBETTE - BREASTWORK of a BATTERY sufficiently low that guns may fire over it without the need for EMBRASURES.

BASTION - Projection from the general line of a FORTRESS from which the garrison can defend by flanking fire the ground between the RAMPARTS. From the mid-sixteenth century, it was generally a four-sided projection.

BASTIONETTE - Small BASTIONS which give local flanking cover but are not the principal defensive element.

BATTERY - Any place where guns or mortars are mounted.

BERM - Level space between the edge of a ditch or moat and the foot of a RAMPART.

BLOCKHOUSE - Small detached FORT at a strategic point, later often a wooden structure.

BULWARK - Early term for a BASTION or BLOCKHOUSE.

CAPONIER - Covered communication way across a dry ditch leading to OUTWORKS usually loopholed. Also a powerful CASE-MATED WORK projecting across a ditch to provide flanking fire.

CASEMATE - Bomb-proof vaulted chamber within the ramparts providing an emplacement for a gun and/or a barrack room

CHEMIN DES RONDES - Passage or sentry path at top of the SCARP WALL with a PARAPET or loopholed wall for cover.

CITADEL - Self-contained FORTRESS usually within a town's fortifications intended as a place of last resort.

COUNTERSCARP - Exterior slope or revetment of a ditch.

COUNTERSCARP GALLERY - Loopholed passage behind the COUNTERSCARP WALL to defend a ditch

COVERED WAY - Continuous communication way on the outer edge of the ditch protected by an earthwork PARAPET from enemy fire.

CRÉMAILLÈRE - Indented or saw-toothed TRACE to allow greater flanking cover, usually applied to fieldworks.

CURTAIN - Length of RAMPART between two BASTIONS on the main line of a defensive work.

DROP DITCH - A deeper section of ditch along the faces of casemates, caponiers or musketry galleries, preventing easy access to them by an attacker.

EMBRASURE - Opening in a PARAPET or wall through which a gun can be fired

ENCEINTE - Also known as 'the body of the place'. The main defensive enclosure of FORTRESS, excluding the OUTWORKS.

ESCARP EN DÉCHARGE - Hollow or counter-arched REVETMENT, constructed so that the earth piled on to the arches can freely fall and be carried away so allowing the scarp to be consolidated.

ENFILADE - Fire coming from a flank which sweeps the length of a fortification.

ESCALADE - The climbing of walls by means of ladders.

ESCARP - Outer slope or revetment of a rampart. Also SCARP.

EXPENSE MAGAZINE - Small MAGAZINE close to a BATTERY in which a small supply of ammunition is kept for immediate use.

FACE (of a BASTION) - Outer sides of a work which meet at a salient angle projecting towards the field. Also used to describe the sides of a polygonal fortification.

FLANK - Side of a work, usually a BASTION, between the FACE and the CURTAIN. The principal defensive element of a BASTIONED fortification.

FLÈCHE - Small arrow-shaped OUTWORK placed at the foot of a GLACIS.

FORT - Position or building designed primarily for defence.

FORTRESS - Major fortified place, often a town, capable of containing a large force.

GLACIS - PARAPET of the COVERED WAY extended in a long slope towards the FIELD.

GORGE - Rear, whether open or closed, of any work.

HAXO CASEMATE - Vaulted CASEMATE for a gun built on the TERREPLEIN of a RAMPART, invented by General Haxo.

KEEP - Principal and strongest tower of a castle and the final point of defence. Also the place of last resort in some later forts.

MACHICOLATION - Projecting gallery corbelled out from a wall.top with openings for vertical defence of the foot of a wall.

MANTLET - Moveable rope screen for a gun, often in a casemate.

PARADE - Ground on which regular muster and exercises are held.

PARADOS - A RAMPART protecting the rear of a WORK from fire.

PLACE OF ARMS - Assembly point at the RE-ENTERING or SALIENT ANGLES of the COVERED WAY to enable the formation of troops for a sortie or for the defence of the OUTWORKS.

PLATFORM - Hard surface of timber, stone, etc. on which guns in a BATTERY can be placed.

POSTERN - (or SALLYPORT). A small entrance or tunnel leading out of the fortifications.

RAMP - Inclined track on the rear slope of a RAMPART to allow the movement of troops and guns on the TERREPLEIN.

RAMPART - Mass of excavated earth on which the troops and guns of the garrison are raised and forming the main defence of the FORT.

REDAN - OUTWORK consisting of two FACES forming a SALIENT ANGLE.

REDOUBT - Small enclosed WORK that does not have flank defences from its own parapet.

RE-ENTRANT - Angle facing inwards from the FIELD as opposed to the SALIENT.

REVETMENT - Retaining wall of a RAMPART or for the sides of ditches.

SALIENT - An ANGLE projecting outwards towards the FIELD.

SALLYPORT - See POSTERN.

SCARP - Outer slope or REVETMENT of a RAMPART or inner side of a ditch. Also ESCARP.

TENAILLE TRACE - Succession of Redans at right angles to each other to form a zigzag front.

TERREPLEIN - Level surface on top of a RAMPART and below the PARAPET where guns are mounted.

TÊTE-DE-PONT - Fortification on the vulnerable side of a bridge.

TRACE - Plan of a fortified place and its angles of fire.

TRAVERSE - Earthwork thrown up to bar enfilade fire along any line of a WORK which is liable to it.

WORK - General term for any work of defence.

INDEX